Education and Youth

EDUCATIONAL ANALYSIS
General Editors: Philip Taylor and Colin Richards

CONTEMPORARY ANALYSIS IN EDUCATION SERIES
General Editor: Philip Taylor

Contemporary Analysis in Education Series

Education and Youth

Edited and introduced by
David Marsland

22 The Falmer Press

(A member of the Taylor & Francis Group)
London and Philadelphia

UK   The Falmer Press, Falmer House, Barcombe, Lewes, East Sussex,
           BN8 5DL

USA   The Falmer Press, Taylor & Francis Inc., 242 Cherry Street,
           Philadelphia, PA 19106-1906

© Selection and editorial material copyright D. Marsland 1987

First published 1987

Library of Congress Cataloging in Publication Data

Education and youth.
   (Contemporary analysis in education series; v. 14)
   1. Youth—Great Britain—Social conditions.
2. Adolescent psychology—Great Britain.   3. Education,
Secondary—Great Britain—Aims and objectives.   4. High
school graduates—Employment—Great Britain.   I. Marsland,
David.   II. Series: Contemporary analysis in education
series; 14.
HQ796.E29   1987   305.2′35′0941   86-29352
ISBN 1-85000-137-5
ISBN 1-85000-138-3 (pbk.)

Jacket design by Leonard Williams

Typeset in 11/13 Garamond by
Imago Publishing Ltd, Thame, Oxon

*Printed in Great Britain by Taylor & Francis (Printers) Ltd,
Basingstoke*

Contents

Contents

The Elusiveness of Youth Policy

Dedicated to the memory of
Leslie Button

General Editor's Preface

The dilemma of youth today is the central issue of this reader. Their dilemma is, at least for very many, to be powerless educationally, economically and socially in a society which endows with power those with high educational achievement from upper social classes, having benefited from the wealth of their backgrounds. In a society where increasingly to the victor go the spoils, many young people see their life chances, where they see them at all, uncertainly and with increasing pessimism.

It is the value of this book that it documents from a variety of perspectives what appears at times to be a social indictment of youth. If this was all the book did, it would be enough but it goes further. It shows what can be done to mitigate, even reverse the conditions with which the young are faced and must cope. In this it is a hopeful and challenging appraisal of the dilemma of youth in our time.

Finally, David Marsland is to be congratulated in bringing together a fine array of contributors who each in their own style make distinctive contributions to our understanding of the young in education and society today.

Philip Taylor
University of Birmingham October 1986

Introduction: Education and Youth

David Marsland

The specifically *youthful* character of young people, and the powerful effects of adolescence on their behaviour are still inadequately
acknowledged generally in Britain. Remarkably, this neglect of
youth extends even to the sphere of secondary education. School
organization, the curriculum, and teaching methods have been designed with scarcely any explicit account being taken of the fact that
secondary school pupils are — young people. Many of the difficulties in the schools arise as a result of this socially structured
blindness. Pupils tend even now to be treated either as overgrown
children or as rather backward adults. Either they are allowed no
choices, responsibility, or initiative — for example the curriculum is
simply given, or they are assumed to be capable of seeing for
themselves, without adequate help and guidance, the sense of this
argument or that procedure.

The result is, for many pupils, either boredom and a sense of
oppression, or mystification and alienation. Overall the consequence
is de-motivation at all levels, and considerably reduced educational
effectiveness. A major source of these difficulties is the very modest
extent to which social scientists or educationists have so far examined the relations between education and youth. It was for this
reason that it seemed useful to prepare a volume specifically focusing on the issue of relations between educational theory, policy, and
practice on the one hand, and the condition and characteristics of
adolescence and youth on the other.

The authors range widely in the contexts of their educational
experience and in the theoretical and value perspectives in terms
of which they make their analyses. They include, in disciplinary
terms, representatives of psychology (Coleman), sociology
(O'Keefe, Smith, and Marsland), education (Dickson, Shaw), and

1

youth work, (Day, Ewen, Williamson). Their practical experience ranges through treatment and provision for young people (Coleman, Dickson), youth service work, including training (Day, Ewen, Mathura, Marsland, Williamson), teacher training (O'Keefe, Shaw), and policy analysis (Ewen, Marsland, Williamson). There is also a considerable variation in the concepts of youth adopted by the several authors. Thus Smith and Williamson evince a fair degree of critical scepticism about the validity of the concept of youth as it has become conventionally established by social scientists. By contrast, Coleman, Day, Kerridge, Marsland, and Mathura largely accept that concept, and urge the acknowledgement of its practical implications for education. Between these two extremes, Dickson, O'Keefe, Shaw, and Ewen operate more pragmatically in conceptual terms, and attend more directly to issues of practice and policy in education. In terms of values, a wide spectrum is covered, from Shaw's scepticism about the whole comprehensive project and O'Keefe's demand for a clearer, tougher, more instrumental regime in the schools on the one side, to Williamson's powerful critique of current trends, as he sees them, in just these directions, and Smith's emphasis on disadvantaged groups.

I hope that this variety does not militate against the coherence of the book. It need not, and indeed it is deliberately intended to demonstrate the complexity of the issues involved, and to provide a stimulus for debate and for further research and analysis. All the authors focus sharply, if in different ways, on inadequacies in the education system and on the relevance of our understanding of young people's needs for finding effective remedies.

Chapters 1 and 2, by Coleman and Smith, establish the basic parameters for analysis of the relations of education and youth, respectively from psychological and sociological perspectives. Author of one of the most useful recent general introductions to the psychology of adolescence,[1] Coleman elucidates and evaluates in 'Adolescence and Schooling' the major theoretical perspectives on adolescence, in particular contrasting psychoanalytic and socio-cultural approaches. On this basis he examines three major topics with a direct bearing on schooling — puberty, cognition, and social relationships. Under the latter heading he focuses on two issues whose importance have been remarkably neglected in the recent history of secondary schooling in Britain: the development of independence in young people, and the significance of adults, including teachers, as role models for young people's development.

In 'Peers, Subcultures, and Schools', Smith examines the extensive literature on peer groups and youth culture, and its implications for education. One of the absurdly few specialists in the sociology of youth in Britain, and the author of a number of important articles which critically examine recent developments in the sociology of youth[2], Smith questions the influence of American research and theorizing about peer groups; challenges the assumption that peers are a more important influence than parents; asserts the importance of social class in the shaping of youth sub-cultures; and explores in detail the relations between peer group values and school objectives. In an important section he deplores the neglect in theories and studies of youth of young women and of black youngsters.

Chapters 3 and 4 proceed to explore two practical ways in which schooling can be improved if more adequate account is taken of young people's special characteristics and needs. In 'The Challenge of Learning to Care', the distinguished founder of Voluntary Service Overseas and Community Service Volunteers, Alec Dickson, urges a massive expansion of community service in the schools. He has for many years argued that schooling is bound to be ineffective and even destructive, so long as the schools fail to take account of young people's deep need to take responsibilities, to offer service, and to participate in positively meaningful and worthwhile activities.[3] In Chapter 3 he describes how the introduction of community service in the schools — not as a mere 'filler' for the weakest pupils, but as a general and basic dimension of the school programme as a whole — can strengthen the effectiveness of education. He provides many practical examples of the benefits of community service — to young people, to schooling, and to the community as a whole.

Leslie Button has developed a method of using group work in secondary schools which is designed to increase pupil awareness, involvement and commitment. His books have been influential and his approach has been widely adopted in the training of youth workers and school teachers. In Chapter 4 Marsland and Day examine the negative impact on many young people of teachers' attitudes and established methods of teaching. They explore, by examining Leslie Button's ideas, the ways in which a more positive effect can be achieved if young people's real and fundamental needs are taken proper account of.[4]

The chapters by Dickson and by Marsland and Day focus in practical terms on the issue of young people's values which has been established earlier by Coleman and by Smith as central to an adequate understanding of youth. In Chapter 5, Mathura, with a background in administration of further and social education, attends explicitly to this question of values. In 'Young People and Values: the Case of the Youth Service' he challenges trenchantly the mischievous neglect and misunderstanding of values which he suggests is common in the Youth Service and in the rest of the contemporary educational system.

Chapters 6, 7, and 8 all deal, in very different ways, with the manifest inadequacies of secondary schooling. In 'Uncharted Youth: Adolescence and the Secondary School Curriculum', O'Keeffe, author of important papers on the raising of the school leaving age and on truancy,[5] argues that young people are being short-changed by the pseudo-academic purposes and curriculum foisted on them in too many schools. He argues for a more instrumental approach providing vocationally relevant preparation more attuned to young people's own expressed wishes, and more appropriate to the demands of the real world.

In 'Tripartism Revisited; Young People, Education, and Work in the 1980s', Williamson criticizes just such developments as O'Keeffe urges. A practised youth worker who has been much involved in research and development on MSC special measures schemes,[6] he detects in policy developments of recent years an attempt to put the clock back — to the period before the introduction of comprehensive schooling, when education was sharply stratified to cater for the three main levels of the labour market. He reaches this conclusion by way of an analysis of government responses to youth unemployment, and a critique of training schemes as mere gap fillers for the 'broken transition' between school and work.

In 'Comprehensive Schooling and Procrustes' Shaw, author of one of the most original recent analyses of comprehensive education,[7] identifies quite different causes of the inadequacies of contemporary schooling from those to which Williamson draws our attention. The main problem, he suggests, is the ideological egalitarianism imposed on the schools and their pupils by the proponents of comprehensivisationism. His historical analysis explores in detail the role of Anthony Crosland's ideas and action in the nineteen sixties, and their influence on a largely sceptical — but quiescent — body of teachers and parents. In relation to contemporary developments, he questions the validity of the arguments of advocates, such as Hargreaves, of further movement down the comprehensive road.

Chapters 9 and 10 turn to broader and deeper aspects of these same issues. In 'Order in an Age of Rebellion', Kerridge, an author and journalist with a reputation for penetrating criticism based on inside knowledge[8], writes about the gross inadequacies of some of our inner city schools and their failure to take young people, especially Afro-Caribbean young people, seriously. He argues that rebelliousness is not a characteristic to be automatically welcomed or encouraged, and that the schools are increasingly crippled by the fawning attention to it of those responsible for young people's education. As a significant example of this general error, he raises some serious, critical questions about the theory and practice of multi-cultural education.

In 'The Elusiveness of Youth Policy', Ewen, first director of the National Youth Bureau, and author of a well-known book on youth policy,[9] examines the contradictions and gaps in legislation and in provision for young people, focusing in particular on consequent weaknesses in the schools. He emphasizes the underestimated impact of structural youth unemployment on the schools and on policy thinking generally. In this context he poses some challenging questions about the extent to which educationists, and others responsible for young people, have recognized as yet the order of innovative adaptation youth unemployment requires of them, and of all of us.

The Concept and Theory of Youth

Underlying each of the ten chapters of the book, as they underlie the policy and practice of contemporary education, are particular and varying conceptions of youth. In everyday discourse and in policy analysis in relation to young people, such conceptions of the nature and needs of young people play a large — and for the most part unexplicated — role.

For the most part, conceptions of youth appear to be negative and critical, with young people viewed, as a category, mainly as a source of trouble.[10] Where corrections to this negative stereotype are made, for example by recognition that it is only minorities of young people who are involved in deviant behaviour, this amendment of the initial error is made at the cost of losing *any* general conception of youth at all. Thus, at the level of public discourse and common sense thinking, we have either a false negative concept of youth — or no coherent concept of youth at all.[11] It is the business of social scientists to salvage from this confusion, on the basis of theoretical analysis and concrete research, a coherent and empirically justifiable concept and theory of youth. This requires consistent work by social scientists at the study of young people and their lives. Since the beginning of the century and the vital contribution of G.S. Hall to the establishment of the psychology of adolescence as a special field of study, psychologists have played their part more than adequately.[12] There is the work of psycho-analysts, from Anna Freud to D.W. Winnicott, which Coleman examines in his analysis of the work of Blos in Chapter 1 of this book.[13] There is the immensely influential work of Jean Piaget and of his followers, notably Kohlberg.[14] And there is the more sociologically inclined tradition of Erik Erikson, which has made the concepts of identity and autonomy essential to any sensible account of young people's lives.[15]

Together with the continuing programme of research on the biological aspects of psychological development, with its sharp focus on puberty and sexuality,[16] these different lines of analysis by psychologists have produced a remarkably full and clear understanding of the psychological dimensions of the life of young people. Its scope and stature is demonstrated by the availability and influence of the (admittedly American, but generally used) *Handbook of Adolescent Psychology* edited by Adelson[17].

Sociological Weaknesses in Relation to Youth

There is characteristically no equivalent to Adelson's Handbook, with its hundreds of pages of reports of research and analysis, for the *sociology* of youth. Sociological analysis of the lives of young people began later and remains, logically and empirically, much weaker than the psychology of adolescence.

The work of Talcott Parsons and S.N. Eisenstadt, particularly through the latter's *From Generation to Generation*, established in the forties and fifties quite powerful foundations for the sociology of youth[18]. This was strengthened up to the period of the sixties by the incorporation into sociological accounts of youth of the social and cultural dimensions of Erikson's work, and by the production of a considerable body of empirical research. This is exemplified in James Coleman's influential *The Adolescent Society* and Feuer's *The Conflict of Generations*, and symbolized by the initiation of the journal *Youth and Society*[19]. The work of anthropologists, including, if with some ambivalence, the popular studies of Margaret Mead, added a further dimension[20].

This tradition, even more than the psychology of adolescence, in which the European contributions of psycho-analysis and Piaget are after all central, was dominated by American work. It incorporated, nevertheless, the important early work of Karl Mannheim on generations, and included Frank Musgrove's valuable British study *Youth and the Social Order*[21].

In the past two decades, this body of work, which I have called elsewhere, 'the conventional sociology of youth' has been increasingly subject in Britain to criticism and challenge[22]. It is in consequence of the success of this critique, I believe, that the development of a coherent sociological concept and theory of youth has faltered and fallen back. The major source of challenge to conventionally established sociological analysis of youth has been Marxist theory. As with sex and race, so with youth, Marxist analysis tends to derogate other differentiating variables aside from class to a position so secondary as to approach invisibility. At the end of the 1960s an analysis by Allen[23] provided a definitive formulation of this characteristically Marxist dismissal of youth. The influence of her analysis, which has been reprinted and cited ubiquitously, can hardly be overestimated. Its influence has been strengthened by two other factors. First, the sociologist's parochial tendency to dismiss anything remotely psychological — as the concept of 'adolescence' has routinely been taken to be. Secondly, sociologists' generalized scepticism of anything so manifestly commonsensical as the concept of 'youth', which has been commonly treated as a concept for journalists and the person in the street and *ipso facto* inadequate for sociological analysis.

During the 1970s the undeniable significance of problems associated with young people — for example unemployment, education, delinquency — has constrained some revision of this *a priori* theoretical dismissal of youth. The Marxist approach remains, nevertheless, antipathetic to any coherent concept of youth, or to allowing it to become a primary focus of attention in sociological analysis. This is exemplified in the most important contribution to Marxist analysis of youth — Hall and associates, *Resistance Through Rituals*.[24] This celebrates and maintains Allen's derogative view of the concept of youth, and of the established approach to the sociological analysis of youth which has its roots in Eisenstadt's work.

The key features of Marxist theorizing about youth are most succinctly expressed in a short paper by Hall *et al.*[25] They conclude, among other things, that to construe youth as a stage of life is problematical; that there can be no 'sociology of youth': that, as they say, 'youth as a concept is unthinkable'; that even as a social category it doesn't make much sense; and that in any case youth at best is a trivial, secondary phenomenon and normally dominated by class relations. In short, as in *Resistance Through Rituals*, they reject the concept and the theory associated with it out of hand. This perspective has been further popularized by two influential books by Brake.[26] He accepts Hall and his associates' theorization of youth as a secondary phenomenon largely controlled by class forces, and on this basis seeks to orient sociological analysis of young people's lives to elucidation of the influence of class inequalities.

This overall approach constitutes at this date the orthodoxy in sociological analysis of youth. Beside the work of Allen, Hall and his associates, including especially Murdock[27] and Brake, it includes also the vividly interesting ethnographic studies of Willis, particularly *Learning to Labour* and *Profane Culture*[28]. Willis' work typifies the strengths of the Marxist approach — but also its weaknesses, in particular the extent to which it distracts attention from youth itself and common aspects of all young people's lives to *some* aspects of the contexts of some young people's lives. It excludes altogether any serious attention either to the bio-psychological foundations of youth, or to the basic aspects of the general characteristics of youth, to which the conventional sociology of youth gives pride of place.

There are some recent signs of dissatisfaction with the Marxist perspective, notably in the criticisms of *Resistance* by Cohen and by Smith.[29] Moreover O'Donnell's *Age and Generation*, while sympathetic to Marxist approaches, at least allows for serious attention to the issues Eisenstadt placed on the agenda of the sociology of youth. He even goes as far (page 1) as admitting — what neither Allen nor Hall ever could — that:

> Few would disagree with S.N. Eisenstadt's comment that 'Age and differences of age are amongst the most basic and crucial aspects of human life and determinants of human destiny'. In everyday life we are, perhaps, as conscious of age differences as we are of those of class or gender.[30]

Despite these corrective trends, British sociological analysis of youth remains in 1986 largely dominated by Marxist and Marxisant perspectives. I find their account of youth less than persuasive. It denigrates the established knowledge we have about youth. It represents an account of youth which is compelled to deny falsely the significance of one set of forces in social life, the psycho-social forces organized in the age system, out of fear that their recognition may challenge the determinative pre-eminence of another set of such forces — those of class. I have attempted to present counterarguments about the concept of youth along the following lines. First, the concept symbolizes and demarcates an aspect of social reality which, without it, would remain uncharted and unexplicated. Secondly, it brings coherently into one analytical category a range of phenomena which, taken separately, would be incomprehensible. Thirdly, the concept provides, when properly constituted, a provisional theoretical model of the processes underlying the meaning and conditions of the life of young people, and of the forces controlling them.

On the basis of such arguments, a coherent rationale for the main theoretical alternative to the Marxist approach can be formulated. This approach grows out of the foundational work of Eisenstadt, Coleman and Erikson. It prescribes and justifies four main areas of requisite analysis in sociological research on young people:

1 the significance of peer groups in the life of young people;
2 the meaning, causes and functions of youth cultures and youth subcultures;
3 the causes, pattern, and consequences of intergenerational relations, or more specifically, of the cultural handling of relations between age groups;
4 the historical and political significance of the involvement of youth in transformational social change.

Overall these issues have not received in recent years the attention which they demand. This is due in large part to Marxist influence, which directs theoretical attention in different directions. It is also, however, due to the effects of the third major theoretical approach in British sociological analysis of young people. This latter, which includes the work of some of the best and most influential researchers, such as Smith and Eggleston is typically empiricist and eclectic[31] It tends to minimize the significance of the level of issues pressed alike by Marxists and by the traditionally established sociology of youth. It could hardly be claimed that the work of the 1970s has attended to the resolution of issues at this level. On my reading of that work, such analysis cannot be postponed further, and must be a crucial item on the agenda for the future.

Towards an Adequate Sociological Concept and Theory of Youth

Marxists argue as if any concept of youth except a Marxist concept of youth is bound to be 'merely' biological, psychologically reductionist, or unexplicatedly 'common-sensical' (the latter a term of opprobrium in such circles). The assumptions involved in this mode of thinking are erroneous. There are well established concepts of youth which are not Marxist, which take account properly (as Marxists do not and cannot) of bio-psychology, which go beyond intelligent common sense without contradicting it, and which are thoroughly sociological. The 'conventional' sociology of youth contains the seeds of this alternative to Marxist thinking about youth. It needs to be further developed and strengthened if it is to be useful — as it should be — to practical men and women concerned about the education of young people.[32] The basis of this approach are as follows.

Basic Dimensions of the Age System

The first issue is how we are to construe and conceptualize youth. Answer: youth is part of the age system, itself a sub-system of society as a whole.

Age is a generally important criterion of social differentiation, a powerful principle in terms of which most, if not all, societies are organized and ordered. The age system is comprised of a set of inter-related categories (cultural definitions) and age groups (structural units). Youth is one of this set: an age category, an age group, a social role institutionalized within society. It refers to the same reality as the psychologist construes under the concept of adolescence.

The basic categories/groups of childhood, adulthood, and old age are certainly universal, appearing in all known societies, of course in varying forms. Youth is a transitional category between childhood and adulthood; it is sociologically speaking a transit camp in life. There is much dispute among sociologists about whether youth is a universal phenomenon or whether it appears only in certain sorts of societies. In my view the former position is correct. In some aspects it varies considerably from one society to another, in other more basic aspects it is a recurrent and persistent feature of all age systems in all societies. Like the rest of the age system, youth is a social and sociological reality, not just a biological or psychological force. It is the social construction (i.e. definition and institutionalization) of biological (growth), psychological (time, learning), and sociological (experience) components. In all societies age categories have a powerful force in people's lives — so much so indeed that we tend to take them for granted and treat them as trivial.

Teachers at least should avoid this error. If young people are treated as children, as adults, or as just plain people without taking account of the specific needs, problems, limitations, and capacities they have in consequence of their youth we are bound to mistreat them.[33]

Youth and Society

Like any other 'bit' of society, the age system interacts with and is influenced by all the other bits. An old, rich woman is at least all three things, and they all matter. She is (quite apart from her unique individuality) importantly different from the *young* rich woman she may once have been — and can never be again. Different also from the *poor* old woman she may become tomorrow if her shares crash, and from the old rich *man* she can probably never be. Similar to *and* different from the rich, *old* man she is probably married to or widowed from. Because the age system is — obviously and undeniably — influenced by the economic system, the political system, the gender system, the religious system, etc., etc., etc., this does not render it trivial. That is how social life is — unless we content ourselves with a very simple theory of one-way causes. Age in turn affects everything else powerfully and reciprocally. A primary task of the sociology of youth is to examine how youth is affected by history (comparisons over time), by culture (comparisons across different societies), and by other social forces within any given society during any given historical period. There are both constancies and variations in youth and its relations with society.[34]

Youth and Development

Because youth is a transition category in the age system, and because the raw material of the age system as a whole is growth and time, the biological and psychological underpinnings of youth are immensely important. Many sociologists too glibly underplay their significance. The beginning of youth in an individual life is signalled by puberty, and its termination is gradually arrived at in terms of working out the problems of sexuality, identity, and responsibility which puberty and its psychological accompaniments inaugurate. These issues are not peripheral to the sociology of youth. On the contrary they are absolutely central to it, since we have to examine how — variously — societies manage to help or hinder young people's negotiation of the developmental tasks which bio-psychological forces set for all of them. The key issues are puberty, growth, self, identity, relationship, aggression, and autonomy.[35]

Peer Groups

The crucial social meaning of youth is withdrawal from adult control and influence compared with childhood. Peer groups are the milieu into which young people withdraw. In at least most societies, this withdrawal into the peer group is, within limits, legitimated by the adult world. Time and space is handed over to young people to work out for themselves in auto-socialization the developmental problems of self and identity which cannot be handled (at any rate in a complex modern society) by the simple direct socialization appropriate to childhood. There is a moratorium on compliance and commitment, and lee-way allowed for a relatively unguided journey with peers towards autonomy and maturity. Peer groups arise in all the spheres of activity in which young people are involved: the family (sibs against parents), schools and colleges (pupils and students against teachers), work (against bosses and older workers); and the community (kids against adults). Because release of control is of the essence, peer groups necessarily have negative consequences as easily as positive effects. They cannot be broken. Handled badly they are a major source of deviance, conflict, and trouble. Handled well — which I assume it is one of teachers' and youth workers' special roles to encourage and facilitate — the peer group can be a massively powerful source of constructive social advance as well as of individual development.[36]

Youth Culture

A culture is an organized set of values, beliefs, norms, and expectations. The concept of youth culture postulates that there is within a society a differentiated sub-culture distinguished in important ways from the culture of adulthood (and childhood). This youth culture is available to, belongs to, and is used by young people as a generalized age category and age group. It is potentially shared by all young people, however many sub-cultures of youth it may also be divided into, and is unavailable to children or adults. However much it may be exaggerated and exploited by the media, by commercial interests, and by adult organized youth organizations, it has a genuine autonomous reality of its own. This youth culture is the stuff which the life of young people in peer groups expresses, the symbols which energize peer group activities, the beliefs and values which young people use to make sense for themselves of their world as they see it. Sociologists need to attend in their analyses of youth simultaneously to peer groups and to youth culture; they are the two sides of the coin of youth.

As well as being one thing over against established adult culture, youth culture is also divided into differentiated youth sub-cultures, with their own particularized ways of believing and patterns of activity. These need to be classified broadly (for example, conformist, deviant, rebellious, and criminal sub-cultures), and also more concretely (for example, hippies, skinheads, mods, punks, etc., etc.) These differentiations into distinct sub-cultures are a product both of forces within the age system, and of forces from outside such as education, class, race, and politics.

With all of what I have said so far in this section, the currently dominant approach to youth culture is in conflict. The best account of this alternative approach is Brake's — *The Sociology of Youth Culture and Youth Sub-Cultures*, which in this respect is largely derivative from Hall and Jefferson's *Resistance Through Rituals*.[37] The two approaches seem to me to be mutually exclusive:

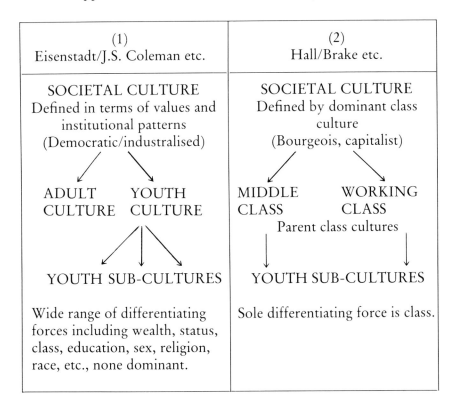

(1) Eisenstadt/J.S. Coleman etc.	(2) Hall/Brake etc.
SOCIETAL CULTURE Defined in terms of values and institutional patterns (Democratic/industralised)	SOCIETAL CULTURE Defined by dominant class culture (Bourgeois, capitalist)
ADULT YOUTH CULTURE CULTURE	MIDDLE WORKING CLASS CLASS Parent class cultures
YOUTH SUB-CULTURES	YOUTH SUB-CULTURES
Wide range of differentiating forces including wealth, status, class, education, sex, religion, race, etc., none dominant.	Sole differentiating force is class.

David Marsland

Relations Within the Age System

Youth is not self-contained. A major focus of the sociology of youth has to be the relations between age groups, particularly relations between young people and adults, generally and in particular spheres (parent/child, teacher/pupil, young worker/ manager, etc.) Because of youth's transitional status, and because of the nature of peer groups and youth culture, these relations are necessarily problematical to a degree. The emphasis in the literature is perhaps too much on difference, conflict, and problems. But there can be little doubt that relations between young people and adults are in almost all known societies fraught with difficulties for young people and for adults alike. Hence in part the Youth Service. Blame and accusation in either direction is naive and unhelpful. What we need is to know about it and to understand it, and in our professional roles to minimize its damaging effects.

In general young people seem to be faced with an arbitrary oscillation between authoritarianism and *laissez-faire* neglect on the part of even the most well-meaning adults, including certainly many teachers. How can just and effective relations be established? Within the family especially, but also more generally, young people have to resist, and establish their independence. There are deep, persistent psychological causes for conflict between youth and adults. These make any once for all solution a fantasy. The difficulty recurs, escalates, subsides, and re-appears throughout history in every sort of society. These issues have commonly been examined in terms of the notion of a 'generation gap'. Usually this really means age group conflict. It passes with the ending of youth, and today's misunderstood young man is tomorrow's uncomprehending adult. Generations as such are only involved if youth age groups carry new and deviant ideas forward beyond their own youth into adulthood. How common, we need to ask, is general disaffection by young people from the values of the 'older generation'? How common and serious does it need to be before we treat it as other than entirely normal? What are the sources and causes of normal and abnormal levels of disaffection and conflict? And what should we do about it?[38]

Youth and Social Change

This is a fundamental theme in the sociology of youth for more and better reasons than the counter-cultural movement of the sixties and the student revolt, important though these were. Young people always have a crucial role in relation to social change. Because of the transitional status of young people, because of the relative freedom compared with children which they have to be allowed, and because their commitment to basic values and involvement in established roles has not yet been tied up — youth is always a weak and crucial link in the chain of social and cultural reproduction. If this process of reproduction fails, then by definition social change occurs.

Time and again, in circumstances of many distinct sorts (for example, in the movement towards socialism in Russia from 1880 to 1917, in the development of national socialism in Germany from 1920 to 1933, in the Arab revolutions of the 1940s and 1950s, in China and Cuba in the decades before their communist revolutions, in Iran since the 1960s in the events leading towards the Islamic revolution, etc.) young people appear to have played a leading role in radical social change — left, right, religious, and so on. In contemporary Britain, the issue seems to be whether and to what extent young people represent a vanguard of disaffection and innovation against the values and institutions of — capitalism, competitive industrialism, perhaps even modernism in any form? Naturally, in this context the significance of large-scale structural youth unemployment (some five million in the Europe of the ten) looms very large. How will it be handled? Where might it lead? What determines the choice between sullen apathy, the fun alternative, and outright revolt?

This area is especially important for those working in the Youth Service and in education more broadly, since the attitudes to society and to social change taken by youth workers and teachers in their influence on the young people may be crucial.[39]

Sociology of Youth

These themes, the sets of issues they point up, and their inter-relations, define the main structure for an adequate sociological analysis of youth. They are illustrated in the diagram below. They need to be worked through in their own right — and applied to the various concrete contexts of young people's lives, including not least of all the school. Past studies of young people and the family, school, work, community, race, etc., which fail to frame their analysis in terms of the ideas raised by this model may be interesting, but they are unlikely to contribute much to an authentic understanding of young people's situation.

David Marsland

Themes in the Sociology of Youth

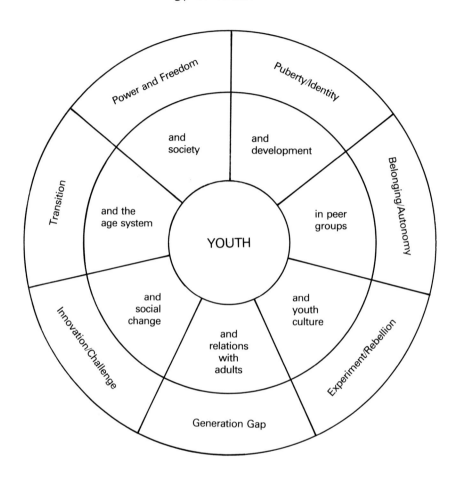

Power and Freedom / and society / and the age system / **Transition** / **Innovation/Challenge** / and social change / and relations with adults / Generation Gap / and youth culture / **Experiment/Rebellion** / in peer groups / **Belonging/Autonomy** / and development / **Puberty/Identity** / **YOUTH**

Education and Youth

Secondary school pupils are all, in bio-psychological and social terms alike, adolescents and members of the age group of youth. This fact matters to young people themselves and to their parents and teachers, who share the responsibility with them for their education. It affects at every turn what is possible, what is desirable and what is optimal in the educational process. I am even more strongly persuaded now than when I began work on this book that to a significant degree current weaknesses in our schools are attributable to our collective failure to acknowledge and to adapt effectively to the fact of school pupils' youthfulness. They are not children and we cannot treat them as if they were with impunity.

They are not adults either, and we do them nothing but harm if we pretend otherwise.

What educationists need from social scientists if they are to take this challenge seriously is the following:-

1 Coherent concepts of adolescence and youth.
2 Sensible, testable, corrigible theories of adolescence and youth.
3 Psychological and sociological knowledge about young people which is reliable and useable in practice.

In my judgment psychology already answers the first two criteria adequately. Sociology, I conclude sadly, does not as yet answer either adequately. It could, and it will: but this will require of sociologists more attention to research on young people, and a greater willingness to sacrifice theoretical dogma when it comes into conflict with evidence. The third criterion is beyond the reach of either discipline except in some specialized areas such as intelligence testing, group work, and cognitive development. Yet this criterion provides, in the long run, the ultimate test of the two earlier criteria. Concepts and theories of adolescence and youth are futile unless and until they provide the basis of reliable knowledge which can be put to practical use. The schools need that knowledge urgently.

There will be some readers, no doubt, who will object against my programme — for extending our knowledge, psychological and sociological, about adolescence and youth, and for enabling teachers to use it in practice in the schools — that it poses grave dangers of oversimplification and over-generalisation. Young people come in every shape and variety, and they are already too much liable, it might reasonably be argued, to negative stereotyping.

I grant the risk, and acknowledge that, of course, variation matters as much as commonality. Sociologists have consistently neglected the study of girls and young women, and established concepts of adolescence and youth take far too little account of gender differences[40]. Again, the special needs of British young people, male and female, of Afro-Caribbean and Asian family origin have not yet been adequately incorporated into our concepts of youth.[41] Nor have class, educational, or regional differences been as yet attended to systematically. And beyond these structural differentiations of adolescence and youth, there is the most important differentiation of all — which marks off each unique individual from the next as just that one particular, and uniquely valuable person.

All this of course has to be acknowledged and accepted. Yet all of them, all of Britain's young people, all of the pupils of our secondary schools, are also every one of them young people, with the common needs and problems of young people everywhere. The better we appreciate and understand this under-acknowledged truth, the better we shall educate them for the difficult days ahead.

Notes

1 COLEMAN, J.C. (1980), *The Nature of Adolescence*, London, Methuen.
2 SMITH, D. (1981) 'New movements in the sociology of youth', *British Journal of Sociology*, XXXII, 2; and (1983) 'Structural-functionalist accounts of youth', *Youth and Policy*, 1, 3.
3 DICKSON, A and M. (1976) *A Chance to Serve*, London, Dobson.
4 MARSLAND, D. (1978) *Sociological Explorations in the Service of Youth*, London, National Youth Bureau.
5 O'KEEFFE, D. (1981), 'Labour in Vain: Truancy, Industry, and the School Curriculum', in FLEW, A. *et al*, *The Pied Pipers of Education*, London, Social Affairs Unit; and 'Market capitalism and nationalised schooling,' *Educational Analysis*, Vol. 3, No. 1.
6 WILLIAMSON, H. (1982) 'Client responses to the Youth Opportunities Programme', in REES, T. and ATKINSON, P. *Youth Unemployment and State Intervention*, London, Routledge and Kegan Paul; and (1983) WEEP: Exploitation or Advantage?', in FIDDY, R. (Ed). *In Place of Work*, Lewes Falmer Press.
7 SHAW, B. (1983) *Comprehensive Schooling: the Impossible Dream?* Oxford, Blackwell.
8 KERRIDGE, R. (1983) *Real Wicked Guy: View of Black Britain*, Oxford, Blackwell; and (1984) *The Lone Conformist*, London, Chatto and Windus.
9 EWEN, J. (1973) *Towards a Youth Policy*, MBS Publications.
10 MUSGROVE, F. (1964) *Youth and the Social Order*, London, Routledge and Kegan Paul. MURRAY, C. and THOMPSON, F. (1985) 'The representation of authority: an adolescent viewpoint,' *Journal of Adolescence*, 18, 3, demonstrates remarkably positive attitudes by young people towards parents, teachers, and policemen.
11 MARSLAND, D. (1979) 'Youth's problems and the problem of youth', in DAY, M. and MARSLAND, D. (Eds.) *Black Kids, White Kids: What Hope?*, London, National Youth Bureau.
12 HALL, G.S. (1904) *Adolescence: Its Psychology and Its Relations to Physiology, Sociology, Sex, Crime, Religion, and Education*, New York, Appleton.
13 FREUD, A. (1958) *Adolescence, Psychoanalytic Study of Children*, and (1982) *Psycho-analytic Psychology of Normal Development, 1970–1980*, London Hogarth; WINNICOTT, D.W. (1974) *Playing and Reality*, Harmondsworth, Penguin; and (1964) *The Child, the Family, and The Outside World*, Harmondsworth, Penguin; BLOS, P. (1962) *On Adolescence*, London, Collier-MacMillan.

14 INHELDER, B. and PIAGET, J. (1958) *The Growth of Logical Thinking*, London, Routledge and Kegan Paul; KOHLBERG, L, (1969) *Stages in the Development of Moral Thought and Action*, London, Holt, Rinehart, and Winston.

15 ERIKSON, E.H. (1977) *Childhood and Society*, London, Triad/Paladin.

16 TANNER, J.M. (1978) *Foetus into Man*, London, Open Books; KAGAN, J. and MOSS, H.A. (1962) *Birth to Maturity*, New York, Wiley, EICHHORN, D. (1974) 'Biological, psychological and socio-cultural aspects of adolescence and youth', in COLEMAN, J.S. (Ed.) *Youth: Transition to Adulthood*; Chicago, Chicago University Press.

17 ADELSON, J. (Ed.) (1980), *Handbook of Adolescent Psychology*, New York Wiley; also CONGER, J.J. and PETERSON, A.C. (1984), *Adolescence and Youth; Psychological Development in a Changing World*, 3rd Edition, New York, Harper and Row.

18 PARSONS, T. (1942) 'Age and sex in the social structure of the United States', *American Sociological Review*, 7; EISENSTADT, S.N. (1956) *From Generation to Generation: Age Groups and the Social Structure*. Glencoe, Free Prees.

19 COLEMAN, J.S. (1961) *The Adolescent Society*, Glencoe, Free Press; FEUER, L.S. (1969) *The Conflict of Generations*, London, Heinemann.

20 MEAD, M. (1972) *Culture and Commitment*, New York, Panther.

21 MANNHEIM, K. (1952) 'The problem of generations', in KECSKEMETI, P. (Ed.) *Essays in the Sociology of Knowledge*, London, Routledge and Kegan Paul; MUSGOVE, F. *op. cit.*

22 MARSLAND, D. (1978) *Sociological Explorations, op. cit.*

23 ALLEN, S. (1968) 'Some theoretical problems in the study of youth', *Sociological Review*, 16, 3.

24 HALL, S. and JEFFERSON, T. (Eds.) (1976), *Resistance Through Rituals*, London, Hutchinson.

25 HALL, S. *et al.*, (1976) 'Youth: a stage of life?', *Youth in Society*, 17, pp. 19–25.

26 BRAKE, M. (1980) *The Sociology of Youth Culture and Youth Sub-cultures*, London, Routledge and Kegan Paul and (1985) *Comparative Youth Sub-Cultures*, London, Routledge and Kegan Paul.

27 MURDOCK, G. and MCCRON, R. (1979) 'Consciousness of class and consciousness of generation', in HALL and JEFFERSON, *op. cit.*; also, HEBDIDGE, D. (1979) *Subculture; the Meaning of Style*, London Methuen.

28 WILLIS, D. (1977) *Learning to Labour*, London, Saxon House; and (1978) *Profane Culture*, Routledge and Kegan Paul.

29 COHEN, S. (1979) *Folk Devils and Moral Panics*, 3rd Edition, London, McGibbon and Kee, and SMITH, D. 1981, *op. cit.*

30 O'DONNELL, M. (1985) *Age and Generation*, London, Tavistock.

31 SMITH, C. (1971) *Adolescence*, London, Longmans; EGGLESTON, J.S. (1976) *Adolescence and Community*, London, Edward Arnold.

32 The argument which follows is developed fully in MARSLAND, D. (1986) *Towards a Sociological Theory of Youth*, London, Routledge and Kegan Paul.

33 ERIKSON, E.H. *Childhood and Society, op. cit.*

34 EISENSTADT, S.N. *From Generation to Generation, op. cit.*

35 COLEMAN, J.C. *The Nature of Adolescence, op. cit.*
36 KAHANE, R. (1975) 'Informal youth organisations: a general model', *Sociological Inquiry*, 45, 4 pp. 17–28.
37 *op. cit.*
38 FEUER, L.S. (1970), *op cit*; BENGTSON V. (1970) 'The Generation Gap,' *Youth and Society*, September.
39 MUSGROVE, F. (1974) *Ecstasy and Holiness*, London Methuen; MARSLAND D. *Sociological Explorations, op. cit.*, chapters 1 and 6.
40 WALKER, S. and BARTON, L. (1983) *Gender, Class, and Education*, Lewes, Falmer Press. McROBBIE, A. (1978) *Women Take Issue*, London, Hutchinson; MARSLAND, D. (1985), Freedom and equality in alternatives to unemployment, *Youth and Policy*, 17, Spring.
41 STONE, M. (1981) *The Education of the Black Child*, London, Fontana; CASHMORE, E.E. (1984) *No Future*, London, Heinemann; CASHMORE, E.E. and TROYNA, B. (1982) *Black Youth in Crisis*, London, Allen and Unwin; DAY, M. and MARSLAND, D. (Eds.) (1979) *Black Kids, White Kids: What Hope?* London, National Youth Bureau; MARSLAND, D. (1986), 'Freedom or new slaveries?' *Social Policy and Administration*, Vol. 20, No. 1.

Adolescence and Schooling

John Coleman

Introduction

Adolescence is a complex stage of human development, for the years twelve to eighteen involve a wide range of major life changes. In fact it is unlikely that the individual undergoes greater changes at any other stage in the life-cycle apart from infancy. During the teenage years the young person experiences puberty, which has an impact on physical, physiological and psychological systems. He or she undergoes a significant maturation of cognitive function. Major changes in the self-concept are likely to occur, and there are radical alterations in all social relationships to be negotiated. How can we understand such fundamental transitions in human development, and make sense of the effects which they have upon the individual? Especially important in the context of the present book are the effects which these changes have upon the way the young person functions in the school setting, and it is primarily to this question that I shall address myself in what follows.

Broadly speaking there are two ways in which we can attempt to make sense of adolescent development. On the one hand we can look to theory. We can study theoretical notions of adolescence, and determine for ourselves the validity or logic of the different approaches. On the other hand we can turn to the research evidence. This will provide us with a factual base upon which to make an assessment of this period of the life-cycle, but will inevitably leave a wide range of questions unanswered. It is my view that neither theory nor research can at present provide a complete answer. Both have limitations, and yet both have valuable insights to offer.

Clearly the scope of the present chapter must be limited. It seems important, however, to provide some form of introduction to the educational issues raised by adolescent development, and to offer a framework for those who wish to pursue further their study of adolescence, aided no doubt by the chapters that follow. I shall therefore review briefly two major theoretical views of adolescent development, and then turn to one or two of the issues which appear most pertinent to the school context. I have chosen to cover puberty, cognition and some aspects of social development, but have deliberately excluded the topic of the peer group, since this will be covered in a subsequent chapter.

Theoretical Approaches

Of all the theories of adolescence it is evident that the psychoanalytic and sociological approaches have had the widest impact. However the two are clearly different from each other. While the psychoanalytic view concentrates on the psycho-sexual development of the individual, and looks particularly at the inner psychological factors which underlie the young person's progress toward maturation, the sociologists concentrate on the social setting of the individual, emphasizing the pressures of social expectation, the relative influence of different agents of socialization, and the nature of roles and role change. Obviously the two approaches represent alternative perspectives, yet in my opinion each are equally important in shedding light on the nature of adolescence.

The psychoanalytic view takes as its starting point the upsurge of instincts which is said to occur as a result of puberty. This increase in instinctual life, it is suggested, upsets the psychic balance which has been achieved by the end of childhood, causing internal emotional upheaval and leading to a greatly increased vulnerability of the personality (Freud, 1937). This state of affairs is associated with two further factors. In the first place, the individual's awakening sexuality leads him or her to look outside the family setting for appropriate 'love objects', thus severing the emotional ties with the parents which have existed since infancy. Secondly, the vulnerability of the personality results in the employment of psychological defences to cope with the instincts and anxiety which are, to a greater or lesser extent, maladaptive.

Blos (1962, 1967), a prominent psychoanalytic writer, has described adolescence as a 'second individuation process', the first having been completed towards the end of the third year of life. In his view both periods have certain things in common: there is an urgent need for psychological change which helps the individual adapt to maturation; there is an increased vulnerability of personality; and finally, both periods are followed by specific psychopathology should the individual run into difficulties. Furthermore, an analogy can be drawn between the transformation in early childhood from a dependent infant to a self-reliant toddler, and the adolescent transition to adult independence. In both there is a process of disengagement involving a loosening of emotional ties and a move towards a new stage of autonomy. Other features of adolescent development which are of significance to the psychoanalytic viewpoint include regression — a manifestation of behaviour more appropriate to earlier stages of development — and ambivalence.

According to the psychoanalysts, ambivalence accounts for many of the phenomena often considered incomprehensible in adolescent behaviour. For example the emotional instability of relationships, the contradictions in thought and feeling, and the apparently illogical shift from one reaction to another reflect the fluctuations between loving and hating, acceptance and rejection, involvement and non-involvement which underlie relationships in the earlier years, and which are reactivated once more in adolescence. Such fluctuations in mood and behaviour are indicative also of the young person's attitudes to growing up. Thus, while freedom may appear the most exciting of goals, there are also moments when, in the harsh light of reality, independence and the necessity to fight one's own battles becomes a daunting prospect. At these times childlike dependence exercises a powerful attraction and is manifested in periods of uncertainty and self doubt, and in behaviour which is more likely to bring to mind a wilful child than a young adult.

A consideration of ambivalence leads us onto the more general theme of non-conformity and rebellion, believed by psychoanalysts to be an almost universal feature of adolescence. Behaviour of this sort has many causes. Some of it is a direct result of ambivalent modes of relating. In other circumstances, however, it may be interpreted as an aid to the disengagement process. In this context if the parents can be construed as old-fashioned and irrelevant then the task of breaking the emotional ties becomes easier. If everything that originates from home can safely be rejected then there is nothing to be lost by giving it all up. Non-conformity thus facilitates the process of disengagement, although as many writers point out, there are a number of intermediate stages along the way.

To summarize, three particular ideas characterize the psychoanalytic position. In the first place adolescence is seen as being the period during which there is a marked vulnerability of personality, resulting primarily from the upsurge of instincts at puberty. Secondly, an emphasis is laid on the likelihood of maladaptive behaviour, stemming from the inadequacy of the psychological defences to cope with inner conflicts and tensions. Examples of such behaviour include extreme fluctuations of mood, inconsistency in relationships, depression and non-conformity. Thirdly, the process of disengagement is given special prominence, for this is perceived as a necessity if mature emotional and sexual relationships are to be established outside the home.

As has been indicated, the sociological view of adolescence encompasses a very different perspective from that of psychoanalytic theory. While there is no disagreement between the two approaches concerning the importance of the transitional process from childhood to maturity, it is on the subject of the causes of this process that the two viewpoints diverge. Thus while the one concentrates on internal factors, the other looks to society and to events outside the individual for a satisfactory explanation. For the sociologist and social psychologist 'socialization' and 'role' are two key concepts. By socialization is meant the process whereby individuals in a society absorb the values, standards and beliefs current in that society. Everyone in a society learns through the agents of socialization, such as school, home and mass media etc., the expectations associated with various roles, although as we shall see these expectations are not necessarily clear cut. Furthermore socialization may be more or less effective, depending on the nature of the agents to which the individual is exposed, the amount of conflict between the different agents and so on. During childhood the individual, by and large, has his or her roles ascribed by others, but as he or she matures through adolescence greater opportunities are available, not only for a choice of roles, but also for a choice of how those roles should be interpreted. As will become apparent it is implicit in the social-psychological view that both socialization and role assumption are more problematic during adolescence than at any other time.

Why should this be so? In attempting to answer this question we may first of all consider roles and role assumptions. It is the belief of most sociologists that a large proportion of an individual's life is characterized by engagement in a series of roles — the sum total of which is known as the role repertoire. The years between childhood and adulthood, as a period of emerging identity, are seen as particularly relevant to the construction of this role repertoire, for the following reasons. Firstly, features of adolescence such as growing independence from authority figures, involvement with peer groups, and unusual sensitivity to the evaluations of others, all provoke role transitions. Secondly any inner change or uncertainty has the effect of increasing the individual's dependence on others, and this applies particularly to the need for reassurance and support for the self-concept. Thirdly, the effects of major environmental changes are also relevant in this context; different schools, the move from school to university or college, leaving home, taking a job, all demand involvement in a new set of relationships, which in turn lead to different and often greater expectations, a substantial reassessment of the self, and an acceleration of the process of socialization. Role change, it will be apparent, is thus seen as an integral feature of adolescent development.

While role change may be one source of difficulty for the adolescent, it is certainly not the only one. Inherent in role behaviour generally are a number of potential stresses, some of which appear to be particularly relevant to young people. Role conflict is one example of such a stress. Here the individual occupies two roles which have expectations associated with them which are incompatible. Thus the individual may be caught in the middle between two people or sets of people who expect different forms of behaviour. Another example is role discontinuity. Here there is a lack of order in the transition from one role to another. One only has to think of the inexperience among school leavers of the work situation, or the grossly inadequate preparation for parenthood in our society to appreciate the point. Thirdly, we may note role incongruence. Here the individual is placed in a position for which he or she is unsuited; in other words the role ascribed by others is not the one the individual would have chosen. Good illustrations of this in the adolescent context would be parents who hold unrealistically high expectations of their teenage children, or who, alternatively, fight to maintain their adolescent sons and daughters in childlike roles.

Implicit in these theoretical notions is the view that the individual's movement through adolescence will be very much affected by the consistent or inconsistent, adaptive or maladaptive expectations held by significant people in his or her immediate environment. Up to this point our discussion has concentrated on the features of role behaviour which lead sociologists and social-psychologists to view adolescence not only as a transitional period, but as one that contains many potentially stressful characteristics.

However, the process of socialization is also seen by many as being fraught with conflict at this stage. Socialization processes inevitably interact with social change, and we may draw attention to two particular changes which have occurred in the last decades or so; the prolonged dependence of young people as a result of increased opportunities for secondary and higher education, and the decline in the role of the family. These phenomena have, in turn, had a number of consequences. In the first place, industrialized societies have witnessed increasing age segregation, with a decline in the time adults and teenagers spend together. Secondly, the peer group has assumed an ever more important role, precisely as a result of the abdication of responsibility by parents in the upbringing of their teenage children. Finally, the adolescent is exposed to a large variety of socialization agencies, including secondary school, the peer group, adult directed youth organizations, the mass media, political organizations and so on, and is thus presented with a wide range of potential conflicts in values and ideals.

To summarize, the sociological or social-psychological approach to adolescence is marked by concern with roles and role change, and with the process of socialization. There can be little doubt that adolescence, from this point of view, is seen as being dominated by stress and tension, not so much because of inner emotional instability, but as a result of conflicting pressures from outside. Thus, by considering the two major theoretical approaches, we have reviewed two mutually complementary but essentially different views of adolescent development. Let us now turn to the topics mentioned earlier which have a direct bearing on schooling. In the course of such a discussion we shall have the opportunity of examining the relevance of each of the two theoretical viewpoints.

Puberty

Puberty, and the physical growth that accompanies it, is important to those involved in education for a number of reasons. In the first place puberty has a range of physiological effects which are not always outwardly apparent to observers, but which can nonetheless have a considerable impact on the individual. Secondly, rates of maturation vary enormously, leading inevitably to questions of normality and comparability between young people. Furthermore, especially early or unusually late developers have particular difficulties to face, which again have marked implications for classroom performance and behaviour. Thirdly, physical development cannot fail to have psychological consequences, often affecting self-concept and self-esteem, factors which themselves play a major part in motivation and learning. Thus it can be seen that an understanding of puberty is essential in making sense of adolescent development as a whole. I shall deal with each of these areas in turn.

Adults often fail to appreciate that puberty is accompanied by changes not only in the reproductive system and in the secondary sexual characteristics of the individual, but in the functioning of the heart and thus of the cardio-vascular system, in the lungs, which in turn affect the respiratory system, in the size and the strength of many of the muscles of the body, and so on. One of the many physical changes associated with puberty is the 'growth spurt'. This term is usually taken to refer to the accelerated rate of increase in height and weight that occurs during early adolescence. It is essential to bear in mind, however, that there are very considerable individual differences in the age of onset and duration of the growth spurt, even among perfectly normal children. This is a fact which parents and adolescents themselves frequently fail to appreciate, thus causing a great deal of unnecessary anxiety. In boys the growth spurt may begin as early as ten years of age, or as late as sixteen, while in girls the same process can begin at seven or eight, or not until twelve, thirteen or even fourteen. For the average boy, though, rapid growth begins at about thirteen, and reaches a peak somewhere during the fourteenth year. Comparable ages for girls are eleven for the onset of the growth spurt and twelve for the peak age of increase in height and weight. Other phenomena associated with the growth spurt are rapid increase in size and weight of the heart (the weight of the heart nearly doubles at puberty), accelerated growth of the lungs, and a decline in basal metabolism. Noticeable to children themselves, especially to boys, is a marked increase in physical strength and endurance (see Tanner, 1978, for a full description).

Sexual maturation is closely linked with the physical changes described above. Again the sequence of events is approximately eighteen to twenty-four months later for boys than it is for girls. Since individuals mature at very different rates, one girl at the age of fourteen may be small, have no bust and look very much as she did during childhood, while another of the same age may look like a fully developed adult woman, who could easily be taken for someone four or five years in advance of her actual chronological age. Such marked physical differences will have particular consequences for the individual's psychological adjustment.

The issue of especially early or late development is one to

which considerable attention has been paid in the literature. Studies have shown that whether puberty occurs early or late bears little relation to abnormality in physical development. Thus, for example, slowness in beginning the growth spurt does not appear in any way to be indicative of later physical difficulty. However, there is good evidence from both Europe and North America to show that those who mature earlier physically score higher on most tests of mental ability and perform better in the classroom than their less mature peers. The differences between the groups are not great but are consistent. One implication of this is that in age-linked examinations physically fast maturers have an advantage over those who develop more slowly (Tanner, 1978).

The age of onset of puberty is also associated with other psychological consequences. Results of work carried out at the University of California (for review see Conger and Petersen, 1984) have shown that where boys are concerned those who were among the slowest twenty per cent to develop physically were rated by adults as less attractive, less socially mature, and more restless, talkative and bossy. In addition they were seen by their peers as being less popular, and few of them were leaders. On a personality test the group revealed more feelings of inadequacy and negative self-perceptions. Many of these difficulties appear to persist over a period of time, for when they were followed up at the age of thirty-three the majority of the group still showed difficulties in personal adjustment.

Whereas for boys it is slow physical development which appears to be associated with poor psychological adjustment, the picture among girls is rather more complicated. Differences between early and late maturing girls are not as great, and furthermore the advantages and disadvantages of early versus late maturation may vary with time. Thus one study showed that among twelve year-old girls early maturation was a definite handicap in relation to social prestige. At this age girls value more highly the personality traits associated with the pre-pubertal stage of development than those related to sexual maturity. However, by fourteen or fifteen the picture had changed, and traits associated with early maturation were, by this time, the more highly valued. Other studies have shown differences in interests between thirteen year olds who have reached puberty and those who have not. Thus there appears to be little doubt that the age of onset of puberty is associated with particular patterns of psychological adjustment. In general, apart from young adolescent girls, early maturation is related to general self-confidence and social maturity. This is hardly surprising given the advantages, both in terms of physique and self image, which stem from early maturation. In view of this the most important task for adults in this sphere is undoubtedly to work to counteract the psychological disadvantages faced by the late maturer.

The changes discussed above inevitably exercise a profound effect upon the individual. The body alters radically in size and shape, and it is not surprising that many adolescents experience a period of clumsiness in an attempt to adapt to these changes. The body also alters in function, and new and sometimes worrying physical experiences, such as the girl's first period, have to be understood. Perhaps most important of all, however, is the effect that such physical changes have upon identity. As many writers have pointed out, the development of the individual's identity requires not only the notion of being separate and different from others, but also a sense of self-consistency, and a firm knowledge of how one appears to the rest of the world. Needless to say dramatic bodily changes seriously affect these aspects of identity, and represent a considerable challenge in adaptation for even the most well-adjusted young person. It is unfortunate that many adults, having successfully forgotten much of their own adolescent anxiety, retain only a vague awareness of the psychological impact of the physical changes associated with puberty.

Experimental evidence has clearly shown that the average adolescent is not only sensitive to, but often critical of his or her changing physical self. Thus, probably as a result of the importance of films and television, teenagers tend to have idealized norms for physical attractiveness, and to feel inadequate if they do not match these unrealistic criteria. Studies have shown that adolescents who perceive themselves as deviating physically from cultural stereotypes are likely to have impaired self-concepts, and the important role that physical characteristics play in determining self esteem, especially in the younger adolescent, has been underlined by many writers (Brooks-Gunn and Petersen, 1983). Other studies have been reported in which young people were asked what they did and did not like about themselves. Results showed that those in early adolescence used primarily physical characteristics to describe themselves, and it was these characteristics which were most often disliked. It was not until later adolescence that intellectual or social aspects of the personality were widely used in self-descriptions, but these characteristics were much more frequently liked than disliked (see Coleman, 1980).

It can be seen therefore that some understanding of puberty and its effects is essential in the school context. Research evidence has certainly underlined the wide ranging implications of physical change in early adolescence but has not, in my view, provided much support for the psychoanalytic notion of psychological upheaval which is supposed to go hand-in-hand with puberty. It is clear that the self concept, particularly that aspect of it associated with physical characteristics, does undergo substantial change which may well result in some temporary instability. Nonetheless this hardly constitutes the sort of vulnerability of personality described in the theoretical literature, and while on the one hand it is obviously extremely important for adults to pay attention to the psychological effects of puberty, particularly for late developers, on the other hand it seems essential not to exaggerate the extent of the effect of these aspects of maturation.

Cognition

Those involved in education will no doubt be more aware than others of the range and significance of cognitive development during adolescence. In a short review such as this it is possible only to draw attention to the major themes, and to highlight one or two of the most significant areas of recent work in this field. For those wishing to read further good general discussions of cognition in adolescence are to be found in Adelson (1980), Serafica (1982) and Conger and Petersen (1984).

Changes in intellectual functioning during the teenage years have implications for a wide range of behaviours and attitudes. Such changes render possible the move towards independence of both thought and action, they enable the young person to develop a time-perspective which includes the future, they facilitate progress towards maturity in relationships, and finally they underlie the individual's ability to participate in society as worker, voter, responsible group member and so on. We cannot consider these changes without looking first at the work of Piaget, for it is he who has laid the foundation for almost all subsequent work on cognitive development. It will be worthwhile also to discuss briefly some work on adolescent reasoning and to review ideas on both moral and political thought in adolescence.

The work of Jean Piaget, the Swiss psychologist, is the most obvious starting place for a consideration of cognitive development during the teenage years. It was he who first pointed out that a qualitative change in the nature of mental ability, rather than any simple increase in cognitive skill, is to be expected at or around puberty, and he has argued that it is at this point in development that formal operational thought finally becomes possible (Inhelder and Piaget, 1958). A full description of Piaget's stages of cognitive growth is not possible here. Most readers will be familiar with his assertion that in early adolescence the individual moves from a stage of concrete operations to one of formal operational thought. With the appearance of this stage a number of capabilities become available to the young person. Perhaps the most significant of these is the ability to construct 'contrary to fact' propositions. This change has been described as the shift of emphasis in adolescent thought from the 'real' to the 'possible', and it facilitates hypothetico-deductive logic. It also enables the individual to think about mental constructs as objects that can be manipulated, and to come to terms with notions of probability and belief.

This fundamental difference in approach between the young child and the adolescent has been neatly demonstrated in a study by Elkind (1966). He showed dramatic differences between eight and nine year-olds and thirteen and fourteen year-olds in their capacity to solve a concept-formation problem by setting up hypotheses and then testing them out in logical succession. However, it is clear that formal operational thought cannot be tested using a single problem or task. Any investigator must use a range of tests, in an attempt to construct some overall measure of the individual's ability to tackle problems of logical thought in a number of areas. In relation to this it is important to bear in mind that the development of formal thinking is certainly not an all-or-none-affair, with the individual moving overnight from one stage to another. The change occurs slowly, and there may even be some shifting back and forth before the new mode of thought is firmly established. Furthermore it is almost certain that the adolescent will adopt formal modes of thinking in one area before another. Thus for example someone interested in arts subjects may use formal operational thinking in the area of verbal reasoning well before he or she is able to utilize such skills in scientific problem solving.

In addition to these points recent research indicates that in all probability Piaget was a little too optimistic when he expressed the view that the majority of adolescents could be expected to develop formal operational thought by twelve or thirteen years of age. While studies do not entirely agree on the exact proportions reaching various stages at different age levels, there is general consensus that up to the age of sixteen only a minority reach the most advanced level of formal thought (Coleman, 1980).

Studies show that intelligence is likely to play a role in the development of formal operational thinking. Yet this variable is not sufficient to explain why formal operations appear in one child at twelve, and in another at sixteen. Inhelder and Piaget (1958) paid remarkably little attention to this problem, contenting themselves simply with some speculation about the relation between intellectual and social development. They appear to suggest that as social pressures operate on the individual, encouraging him or her towards maturity and independence, so intellectual skills develop, enabling the young person to cope with the new demands of a more adult life. This is hardly a very satisfactory explanation, although it may indeed turn out that social and intellectual maturation are correlated.

Surprisingly there is little in the literature which sheds much light on such an important topic, as Niemark (1975) indicates. We may ask what other factors might be involved. Intelligence only contributes a small proportion of the total variance. Perhaps attention should be paid to the type of school and the attitudes of teachers. Studies have indicated that self-image might be important, but what about achievement motivation, or position in the peer group? Also, the impact of parental attitudes and the home environment should undoubtedly be examined. At this point, it must be accepted that there are no definite answers to the question of what it is which determines the appearance of formal operational thinking. It is already clear that many factors will be involved, and the solution is unlikely to be a simple one. However, one thing is certain; this is a question which needs to be answered as soon as possible if the psychology of Piaget is to remain relevant to the education of young people today.

To study adolescent reasoning is obviously another way of looking at cognitive development. David Elkind (1967) represents a good example of someone seeking to extend Piaget's original notions in this way. He argues that while the attainment of formal operational thinking frees the individual in many respects from childhood egocentrism, paradoxically at the same time it entangles him or her in a new version of the same thing. This is because the achievement of formal operational thought allows the adolescent to think about not only his own thought, but also about the thought of other people. It is this capacity to take account of other people's thinking, argues Elkind, which is the basis of adolescent egocentrism. Essentially the individual finds it extremely difficult to differentiate between what others are thinking about and his own preoccupations. He assumes that if he is obsessed by a thought or a problem then other people must also be obsessed by the same thing. One example given by Elkind is that of the adolescent's appearance. To a large extent teenagers are preoccupied with the way they look to others, and they make the assumption that others must be as involved as they are with the same subject. Elkind ties this type of egocentrism in with the concept of what he calls 'the imaginary audience'. Because of this egocentrism the adolescent is, either in actual or fantasized social situations, anticipating the reactions of others. However, these reactions are based on a premise that others are as admiring or critical of him as he is of himself. Thus he is continually constructing and reacting to his 'imaginary audience', a fact which, according to Elkind, explains a lot of adolescent behaviour — the self-consciousness, the wish for privacy, and the long hours spent in front of the mirror. Recent work (reviewed in Conger and Petersen, 1984) has provided strong corroboration for Elkind's views.

Another area of interest to researchers in the field of cognitive development is that of moral and political thought. How is this changed by formal operations? Do young people pass through different stages of thinking where morals and politics are concerned, and if so, what is the nature of such stages? As far as moral thinking is concerned it is once again Piaget's notions which have formed the springboard for later thinking on this subject, and although there have been a number of different theories put forward to explain the development of concepts of morality in young people, the 'cognitive-developmental' approach of Piaget and Kohlberg has undoubtedly been the most influential. In his work on the moral judgment of the child, Piaget described two major stages of moral thinking. The first, which he called 'moral realism', refers to a period during which young children make judgments on an objective basis, for example by estimating the amount of damage which has been caused in an accident. Thus a child who breaks twelve cups is considered more blameworthy than one who only breaks one cup, regardless of the circumstances. The second stage, applying usually to those between the ages of eight and twelve, has been described as that of the 'morality of cooperation', or the 'morality of reciprocity'. During this stage, Piaget believed, decisions concerning morality were usually made on a subjective basis, and often depended on an estimate of intention rather than consequence.

Kohlberg (1969) has elaborated Piaget's scheme into one which has six different stages. His method has been to present hypothetical situations concerning moral dilemmas to young people of different ages, and to classify their responses according to a stage theory of moral development. Some of Kohlberg's most interesting work has involved the study of moral development in different cultures. He has shown that an almost identical sequence appears to occur in widely different cultures, the variation between cultures being found in the rate of development, and the fact that in the more primitive societies later stages of thinking are rarely used.

As in the case of moral judgment the young person's political ideas are likely to be significantly influenced by his or her level of cognitive development. In recent years a number of writers have become interested in the shift which takes place during the adolescent years, from a lack of political thought to — in many cases — an intense involvement in this area of life. How does this occur and what are the processes involved? At what age do adolescents begin to show an increasing grasp of political concepts, and what stages do they go through before they achieve maturity of political judgment? One of the most important early studies was that undertaken by Adelson and O'Neill (1966). They approached the problem of the growth of political ideas in an imaginative way by posing for young people of different ages the following problem: 'Imagine that a thousand men and women, dissatisfied with the way things are going in their own country, decide to purchase and move to an island in the Pacific; once there they must devise laws and modes of government.' They then explored the adolescents' approach to a variety of relevant issues. They asked questions about how a government would be formed, what would its purpose be, would there be a need for laws and political parties, how would you protect minorities, and so on. The investigators proposed different laws, and explored typical problems of public policy.

The major results may be discussed under two headings — the changes in modes of thinking, and the decline of authoritarianism with age. As far as the first is concerned, there was a marked shift in thinking from the concrete to the abstract, a finding which ties in well with the work discussed above.

The second major shift observed was the decline in authoritarian solutions to political questions. The typical young adolescent appeared unable to appreciate that problems can have more than one solution, and that individual behaviour or political acts are not necessarily absolutely right or wrong, good or bad. The concept of moral relativism was not yet available for the making of political judgments. In contrast the fourteen or fifteen year old is much more aware of the different sides of any argument, and is usually able to take a relativistic point of view. Thinking begins to be more tentative, more critical and more pragmatic.

Although there have been a few later studies in this area the field has by and large been very much neglected. Schaffer and Hargreaves (1978), in their statement on research priorities in the United Kingdom, point to the topic of political thought and political socialization in adolescence as being in urgent need of further consideration. It is a topic of particular interest, not only because of its obvious implications for education and government, but also because of the manner in which intellectual change can be seen to interact with social behaviour. This is not to say that other areas of cognitive development are not of equal value and importance, and it is to be hoped that this section may have acted as a signpost, if nothing more, towards issues of general interest.

Social Relationships

I intend in this section to concentrate particularly on the role of adults, and on the nature and significance of relationships between young people and parents, teachers and important others. Peer relationships will be dealt with in the next chapter. In selecting issues which will be of relevance to the educational context, I have chosen the development of independence, and adults as role models, since out of the many available these seemed to me to be two of the most obviously pertinent.

One of the central themes of adolescent development is the attainment of independence, often represented symbolically in art and literature by the moment of departure from home. However, for most young people today independence is not gained at one specific moment by the grand gesture of saying goodbye to one's parents and setting off to seek one's fortune in the wide world. Independence is much more likely to mean the freedom to make new relationships, and personal freedom to take responsibility for oneself in such things as education, work, political beliefs and future career choice.

There are many forces which interact in propelling an individual towards a state of maturity. Naturally both physical and intellectual maturation encourage the adolescent towards greater autonomy. In addition to these factors there are, undoubtedly, psychological forces within the individual as well as social forces within the environment which have the same goal. In the psychoanalytic view, mentioned earlier, the process of seeking independence represents the need to break off the infantile ties with the parents, thus making new mature sexual relationships possible. From the perspective of the sociologist, more emphasis is placed on the changes in role and status which lead to a re-definition of the individual's place in the social structure. Whatever the explanation it is certainly true that the achievement of independence is an integral feature of adolescent development, and that the role of the adults involved is an especially important one.

In understanding this process it is necessary to appreciate that the young person's movement towards adulthood is far from straightforward. While independence at times appears to be a rewarding goal, there are moments when it is a worrying, even frightening, prospect. Childlike dependence can be safe and comforting at no matter what age, if for example one is facing problems or difficulties alone, and it is essential to realize that no individual achieves adult independence without a number of backward glances. It is this ambivalence which underlies the typically contradictory behaviour of adolescence, behaviour which is so often the despair of adults. Thus there is nothing more frustrating than having to deal with a teenager who is at one moment complaining about adults who are always interfering, and the next bitterly protesting that no one takes any interest. However, it is equally important to acknowledge that adults themselves usually hold conflicting attitudes towards young people. On the one hand they may wish them to be independent, to make their own decisions, and to cease making childish demands, whilst on the other they may be anxious about the consequences of independence, and sometimes jealous of the opportunities and idealism of youth. In addition it should not be forgotten that the adolescent years often coincide with the difficulties of middle age for parents in particular. Adjusting to unfulfilled hopes, the possibility of retirement, declining physical health, marital difficulties and so on, may all increase family stress, and add further to the problems faced by young people in finding a satisfactory route to independence.

Research evidence has not provided much support for the notion that wide ranging conflict between adults and young people is the order of the day. Coleman (1980) and Conger and Petersen (1984), in reviewing the data available, come to the conclusion that the general picture that emerges from experimental studies is that of relatively harmonious relationships with adults for the majority of young people. Of course adolescents do seek independence, of that there is no dispute, and so the question arises as to how common sense and research evidence can be fitted together. In the first place it is clear that some adolescents do, temporarily at least, come into conflict with or become critical of adults. In addition there is no doubt that some adults do become restrictive, attempting to slow down the pace of change. Research has shown that there are a number of factors which affect the extent of the conflict occurring between the generations. Cultural background, adult behaviour, age and social class all need to be taken into account.

Other aspects of the situation need also to be borne in mind. For example there is undoubtedly a difference between attitudes towards close family members, and attitudes to more general social groupings, such as 'the younger generation'. Thus, for example, teenagers may very well approve of and look up to their own parents while expressing criticism of adults in general. Similarly, parents may deride 'drop-outs', 'skin-heads', or 'soccer hooligans' while holding a favourable view of their own adolescent sons and daughters. Another fact that needs to be stressed is that there is a difference between feeling and behaviour. Adolescents may be irritated or angry with their parents as a result of day-to-day conflicts, but issues can be worked out in the home, and do not necessarily lead to outright rejection or rebellion. Furthermore too little credit is given to the possibility that adults and young people, although disagreeing with each other about certain things, may still respect each other's views, and live or work together in relative harmony. Thus there seems to be little doubt that the extreme view of a generation gap, involving the notion of a war between the generations, or the idea of a separate adolescent sub-culture, is dependent on a myth. It is the result of a stereotype which is useful to the mass media, and given currency by a small minority of disaffected young people and resentful adults. However, to deny any sort of conflict between teenagers and older members of society is equally false. Adolescents could not grow into adults unless they were able to test out the boundaries of authority, nor could they discover what they believed unless given the opportunity to push hard against the beliefs of others. The adolescent transition from dependence to independence is almost certain to involve some conflict, but its extent should not be exaggerated.

Adults fulfill many different functions for the developing adolescent, and one of these functions, one that is less visible than many others, is the provision of role models. Here the adult represents an example of the way such things as sex roles and work roles may be interpreted. The adult provides a model or an image, which the young person, in a partly conscious and partly unconscious manner, uses to develop his or her own role behaviour. It is of course true that children throughout their early lives depend on their parents and other adults for primary knowledge of such role behaviour, but obviously these models become crucial during adolescence, since it is at this time that the young person begins to make his or her own role choices. Thus, for example, while parents' attitudes to work will be pertinent all through childhood, these will become relevant in a somewhat more direct and more immediate way when the teenager is facing questions about what he or she is going to do after leaving school. As we have seen earlier role change is likely to be a major feature of adolescent development, and it will be evident therefore that the role models available to the young person at this stage in life will be of great significance.

It is important to be clear, however, that the likelihood of role decisions or role choices being influenced by adults will be determined not only by the nature of the role model, but also by the type of relationship between adult and young person. We cannot here enter into a discussion of identification, but we should note the obvious fact that role modelling is likely to be enhanced by a positive emotional quality in the relationship between the individuals concerned, as well as by the structure of the family, school or other institution, and the young person's involvement in decision-making processes.

It is unfortunate that almost all research on role modelling has concentrated on the family, since it is undoubtedly true that teachers, as well as other significant adults, have an important part to play in this sphere. To give one example of sex role modelling, research has indicated that boys whose fathers provide a moderately masculine role model, but who are also involved in the feminine, caring side of family life, adjust better as adults and experience fewer conflicts between their social values and their actual behaviour. Boys whose fathers provide role models which are at either extreme — excessively masculine, or predominantly feminine — appear to adjust less well (see Conger and Petersen, 1984).

Where work role models are concerned, research has shown that close positive relationships are most likely to facilitate the use of the parents as a role model, although this does not necessarily mean taking the same type of job as the mother or father. Much more important here are the transmission of attitudes to work, and the general area of work interests. In one study women's attitudes to work were assessed as a function of their mothers' own attitudes and experiences. Results showed that women between the ages of nineteen and twenty-two held attitudes towards work and everything associated with it which were directly related to (although not necessarily the same as) their mother's attitudes and experiences. In brief, where the mothers had had positive experiences — in whatever work role they had chosen, including that of mother and housewife — then their daughters were likely also to be well adjusted in their attitudes to work and career. Where mothers had experienced conflict over work, or were dissatisfied with their own work experiences, it was likely that their daughters would have similar adjustment difficulties (Coleman, 1980).

Thus it can be seen that adults have a critical part to play in this sphere. Because the nature of the influence involved is usually indirect, the force of the impact that significant adults have in this respect is rarely fully acknowledged. What is certain is that more research is needed since, as all the reviews indicate, we are only just beginning to discover something of the process which occurs. Even in situations of unemployment role modelling is crucial. Here it has been shown that the attitudes that young people hold towards work, and the determination and persistence they apply to overcoming the enormous problems of being without work, are directly related to the behaviour of the role models they have available. Teachers and educationalists in particular should bear in mind that schools offer powerful, influential adult role models at just the time in the young person's life when role models are most needed. In my view it is part of the adult's responsibility, in his or her work with adolescents, to be aware of this aspect of the relationship that is created between them.

In brief, then, two aspects of social relationships between adults and young people have been reviewed. Conclusions from both areas underline the critical part that parents, teachers and others have to play in facilitating the major transitions which occur during adolescence. Both theory and research provide support for this argument, and it is one which has a special relevance in the educational context. Here teenagers are in constant interaction with adults, and yet all too frequently this interaction is perceived, by both sides, as having a narrow and rather specific focus. As this chapter has tried to indicate, adults in the school setting are inevitably involved in far more than the conveying of information. It is to be hoped that the comments made here will encourage readers to consider the psychology of adolescence, and the lessons it has for all within education.

References

ADELSON, J. (Ed.) (1980) *Handbook of Adolescent Psychology*, New York, John Wiley.

ADELSON, J. and O'NEILL, R. (1966) 'The development of political thought in adolescence', *Journal of Personality and Social Psychology*, 4, pp. 295–308.

BLOS, P. (1962) *On Adolescence*, Collier-Macmillan, London.

BLOS, P. (1967) 'The second individuation process of adolescence, ' *Psychoanalytic Study of the Child*, 22, pp. 162–86.

BROOKS-GUNN, J. and PETERSEN, A. (Eds.) (1983) *Girls at Puberty*, New York, Plenum.

COLEMAN, J.C. (1980) *The Nature of Adolescence*, London, Methuen.

CONGER, J. and PETERSEN, A. (1984) *Adolescence and Youth*, 3rd Edition. New York, Harper and Row.

ELKIND, D. (1966) 'Conceptual orientation shifts in children and adolescents', *Child Development*, 37, pp. 493–8.

ELKIND, D. (1967) 'Egocentrism in adolescence,' *Child Development*, 38, pp. 1025–34.

FREUD, A. (1937) *The Ego and the Mechanisms of Defence*, London, Hogarth Press.

INHELDER, B. and PIAGET, J. (1958) *The Growth of Logical Thinking*, London, Routledge and Kegan Paul.

KOHLBERG, L. (1969) *Stages in the Development of Moral Thought and Action*, New York, Holt, Rinehart and Winston.

NEIMARK, E.D. (1975) 'Intellectual development during adolescence,' in HOROWITZ, F.D. (Ed.), *Review of Child Development Research*, Vol. 4, Chicago, University of Chicago Press.

SCHAFFER, H.R. and HARGREAVES, D. (1978) 'Young people in society: A research initiative by the SSRC,' *Bulletin of the British Psychological Society*, 31, pp. 91–4.

SERAFICA, F.C. (Ed.) (1982) *Social-Cognitive Development in Context*, London, Methuen.

TANNER, J.M. (1978) *Foetus into Man*, London, Open Books.

Peers, Subcultures, and Schools

David M. Smith

Introduction

Youth is said to differ from other age categories in its relationship to
a number of key institutions. A wide theoretical spectrum of writers
argue that what makes youth different is that it is less tightly
attached to the institutions of family and work than are adults, and
less tightly attached to education and the family than are younger
children. Children are firmly integrated into the family in subordinate roles, adults through their dominant roles. Youth, on the other
hand, are no longer expected to play the submissive roles of childhood, neither do they yet have the adult status which allows them
access fully to adult roles. In Britain *all children* are obliged to
attend school until the age of sixteen and traditionally most have
then gone into apprenticeships, training or further and higher education. In school they retain the subordinate status of children. In
other fields they are able to experiment with a wider range of adult
roles — but still it is experiment. What is more since they are either
learning a trade or profession (even if it is only YTS), or in a
deadend job, or in school which retains some of the discipline and
non-responsible status of childhood, they are less integrated (it is
argued) into any of these institutions than are members of other age
categories.

Yet, in order to learn adult roles and acquire adult status they
necessarily must have freedom to experiment, and the freedom, at
least initially, to get adult roles wrong. It is in this sense that youth
status is often described as 'irresponsible'. They are obliged in
seeking adult status to move from the non-responsibility of childhood to the supposed responsibility of adults.[1] Given this analysis,
it is hardly surprising that it is their relations with their peers,

particularly in the context of leisure, which is so central to the study of youth. The peer group provides both the support and the opportunity for experiment. Leisure provides a context within which youth — and youth alone — has the time and relative affluence to experience.[2]

There is little disagreement, in general terms, about the peculiar relationship which youth has to these institutional arrangements. Eisenstadt[3] sees the functionality of youth groups in filling precisely these gaps left by other institutions. Parsons defines youth as 'more or less irresponsible' with its emphasis on 'having a good time' which may lead to 'at least a certain recalcitrance to the pressure of adult expectations and discipline'.[4] From a very different theoretical viewpoint Clarke *et al*[5] argue that youth subcultures should be seen in terms of what they call generational experience.[6] 'Generational experience', they claim, is to be understood in terms of 'different sets of institutions and experiences from those of its parents'.[7] The institutions concerned are those of education, work and leisure. Their experiences are developed in relation to peers and in the context of various 'youth subcultures'. Any disagreement is not about the significance of these institutions or the central role of the peer group, it is rather, about the generality of the status of youth. Much of the American work on youth[8] sees youth as a relatively homogeneous category which has a central role in social change or social conformity. The Neo-Marxist (mostly British) view is that youth is certainly not homogeneous and much less centrally significant (in some cases not at all). The significance and nature of youth as a category is an issue which dogs all aspects of the Sociology of Youth. It has significance for how we see the peer group, how we see the educational experience of young people, and how we see the significance of the peer group for education.

Peers, peer groups and gangs

Peter Musgrave, in what was surely the most influential book of the 1960s for British educational practitioners, defines the peer group as 'a homogeneous age group', and argues that 'in such a group a child can gain certain experiences that he cannot possibly have in the normal family, particularly the small sized nuclear family usual in contemporary industrialized society'.[9] This is the traditional, essentially structural-functionalist, view of the influence of peers. Peers affect secondary socialization in the spaces left by other institutions, particularly the family and the school. This literature uses a number of distinct terms to refer to the size and structural complexity of peer groups.

The 'largest of the social units formed by adolescents'[10] is THE CROWD. Crowds are seen to be made up of a number of cliques which are 'smaller and more purposefully organized than is the crowd'[11] However, as Dunphy in a thorough analysis of the terminology, has argued, 'A wide survey of the use of these terms in the literature reveals no clear indication of the relative size limits of the two types of group or agreement on what different functions, if any, these two groups perform for their members'[12] He attempts to correct this lack of coherence in his own study of Australian adolescents, in which he claims that 'the crowd is essentially an association of cliques'[13], but that while the 'clique centers mainly around talking'[14], the crowd 'is the center of larger, more organized social activities, such as parties and dances which provide for interaction between the sexes'[15]. The function of the peer group is largely concerned with managing the move from same sex to hetero-sexual social relations, and he plots stages in the structure of the peer groups to this end. As Musgrave says: 'It is whilst amongst their peers and usually away from the control of their elders that adolescent boys and girls can try out the behaviour expected of them towards the opposite sex and move from apparent gaucheness to greater sophistication'[16].

Dunphy's emphasis on crowds and cliques refers to structured but informal settings. A good deal of the American literature refers to peer relations in the more formal setting of the American High School. Coleman[17] sees adolescent peer group relations as the Adolescent Society. He stresses the, similar, values of athleticism for boys and sexual attractiveness for girls in the culture of this adolescent society. For Coleman, and many other writers[18], the consequences of these peer group relations and their values are often deletereous, despite being highly integrated into the social structure of the school.

There is evidence from a number of societies that the nature and organization of peer groups varies with age. Blyth's early British study[19] showed that even in primary school the division into unisex groups begins to develop up until about nine years old by which time sex divisions are pretty rigid. Dunphy refers to this as the 'initial stage of adolescent group development' which changes to a gradual movement towards 'heterosexuality in group structure'[20], though interaction across sexes is still regarded as very daring.

The next stage, he argues, is the formation of actually heterosexual groups in which 'upper status members of unisexual cliques initiate individual-to-individual heterosexual interaction and the first dating occurs'.[21] Dunphy claims that it is the crowd which is central to this transition because 'membership in the crowd offers opportunities for establishing a heterosexual role'[22]. However, 'membership of the crowd is dependent upon prior membership in a clique'[23]

Dunphy's respondents were from 'differing socio-economic backgrounds', though mostly middleclass. Most were connected in some way with sponsored youth organizations, so his informal groups may in fact be more closely related to formal organizations than at first appears. A considerable amount of other research suggests that these, largely unisex cliques differ considerably in their activities by sex. A different Australian study, for example, noted that whilst boys 'took an active delight in companionship'[24], girls wanted to talk to friends about themselves. Research done by the present author and Peter Musgrave in Scotland[25] suggests that young adolescents have different criteria for entry into peer groups, which closely relate to traditional gender roles. The general conclusion to be drawn from this literature is that sexual-social relations in leisure are central to peer group activity. Sex first differentiates cliques and subsequently brings them together to structure dating and other patterns of sexual relations[26].

There is a quite different literature, using different concepts, which leads to quite different conclusions about the focus of adolescent relations with peers. I refer to the criminological literature on juvenile delinquency, whose central concept has been the gang. The term 'gang' has been reserved almost exclusively for working class adolescent groups. As Block and Neiderhoffer wrote as early as 1958: 'Rarely in sociological literature are middle class adolescent groups referred to as gangs, irrespective of their similarity to their lower economic-class counterparts'.[27] This is undoubtedly related to two assumptions common to the field: that delinquency was a predominantly working class activity; and that juvenile delinquency was largely to be explained as gang activity. The ideological assumptions about working class crime and the over-reliance on official crime-rate statistics have received serious challenges from criminologists since, as also the assumption that gangs are necessarily deviant in one form or another. As Furfey says: 'One point to grasp about gangs is that they are not necessarily anti-social. Even in New York City which is all too well known for its fighting gangs, many, many other gangs are entirely law abiding'.[28] That argument aside a wide range of deviant gangs were discovered by professional researchers. What is more, whilst Cohen's[29] view of gang subcultures as group problem solving might conceivably be extended to non-hedonistic groupings, Yablonski argues for a quite distinct function of the violent gang for its members compared to peer group, clique or crowd. He sees the gang as 'a convenient and malleable structure quickly adaptable to the needs of emotionally disturbed youths who are unable to fulfill the demands required for participation in more normal groups. They join gangs because they lack the social ability to relate to others not because the gang gives them the feeling of belonging'.[30] So, he claims, the violent gang is only a 'near group'.

American Theorizing — British Kids

One overriding difficulty with this massive amount of literature is that serious doubts have been raised about its applicability to the British experience. Whether Thrasher's conception of the gang 'integrated through conflict'[31] or Yablonski's 'near-group'[32] or the various positions in between, there seems very little evidence that gangs of any sort exist in any numbers in Britain. Downes in his now classic study[33] found no evidence for their existence. Scott[34] in a more specific study of London found not gangs but loosely organized delinquent groups, often short-lived. The only major study in recent times to suggest the existence of gangs is Patrick's study of Glasgow, though informants have suggested the growth of 'utilitarian gangs' in some London suburbs in recent years.[35] At most, it would seem, gangs, if they exist, are rare, and probably specific to certain cities.

A similar problem exists with the concept of 'youth culture'. Although some contributions to the debate about the functionality of youth groups and values have been very sophisticated,[36] much of the 'Youth Culture' debate has been presented more simplistically. This literature is summarized in Sebald's textbook on adolescence in the form of three statements:

1 The typical adolescent is characterised by symptoms which can be described as socially-caused 'storm and stress'.
2 ... a teenage subculture exists and is a widespread and powerful pattern among American adolescents.
3 The third assumption suggests a causal relationship be-

tween the adolescent subculture and the 'storm and stress' of the young individual, implying that the peer culture is a compensation providing a sense of security and belonging during the period of adolescent discontinuity.[37]

This position was rapidly modified to accommodate evidence of a wide variety of values amongst adolescents. Thus, the 'Youth Culture' became youth subcultures, each a specific solution to the general problem of youth.

Several attempts have been made to apply the position to the British experience. Perhaps the best known argument for a British Youth Culture is that made by Brian Wilson[38], though his 'Youth Culture' was exclusively a culture of students. For school age children/adolescents it was related to the concept of 'generation gap'. As Ashley *et al* argue: 'The generation gap plus the economic independence of many modern adolescents and the development of commercial interests to serve the emerging needs of the adolescent, gives rise to the development of a youth culture'[39]. Whilst there was evidence for the relative independence of adolescents and certainly their exploitation by commercial interests in the post-war period[40], poverty surveys revealed that class divisions in economic well-being remained very similar to pre-war levels, so that for some working class adolescents the view of 'Affluent Teenagers' was singularly inappropriate,[41] a proposition even less convincing with the unemployment levels of the 1970s and 1980s.

A great deal of other work raised serious doubts about the 'generation gap' itself, at least as far as values were concerned. The Eppels[42] major study of young people's values found them to be conventional, humane, socially concerned, anti-authoritarian and valuing the family. Veness[43] observed very similar values in her study of school leavers. Even in the matter of sexual relations adolescents were not very far from the attitudes of their parents. Despite the so-called 'sexual revolution' of the 1960s Schofield's findings[44] claimed only one-third of boys and 11 per cent of girls were sexually experienced; though Farrell's figures for the 1970s show a marked increase in sexual activity. Even so, Farrell observes that 'The attitudes of the young people in this study to sex before marriage are in line with what has been described as the "widespread" view in this country — approval in the context of a stable relationship and if care is taken to avoid unwanted pregnancy'[45].

However, it is not just the inappropriateness of these literatures in the light of empirical evidence which must concern us, it is also

the theoretical adequacy of the arguments. There is a real disjunc-
tion in these literatures between the study of youth subcultures —
largely middleclass — and the delinquency/gang literature — largely
working class. The presumption of much of the youth subculture
literature is that youth constitutes a distinctive age-category: an age
status; the culture or subcultures representing the values associated
with that age-status, yet it is premised on the rating and dating
behaviour of the white, middleclass, American High School. A
visitor from Mars only versed in this literature might be forgiven for
believing that youth were white and middleclass. What is more,
whilst girls are mentioned in this literature, they are so almost
entirely in terms of their traditionalist sex roles and in submissive
roles within the peer group. This is, of course, not entirely unsup-
ported by the empirical evidence and, at least in part, is a reflection
of the genuine oppression of women.

The delinquency and gang literature, on the other hand, contains no discussion of conformity, more or less ignores middle-class
deviance, and totally avoids any discussion of females except as
objects in a male universe. The same Martian visitor, on reading this
literature might assume that crime was the province, almost exclusively of black, working class boys, whilst females only exist as
cultural objects between the ages of thirteen and eighteen, when
they miraculously re-emerge in physical form in the sociology of the
family literature.

Peer Groups Versus Parents

What these literatures do share as a common assumption is the
central importance of peers to young people. Eisenstadt argues that
youth groups 'arise and exist only under very specific conditions'[46].
He sees age groups as an interlinking sphere between the family and
other institutional spheres. Within this institutional void youth
groups function to decrease inter-generational conflict. Only under
very special circumstances do youth develop 'deviant' characteristics. This may be surprising to anyone reading the American
Structural-Functionalist literature which is almost exclusively concerned with the dangers of peer group influence and youth subcultures posed either as anti-school, anti-parent or both. Much of this
probably stems from Parsons original analysis[47] locating adolescent
roles as largely irresponsible and limited to the field of leisure. The
problem of youth subcultures and youth peer group influence for

the Structural-Functionalist, then, is that whilst they serve positive functions for stability and order in the absence of other institutional constraints, inadequate socialization or a failure of local social control may lead them to become disruptive influences in the smooth process of transition to adult roles.

Perhaps oddly, Left-Idealism/Neo-Marxism would substantially agree. The Birmingham School[48] see ephemeral youth subcultures, based largely in neighbourhood peer groups, as being a youthful response to a situation of class domination which allows them to temporarily win space but which is substantially shaped by the parent class culture.

Coleman, in his study of the American High School argues that the adolescent subculture, as operated through the adolescent peer group, is both substantially anti-school and anti-parent, leaving the outstanding athlete at the centre of the status system with the outstanding academic student with 'little or no way to bring glory to the school'[49] He concludes that it is no wonder that the academic students' 'accomplishments gain little reward and are often met with ridiculing remarks'.[50] For Coleman, the peer group is a central influence on educational performance. Epperson[51] has argued with some force that the nature of Coleman's methodology has underplayed the influence of parents and that whilst it might be anti-teacher to a degree, the peer group social system is not anti-parent. Whilst some other studies[52] have argued for the existence of values similar to those observed by Coleman, still others have strongly suggested that parental influence remains important alongside that of peers. Remmers and Radler[53], for example, observed that whilst peers were important as a source of information about leisure/social activities, Parents remained important where politics, finance or personal problems were concerned. Similar conclusions were reached by Brittain[54], Turner[55], and Rosenmayer[56]. My own research on Scottish young people[57] also showed different areas of influence for parents and peers, though the areas were not identical to the American studies. What it demonstrates is a general movement with age away from the influence of parents towards their conception of their own ideas rather than those of peers. What is more, this study shows clear differences by sex, with girls showing far greater influence of parents on some aspects of their leisure time — when to be in at night, how to behave when out — whereas boys accept parental influence only on their appearance. All of this suggests that young people do not see themselves as rejecting parents in favour of peers but rather of an increasing influence of peers upon certain aspects of their lives, alongside the continuing influence of their parents.

Peers and Class

The early 'Youth Subculture' literature was overly concerned with emphasizing the unity of youth as a category and thus its distinctiveness from parents. Yet, as Clarke *et al* argue:

> When we look at some of these writers who subscribe to notions such as the generation gap, distinctive youth culture, welfare state youth, the 'classlessness of youth culture', and so on, we find that the evidence they bring forward actually undermines the interpretation of it which they offer. Within the 'classlessness' interpretation, there is often a contradictory stress, precisely upon the class structuring of youth.[58]

Once variables such as class, and also ethnic origin and gender, are taken into account a much closer correspondence between adult and adolescent values can be observed. Hollingshead[59] in his 1940s study of a small American town suggests that similarities of behaviour by age and sex are hardly surprising. What, he claims, is more interesting is 'that the position the adolescents' family occupied in the status structure contributed in significant ways to the behaviour the adolescents exhibited in their relations with the schools, the church, the job, recreation and their peers'[60]. What is more, on his return in the 1970s he noted, 'in spite of three wars, prolonged prosperity and increasing industrialization, the status structure of Elmtown has been highly resistant to change'.[61]

Although Elmtown was regarded as a major contribution to community studies, its conclusions about adolescents were largely ignored by students of youth. More influential in this respect was a small scale study of Canadian Upper Middle class youth completed in the mid 1950s by Elkin and Westley[62], who observed a high level of continuity in socialization during adolescence with very few sharp conflicts with parents. This study was widely quoted but subjected to quite vitriolic attacks by supporters of the youth culture thesis.[63]

In Britain the concept of class has been more openly on the agenda, at least as far as empirical work is concerned. It was David Sugarman[64] more than anyone who attempted to apply Coleman's view of youth to the British scene. Sugarman claims clear evidence for the existence of a British 'Youth Culture'; but, in Britain, he claims, it operates outside the school and is strongly associated with working class, not middle class, youth. For him, British youth culture is an anti-school culture indulged in by working class youth drop-outs.[65] From a quite different theoretical perspective Murdock and McCron[66] agree that youth subcultural styles are reflections of working classness. They are made up, they insist, of 'situated class cultures embedded in the family and the local neighbourhood, and the "mediated" symbol systems sponsored by the youth orientated sectors of the entertainment industry' so that subcultural styles can be seen as 'Coded expressions of class consciousness transposed into the specific context of youth and reflective of the complex way in which age acts as a mediator both of class experience and of class consciousness.'[67]

There is good reason, then, to believe that youth culture is not an independent set of values, norms and behaviour operated through the peer group, but rather that peers constitute in adolescence an increasingly important influence alongside particularly parents, and that even so, that influence is for the most part limited to certain aspects of life — largely those surrounding leisure. Yet, whilst there is general empirical support for a 'fit' between youth and parental subcultures, there is disagreement on the nature of the parental subculture, and hence on the youth subcultures. On the one hand, youth subcultures are seen to be influenced by parental class subcultures which are specifically structurally-located interpretations of the consensus. On the other hand, the dominant culture is seen not as a consensus but as the basis of the dominant ideology, so that the world is viewed in terms of cultures which 'always stand in relations of domination — and subordination — to one another'[68] It is within these cultures — which are class cultures — that subcultures exist. This includes youth subcultures, so, youth subcultures must be a reflection, at least in part, of parental (class) cultures.

Peer Groups, Subcultures and Schools

The debate has been substantially about values. If peer groups of young people have come to constitute a problem, it is because they have developed in gaps in the institutional structure sets of values which differ in some measure from the *status quo*, whether that *status quo* be seen as a genuine consensus or a set of class values. In America the problem is posed as essentially WASP kids getting into counter-cultures: the hippie, the student activist threatening a genuine consensus. In Britain, it is posed as essentially working class kids dropping out of school, and often into delinquency and deviance. British kids either didn't want the education which was provided or didn't want education *per se*; so some of them wouldn't go to school, and the ones that did go didn't want to learn. What they wanted to do instead was to listen to pop music, watch football or hang around on street corners. Either this subculture, generated amongst their peers, led them to seek dead-end jobs or the fact that they would only get dead-end jobs or no jobs at all, led them to reject all else but this subculture. This is the basis of Hargreaves' 'Delinquescent subculture'[69]. If the structure of education is such that working class people in school cannot be ambitious in the schools' terms, then they will develop a set of values and practices which are deliberately unambitious. However, they will not do this individually, for the whole group is 'failing', and consequently the formation of values to fit their behaviour takes place within the group. So subculture is group-problem solving made possible by the recognition that the problem is being suffered by certain sorts of people all requiring a similar solution. So, working class boys in particular, develop a group subculture which is anti-school. What is more, Hargreaves is arguing, this 'Delinquescent subculture' is far more relevant to their needs than anything offered in the school. Indeed, he sees them to some extent as attempting to apply adult working class roles in a school context which cannot handle or even recognize them.

Lacey's 1970 study of a grammar school[70] is largely compatible with Hargreaves'. In the different 'academic' atmosphere of the grammar school, Lacey observes differentiation on an academic scale which leads to polarization. At the top end the problem becomes the problem of success. At the bottom end, the problem of failure. He claims that at either end of the academic dimension subcultures develop. What is more, though arising from the ethos of the school they closely relate to social class, for it is the grammar school pupils of working class origin who tend to end up in the lower streams, whereas middle class pupils disproportionately fill the higher streams. So the grammar school produces its own academically-orientated normative group; largely middle class; and its 'anti-group' culture; largely working class. What is perhaps most remarkable about Lacey's findings is that in a grammar school, taking only 11-plus successes an 'anti-group' culture is seen to develop so quickly. Yet it appears to make little difference whether they attend traditional grammar schools or comprehensive schools. Ball's recent study of Beachside Comprehensive[71] shows the development of a similar anti-school group in the lowest academic positions. Ball claims that changes in 'clique' membership, friendship choices and changes in the distribution of academic success are all closely related.

It seems that the explanation lies not so much in the schools as in the context of school in working class culture. Certainly, if Willis[72] is to be believed, the anti-school pupils develop what he describes as a counter-school culture within the school which derives from the larger working class culture and shares many features with what he calls 'shop-floor' culture. So, argues Willis, how working class kids get working class jobs is that the similarity of 'cultures' leads them to choose a life of manual labour.

This view of the centrality of values has been seriously questioned by Paul Corrigan.[73] Corrigan is dealing exclusively with working class children and claims to have begun his own research with a hypothesis about the rejection of school values. However, as his research developed 'the whole theory seemed totally *irrelevant* to the boys' experience ... it does not seem that truancy is an action which is meant to *attack the school values* in any way, rather the action seems to have something to do with the boys' protection of themselves from things that they don't like'.[74] For Corrigan the boys' 'actions were not created by such consistent things as "values"; the crucial factor ... seemed to be much more to do with the power differential'[75] The reason why working class boys play truant, miss classes, talk, eat and disrupt classes, take dead-end jobs and concentrate their leisure time either in the commercial youth subculture or in unstructured street corner activity is because they lack power in all formally structured institutionalized contexts. Only mixing with their group on 'the street', or fighting on the football terraces, or going to dances to 'chat up the lasses ... (or) ... have a scrap'[76] do they feel less oppressed by institutionalized power; only in these contexts are there 'the social institutions that we can create out of the freedom that we are allowed'.[77]

This emphasis on freedom is also to be found in Robins and Cohen's work: 'as long as you aren't washing floors in a detention centre, as long as you have still got a few bob in your pocket, and you can go out and have a good time with your friends, then you are still free'.[78] However, it is a limited freedom. It is a freedom 'from school, from the parental nags.... You're a young worker, not a school *kid* living on pocket money and paper rounds'.[79] It is not even a real escape from parents. 'Relative affluence shrivels up

the moment they walk out of the parental home'.[80] They do not
have enough money for real independence, merely enough 'to buy
substitutes for the thing they lack'.[81] This is clearly part of the
explanation for the continuing influence and respect for parents
shown elsewhere in the literature. But, it is not all. There are also
genuinely common responses to a similar relation to class power.
Robins and Cohen see territoriality as one such common response.
However, it functions differently for different ages, operating
through different institutions. For adults, there is the 'pub and
shops, the local political, religious and cultural associations of every
kind. But the kids have only one institution to support this function
and a fragile one at that — "the gang".... So the street becomes the
area where the Growing Up game is played'.[82] There are also
genuinely generational differences to be taken into account. 'Girls in
the 8–14 age group were increasingly rejecting their role as child-
minder (and) ... were breaking away to form their own distinctive
peer group, parallel to but independent of the boys',[83] which resulted in 'the creation of a new peer group of pre-adolescent girls
outside the family'.[84]

Not all peer groups, nor all members of peer groups even
amongst the working class are anti-school in one way or another.
Indeed, many of the sociologists writing about working class youth
would never have made it as sociologists if this were the case. The
youth subculture literature distinguishes between the upwardly
mobile styles, like Mods, and the firmly working class, like skin-
heads. Hargreaves[85] and Ball[86], as we have seen recognize 'academic
subcultures'. Corrigan, however, is also critical of this. Some boys
do well but even here, he says:

> There is no evidence at all of these boys seeing education as
> useful for its own sake; as seeing learning and knowledge as
> important, or, indeed, of their learning a set of moral rules
> by which they will live their lives. Instead, those that found
> these experiences rewarding found it rewarding in a *specific
> way*; they saw that through education they could get better
> jobs.[87]

This he claims was most obvious in their clear distinction between
co-operation in school when it was in their interests and non-co-
operation when it was not.

Furlong,[88] from a very different theoretical position, also sees
pupils' reaction to the school very much in terms of the relevance of
school to their own concerns. This study is equally critical of

anti-school subcultural explanations, but argues for the existence of interaction, set composed of a group of students who perceive what is happening in a similar way, communicate this to each other and define appropriate action together. This seems to be much more situationally specific, as indeed one might expect from its Interactionist theoretical roots, yet the common concerns of pupils — who are soft and who are hard teachers, which are learning and which non-learning situations — are not dissimilar from those described by Robins and Cohen.[89] This is in itself interesting since Furlong is, unusually, studying lower stream, black girls.

Another recent British study has also raised serious doubts about locating explanations of school deviancy and conformity of adolescents in subcultures. Glen Turner's study of the social world of the comprehensive school[90] is unusual in that it began by concentrating on the study of conformist youth. Subcultural explanations, he argues, are one-sided in that they fail to deal with the problem of 'pupils being subjected to competing demands made upon them by, on the one hand, their examination courses, and on the other hand, by their peer group'.[91] 'Clearly,' he writes, 'pupils had a variable commitment to both demands.[92] At the same time, he claims, there is a difference between long term goals, such as examination success and 'goals related to shorter term features, such as "having a laugh", combating boredom and so on.'[93] So the explanation of student careers is probably better explained, he argues, in terms of Matza's concept of drift[94] than by a commitment to explicit values either within a school peer group or in wider class cultures. So, he concludes,

> if pupils do adopt a pro-school or an anti-school career pattern:
> a) They conform or deviate in only certain respects and by no means on all occasions.
> b) There is a variety of motivations to be found among 'pro-school' and 'anti-school' pupils.
> c) Career decisions are made continually and pupil orientations are subject to the possibility of change and drift.[95]

This is not to suggest that Turner rejects subcultural explanations entirely. He acknowledges that 'commitment to certain values and conformity to particular norms does in part characterise pupil orientations'.[96] His point is, rather, that 'pupils do not accept or reject school values in toto but react to them selectively on the basis of their own goals and perceived interests'.[97] Nevertheless, his pupils are mostly from a local council estate and he acknowledges both that 'there is some connection between the low commitment of most pupils to academic achievement and their home background ... (and that) ... those pupils who are most highly committed to success in external exam are mostly middle class'.[98] Turner also notes an additional element: that of teacher orientations, which he sees as relevant to pupils' careers. The constraints of the institution have often been underplayed in studies of state schools, though Wakeford's study[99] of a public school as a total institution has been used as a model for the study of a state secondary school by Woods.[100] Clearly, state schools are not total institutions. Nevertheless, the nature of the institutional demands should not be ignored. Much of the British literature possibly overemphasizes the impact of the peer group by not taking cognisance of the difference between 'middle class' and 'working class' school demands.

Where Have All The Black Girls Gone?

Most of the above studies do seem to agree on the centrality of the peer group in adolescent careers, whether these lead to the ideal-typical middle class 'conformist', working hard in school and shunning excessively deviant behaviour, or to the ideal-typical working class school truant/dropout come delinquent, rejecting school in preference to 'working class' conceptions of careers. Of course, these are ideal types, and detailed studies of adolescent interaction patterns show a much more complex situation with a much more active factor. Structural factors are seen to influence power, values, norms, their relation to school, the nature of the available peer groupings and the availability of alternative subcultures. However, within this structural-determinism choices are made. For the most part, the nature of the choice is severely constrained but not for all; and the school is the main institutional context in which cross-class choices of peers can be made.

Yet, if peer groups are so important to accounts of both school conformity and deviance, how are we to explain the very different experiences of girls? Most studies are exclusively of boys. Those that do include girls tend to characterize them as more conformist, less likely to engage in more than the most mundane acts of deviance. Is this the case? If it is, does it mean that girls' peer groups are more conformist, or structured differently from boys, and, if so, why?

Perhaps the first thing to be said is that there is evidence to show that the structure of peer relations amongst girls is different from boys. Though there is disagreement over the age-ranges involved, there is plenty of evidence for single-sex peer groups (i.e. cliques) which gradually come together to form heterosexual crowds and eventually heterosexual cliques before breaking up into marriage partners. For much of adolescence close friends are different by sex.[101] Other evidence points to different activities being central to the peer group according to sex.[102] Even the size of peer group may be different by sex. My own unpublished research in Aberdeen[103] showed distinctly different ways of structuring peer relations by sex and social class. This research showed that whilst about a third of all young people identified with a single friend rather than a group of friends, the proportion of working class girls to whom this applied increased with age, so that by fifteen to sixteen years old half of working class Aberdonian girls preferred to organize their social life around one close friend rather than the wider clique. This is not to say that they were not members of a clique but that they valued a specific peer relation over the value of the group.

These apparent differences in the structure of girls' friendships do seem to relate to their conformism in and out of school, at least as far as Control Theorists are concerned. Numerous empirical testings of Hirschi's control theory thesis[104] appear to demonstrate both that girls are more typically constrained by their social locations so that they are as adolescent daughters and subsequently as mothers more encapsulated within the nuclear family;[105] and that those girls who do engage in delinquent acts are more closely associated with already delinquent peers.[106] The evidence for girls doing consistently better than boys in school examinations is also clear in the education literature. So girls may well be different precisely because of the nature of their peer groups which, as Hogan, Simpson and Gillis argue: 'reinforce dependence, compliance, and passivity among their members';[107] precisely the opposite of peer groups for working class adolescent boys.

The other major area of study to be underemployed in the literature is ethnicity. There are some studies of black youth. Probably best known is Hebdidge's 'Reggae, Rastas and Rudies'.[108] Hebdidge provides an account of 'stylistic interaction' between West Indian and white lower working class males. Yet Asian youth hardly appear at all in the literature except in terms of their relative success in schools. Most books and articles on youth subculture now contain a reference to the need to take account of race, but the trouble with studying ethnicity is that the convenience of a black/white methodology does not hold up in practice. As D. Smith observes:

'From the point of view of the receiving society, they may all be lumped together as 'coloured people'. From the point of view of the different minorities that is a bizarre terminology.... To the extent that they are treated in the same way they may come to see themselves as a single group of 'coloured' people or 'blacks' — at present Asians do not regard themselves as 'blacks' and West Indians do not regard themselves as 'coloured'.[109]

Hebdidge's account of West Indian youth which explores at least the possibility of stylistic interaction with elements of white working class youth is unlikely to be mirrored in the Asian community, amongst whom both parents[110] and the boys themselves[111] see little value in multi-racial organizations.

If the literature on black and brown boys is scarce, that of black and brown adolescent girls is scarcely existent. We know from the structure of marriage and the family in both societies that the traditional roles for women are restricted. The matriarchal structure of West Indian society, based on a relative economic independence from men places women at the centre of familial control.[112] The less formal conception of marriage in West Indian culture does not, however, lead to a liberated view of sex amongst adolescent girls. On the contrary, Sharpe[113] notes a tight control over girls' social activities, especially boy friends. At the same time, the traditional view of women's economic independence and the developing emphasis upon the familial role once in Britain, does lead West Indian girls to a degree of freedom, so that although three-quarters of them said that their parents seldom or never allowed them to go out with boys, half of them did so anyway. Yet, there is nothing to show us how they relate to even West Indian boys, rastas or otherwise.

Asian girls are even more restricted within the structure of the family. The combination of a value of great deference to parental wishes and the continuing practice of arranged marriage, plus religious taboos, severely restricts the girls' social relations, not just with whites, but with other religions, other castes, and, within their own caste with boys. Given the peculiar circumstances of these girls within British society, one might expect them to be a prime target of study. Their culture encourages them to be conformist and hardworking in school[114], yet their restricted home life makes school the only context in which they can associate with others, and especially boys, of their own age, out of the highly structured ethnic community. The question of how their peer group relations are structured, of whether and how they relate to wider cliques and crowds must be of considerable interest. Yet, in the literature it barely exists. Where have all the black (and brown) girls gone?

Conclusions

What I have tried to show in this chapter is that there is good evidence for the importance of the peer group as an informal institution around which much adolescent activity is organized, and that this has implications for how young people relate to' school. However, much of this literature has greatly exaggerated the distinctiveness of youth values and consequently overemphasized the significance of the peer group as an influence on many aspects of adolescent life. This is particularly so in the context of education. What a considerable body of evidence shows is that parents continue to be an important influence on adolescents across a wide range of their activities and concerns. This should come as no surprise to anyone reading the literature on education and social class, but it is worth stressing in this context. If working class kids fail in schools, it is not primarily because they are members of disruptive peer groups or delinquent gangs. It is because their classness (or sex or ethnicity, etc.) locates them securely in a system of power and that this leads them to adopt class values not too dissimilar from their parents. How adolescents, through their peer groups, interpret those values, or how as a group of peers they react to a particular situation of powerlessness, will of course be distinctive. Since most with the same class location will experience similar powerlessness and similar values their responses are likely to be distinctly adolescent across peer groups.

Nor should we assume that peer group responses to education are merely class responses. The rejection of youthfulness seems to me to have gone too far. The 'youth subculture' is not merely the creation of commercial interests. It is usually argued[115] that youth only becomes significant as a category with the extension of compulsory education, but that extension applied as readily to middle class youth as it did working class. What is more, historically the extension of education for middle class children pre-dates that for working class, as does the craft apprenticeship for the skilled artisans. *Tom Brown's Schooldays* can be analyzed in terms of peer group values and adolescent irresponsibility just as readily as can 'the lads'.

I have also tried to point to some glaring omissions in our knowledge of young people. Most British literature is a literature of working class males, particularly those who are already deemed to have failed in the education system. In recent years this has been somewhat remedied by a number of studies of comprehensive schools with much wider class intakes. However, there remains a paucity of studies of girls and we still know very little about the structure of their peer relations and how they relate to youth subcultures, if indeed they do[116]. There is some reason to suppose that most girls are more normative precisely because they are more tightly integrated into formal institutional arrangements than are boys. If so, this may explain why peer groups are less developed, if they really are?

We also know very little about black youth. The claim that black Britons are the new phenomenon no longer holds. The last World War was forty years ago, so black Britons are in their second and third generations. What is more, they could provide a crucial test both for the concept of youth subculture and for the significance of parental cultures. If youth subculture really is defined largely in 'youth' terms then it must refer to black youth as much as to white. So it is important to know if black youth operate similar youthful responses in their peer groups as do white youth. Also, we know that their parents, as immigrants to this country, necessarily brought with them aspects of different cultures which have been retained in the form of ethnic subcultures. If class cultures are a major influence on youthful peer responses then so will ethnic subcultures be. So the precise nature of black youth's responses in relation to their ethnic and class cultures is of the greatest importance.

What we do know about black youth in Britain is almost exclusively about black boys. Very little information indeed is available about black girls. Yet what we do know about both West Indian and Asian subcultures gives girls within these subcultures quite distinctive roles in relation to family, leisure activities — particularly social-sexual relations — and education. Once again, then, we would expect the relation between peers and school to be quite distinctive.

It is becoming a cliché in sociological writings to end your paper with a call for further research. However, I will risk the cliché in order to call for a filling of some of the gaps. In particular we

need to identify the relationship between peer relations and structures within and outside school, and the socio-structural locations of
adolescent peers.

Notes

1 SMITH, D.M. (1970) 'Adolescence: a study of stereotyping', *Sociological Review*, 18, 2, July, pp. 197–211.
2 The old have similar opportunities but structure their leisure differently. Whilst youth is used here as a social category not a biological or
psychological one, the onset of puberty and the way in which sexual
relations are institutionally organized will be of importance in defining
the central concerns of their leisure.
3 EISENSTADT, S.N. (1956) *From Generation to Generation: Age groups
and Social Structure*, London, Collier-Macmillan.
4 PARSONS, T. (1942) 'Age and sex in the social structure of the United
States', *American Sociological Review*, 7, Oct. pp. 604–16.
5 CLARKE, J. *et al.* (1976) 'Subcultures, cultures and class', in HALL, S.
and JEFFERSON, T., (Eds.), *Resistance Through Ritual*, London,
Hutchinson.
6 Though note the problems with their 'generational' analysis: see:
SMITH, D.M. (1981) 'New movements in the sociology of youth',
British Journal of Sociology, 32, 2, June.
7 CLARKE *et al. op. cit.*.
8 Not just Structural-Functionalist but Counter-Cultural and Youth
Class literatures as well.
9 MUSGRAVE, P. (1972) *The Sociology of Education*, 2nd Ed., London,
Methuen.
10 HURLOCK, E.B. (1949) *Adolescent Development*, New York, McGraw-
Hill.
11 HOLLINGSHEAD, A.B. (1949) *Elmtown's Youth*, New York, McGraw-
Hill.
12 DUNPHY, D.C. (1963) 'The social structure of urban adolescent peer
groups', *Sociometry*, 26, 2, June, p. 23.
13 *Ibid.*, p. 233.
14 *Ibid.*, p. 235.
15 *Ibid.*
16 MUSGRAVE, P. *op. cit.* p. 105.
17 COLEMAN, J.S. (1961) *The Adolescent Society*, Glencoe, Illinois, The
Free Press.
18 See, for example, CARTWRIGHT, D.S. and ROBERTSON, R.J. (1961)
'Membership in cliques and achievement', *American Journal of Sociology*, 66, 5 March. pp. 441–5; MIRANDE, A.M. (1968) 'Reference group
theory and adolescent sexual behaviour', *Journal of Marriage and the
Family*, 30, 4, Nov., pp. 572–7; LARSON, R.F. and LESLIE, G.R. (1969)
'Prestige influence in serious dating relationships of university students', *Social Forces*, pp. 195–201; SCHWARTS, G. and MERTEN, D.

(1968) 'Social identity and expressive symbols: the meaning of an initiation ritual', *American Anthropologist*, 70, pp. 1117–31.

19 BLYTH, W.A.L. (1960) 'The sociometric study of children's groups in English schools', *British Journal of Educational Studies*, May, see also: BLYTH, W.A.L. (1965) *English Primary School Education*, London, Routledge and Kegan Paul.

20 DUNPHY, *op. cit.* p. 235.

21 *Ibid.*, p. 237.

22 *Ibid.*

23 *Ibid.*

24 CONNELL, W.F., FRANCIS, E.P. and SKILBECK, E. (1957) *Growing Up in an Australian City*, Melbourne.

25 Unpublished research from the Aberdeen Mass Media Project.

26 Note the vast literature on American Dating Patterns. See For example: McDANIEL, C.O. (1969) 'Dating roles and reasons for dating', *Journal of Marriage and the Family*, Feb pp. 97–107; WALLER, W. (1967) 'The rating and dating complex', in VAZ, E. (Ed.) *Middle Class Juvenile Delinquency*, London, Harper-Row; DOUVAN, E. and ADELSON, J. (1966) *The Adolescent Experience*, New York, John Wiley. LOWRIE, S.H. (1951) 'Dating theories and student responses', *American Sociological Review*, 16, pp. 334–40, GRINDER, R.E. (1966) 'Relations of social dating attractions to academic orientation and peer relations', *Journal of Educational Psychology*, 57, pp. 27–34.

27 BLOCH, H.A. and NIEDERHOFFER, A. (1958) *The Gang*, New York, Philosophical Library.

28 FURFEY, P.H. (1963) 'Peer group influences in adolescence', in BIER, W.C. (Ed) *The Adolescent: His Search for Understanding*, New York, Fordham Press.

29 COHEN, A. (1955) *Delinquent Boys: The Subculture of the Gang*, London, Collier-Macmillan.

30 YABLONSKI, L. (1967) *The Violent Gang*, Harmondsworth, Penguin.

31 THRASHER, F. (1927) *The Gang*, Chicago, Univ. of Chicago Press.

32 YABLONSKI, *op. cit.*

33 DOWNES, D. (1966) *The Delinquent Solution*, London, Routledge and Kegan Paul.

34 SCOTT, P. (1956) 'Gangs and delinquent groups in London', *British Journal of Delinquency*, 7, July. pp. 4–25.

35 PATRICK, J. (1973) *A Glasgow Gang Observed*, London, Eyre Methuen; see also WELSH, S. (1981) 'The manufacture of excitement in police-juvenile encounters', *Brit. J. Criminology*, 20, 3, pp. 25–26.

36 See EISENSTADT, S.N. and PARSONS, T., *op. cit.*

37 SEBALD, H. (1968) *Adolescence: a Sociological Analysis*, New York, Appleton-Century-Crofts.

38 WILSON, B. (1970) *The Youth Culture and The Universities*, London, Faber and Faber.

39 ASHLEY, B. COHEN, H.S. and SLATTER, R.G. (1968) *An Introduction to the Sociology of Education*, London, Macmillan.

40 ABRAMS, H. (1959) *The Teenage Consumer*, London, Press Exchange, Paper 5, Routledge and Kegan Paul.

41 TITMUS, R. (1962). *Income Distribution and Social Change*, London,

Allen and Unwin; TOWNSEND, P. and ABEL-SMITH, B. (1965) *The Poor and the Poorest*, London, Bell.

42 EPPEL, E.M. and EPPEL, M. (1966) *Adolescence and Morality*, London, Routledge and Kegan Paul.

43 VENESS, T. (1962) *The School Leavers: Their Expectations and Aspirations*, London, Methuen.

44 SCHOFIELD, M. (1965) *The Sexual Behaviour of Young People*, London, Longmans.

45 FARRELL, C. (1978) *My Mother Said*, London, Routledge and Kegan Paul.

46 EISENSTADT, *op. cit.*

47 PARSONS, *op. cit.*

48 CLARKE, J. *et al., op. cit.*, p. 29.

49 COLEMAN, J.S. (1972) 'The Adolescent Subculture and Academic Achievement', in SCOTT, W.R. (Ed.), *Social Process and Social Structures*.

50 *Ibid.*

51 EPPERSON, D.C. (1964) 'A re-assessment of indices of parental influence in "adolescent society"', *American Sociological Review*, 29, 1, pp. 93–6.

52 For example, VAZ, E.W. and CASPARIS, J. (1971) 'A comparative study of youth culture and delinquency in upper middleclass canadian and swiss boys', *International Journal of Comparative Sociology*, 12, pp. 1–23. INOUE, S. (1973) 'Japanese youth culture, today: play as a way of life', *Diogenes*, 84, pp. 84–100.

53 REMMERS, H.H. and RADLER, D.H. (1957) *The American Teenager*, New York, Bobbs-Merrill.

54 BRITTAIN, C.V. (1963) 'Adolescent choices: parent-peer cross choices', *American Sociological Review*, 28, pp. 385–91.

55 TURNER, R.H. (1964) *The Social Context of Ambition*, San Francisco, Chandler.

56 ROSENMAYER, L. (1964) 'Economic and social conditions influencing the lives of young people', *Annex. V. Final Report*, International Conference on Youth, Grenoble, 23rd Aug — 1st Sept., UNESCO.

57 SMITH, D.M. (1985), 'Perceived peer and parental influences on youth's social world', *Youth and Society*, 17, 2, pp. 131–56.

58 CLARKE *et al., op. cit.*, p. 37.

59 HOLLINGSHEAD, A.B. (1949) *Elmtown's Youth* and (1975) *Elmtown Revisited*, London, John Wiley.

60 *Ibid.*, pp. 383–4.

61 *Ibid.*, p. 385.

62 ELKIN, F. and WESTLEY, W.A. (1955) 'The myth of adolescent culture', *American Sociological Review*, 20, pp. 680–4.

63 See SEBALD, *op. cit.*

64 SUGARMAN, D. (1967) 'Involvement in youth culture, academic achievement and conformity in schools', *British Journal of Sociology*, 18, pp. 151–64.

65 N.B. The present author's critique in SMITH, D.M. (1976) 'The concept of youth subculture: a re-evaluation', *Youth and Society*, 7, 4, pp. 354–55.

66 MURDOCK, G. and McCRON, R.M. (1976) 'Youth and class: the career of a confusion, in MUNGHAM, G. and PEARSON, G. (Eds.), *Working Class Youth Culture*, London, Routledge and Kegan Paul.

67 *Ibid.*, p. 203.

68 CLARKE, J. *et al.*, *op. cit.*, pp. 12–13.

69 HARGREAVES, D. (1967) *Social Relations in a Secondary School*, New York, Routledge and Kegan Paul.

70 LACEY, C. (1970) *Hightown Grammar*, Manchester, Manchester University Press.

71 BALL, S. (1981) *Beachside Comprehensive: A Case Study of Secondary Schooling*, Cambridge, Cambridge University Press.

72 WILLIS, P. (1977) *Learning to Labour: How Working Class Kids Get Working Class Jobs*, Farnborough, Saxon House.

73 CORRIGAN, P. (1979) *Schooling the Smash Street Kids*, London, Macmillan.

74 *Ibid.*, pp. 28–9.

75 *Ibid.*, p. 47.

76 *Ibid.*, p. 110.

77 *Ibid.*, p. 110.

78 ROBINS, D. and COHEN, P. (1978) *Knuckle Sandwich: Growing Up in the Working Class City*, Harmondsworth, Penguin.

79 *Ibid.*, p. 8.

80 *Ibid.*, pp. 8–9.

81 *Ibid.*, p. 9.

82 *Ibid.*

83 *Ibid.*, p. 50.

84 *Ibid.*, p. 51.

85 *Op. cit.*

86 *Op. cit.*

87 *Op. cit.*, p. 50.

88 FURLONG, V.J. (1976) 'Interaction sets in the classroom: towards a study of classroom knowledge', in STUBBS, M. and DELAMONT, S. (Eds.) *Explorations in Classroom Observation*, New York, John Wiley.

89 *Op cit.*

90 TURNER, G. (1983) *The Social World of the Comprehensive School*, London, Croom Helm.

91 *Ibid.*, p. 158.

92 *Ibid.*

93 *Ibid.*

94 MATZA, D. (1964) *Delinquency and Drift*, New York, John Wiley.

95 TURNER, G. *op. cit.*, p. 147.

96 *Ibid.*, p. 148.

97 *Ibid.*

98 *Ibid.*, p. 151.

99 WAKEFORD, J. (1969) *The Cloistered Elite*, London, Macmillan.

100 WOODS, P. (1979), *The Divided School*, London, Routledge and Kegan Paul.

101 See DUNPHY, *op. cit.*, and BLYTH, *op. cit.*

102 See CORNELL *et al.*, *op cit.*, and SMITH and MUSGRAVE, *op, cit.*

103 SMITH, D.M. Unpublished research from the Aberdeen Mass Media Project.

104 HIRSCHI, T. (1969) *Causes of Delinquency*, California, University of California Press.

105 For a review of much of this research, see: BOX, S. (1983) *Power, Crime and Mystification*, London, Tavistock.

106 JOHNSON, R.E. (1979) *Juvenile Delinquency and Its Origins*, Cambridge, University of Cambridge Press.

107 HAGAN, J. SIMPSON, J.H. and GILLIS, A.R. (1979) 'The sexual stratification of social control: a gender-based perspective on crime and delinquency', *British Journal of Sociology*, 30, p. 35.

108 HEBDIDGE, D. (1976) 'Reggae, rastas and rudies', in HALL, S. and JEFFERSON, T. (1976) *Resistance Through Rituals*, Hutchinson.

109 SMITH, D.J. (1977) *Racial Disadvantage in Britain*, Harmondsworth, Penguin.

110 See ANWAR, M. (1976) *Between Two Cultures*, London, Community Relations Commission.

111 LIVINGSTONE, P. (1978) *The Leisure Needs of Asian Boys Aged 8–14 in Slough*, London, Scout Association.

112 HIRO, D. (1973) *Black British, White British*, Harmondsworth, Penguin.

113 SHARPE, S. (1976) *Just like a Girl*, Harmondsworth, Penguin.

114 See, for example, THE SWANN REPORT (1985) *Education for All*, Report of the Committee of Enquiry into the Education of Children from Ethnic Minority Groups, London, HMSO.

115 GILLIS, J.R. (1974) *Youth and History: Tradition and Change in European Age Relations, 1770-Present*, New York, Academic Press.

116 The few recent studies of girls and delinquency which have been published seriously question the traditional view. For a summary of much of this literature see; HEIDENSOHN, F. (1985), *Women and Crime*, London, Macmillan.

The Challenge of Learning to Care

Alec Dickson

In the early seventies Neil Postman, co-author of *Teaching as a Subversive Activity*, wrote in the old *New York Times* an article, 'Once upon a time', which he subtitled 'A fable of student power'. The streets were strewn with garbage, the air polluted, strikes, crime and racial troubles were rampant. There was nothing for the Mayor to do save to declare a state of emergency, as he had done before during snowstorms and power failures. Here, further ideas ran out.

At this point, one of the Mayor's aides, who had been re-reading Thoreau's *Walden*, came upon the passage: '*Students should not play life, or study it merely, while the community supports them at this expensive game, but earnestly live it from the beginning to end.*' So the curriculum of the public schools of New York City became known as Operation Survival. Every Monday 400,000 children helped clean up their own neighbourhoods, removing litter and graffiti. Wednesdays were reserved for beautifying the city, planting trees, painting subway stations and repairing broken-down public buildings, starting with their own schools. Each day 5000 students, the equivalent of our sixth-formers, directed traffic, releasing police to look after serious crime. Each day another 5000 students were asked to help deliver the mail, restoring the service to what it once had been decades earlier. Some helped to run day-care centres, whilst others assisted in hospitals. Every high school pupil helped two elementary school children on Tuesday and Thursday afternoons to learn to read, write and do arithmetic.

Postman observed:

'Because this is a fable and not a fairy tale, not everyone was happy. For example, thousands of children failed to learn the names of the principal rivers of Uruguay. There were hundreds of teachers who felt their training had been wasted because they could not educate children unless it were done in a classroom — and because it became so difficult to grade students on their activities, almost all tests ceased — so that no one could tell the dumb children from the smart children anymore.'

Of course this *jeu d'esprit* dates from the period of the de-schooling movement presently to be answered by the back-to-basics drive and much more recently by a doom-laden report on 'A Nation at Risk', advocating amongst other measures more homework, longer school days, and greater emphasis on technology. Nevertheless 'Once upon a time' focused for a moment on *young people's potential for enriching the community*.

More recently, Ernest Boyer, formerly US Commissioner of Education and now President of the Carnegie Foundation for the Advancement of Teaching, urges as one of four essential goals in the High School, a new 'Carnegie Unit' — not measuring hours spent in the classroom but emphasizing community service. Cynthia Parsons, for years the Education Correspondent of *The Christian Science Monitor*, in 'SEEDS — some good ways to improve our schools' is advocating a form of national service to be conducted through the schools. And Mayor Koch has established the New York City Volunteer Corps who — initially in hundreds rather than hundreds of thousands — are tackling at least some of those tasks touched upon in Postman's article.

So to Britain. Back in the early sixties, triggered off to some extent by what individual sixth form-leavers were doing, full-time, for a period of approximately a year either abroad in VSO or within this country in Community Service Volunteers, schools began to set up their own programmes to involve pupils in help to their immediate neighbourhood, here and now, on a wet Wednesday afternoon in Wolverhampton or Wimbledon, whether as an alternative (generally in the independent sector) to the Cadet Force or Games, or (more often in the statutory sector) as part of the curriculum.

Those were heady days. Imagination and concern resulted in sighted teenagers taking pupils from a nearby blind school out into the country on tandem bikes. A group of London sixth formers would meet immigrants from the West Indies arriving at Waterloo Station and see them to Euston and other main line termini, or direct them to Brixton or Lewisham, sometimes keeping in touch with them subsequently. A factory worker — threatened with the loss of his job by a rare blood deficiency which led to his fingers growing so cold that after a few hours he could not handle his tools

— was equipped by seventeen year-olds on Day Release classes in electricity with battery-operated, transistorized mittens. Practical morality plays — whose message might aim no higher than the desirability of brushing teeth or running errands — were performed by secondary school pupils in primary schools. Big stores were persuaded to stay open one particular evening in early December so that the physically handicapped could be brought in, on stretchers or in wheelchairs, to buy Christmas presents. Elderly ladies in Southall were persuaded to welcome pairs of recently arrived Asian youngsters to help them practice their English; the Punjabi boys were told that they were needed to befriend our lonely old people — a nice instance of reciprocity or mutual aid.

Matrons were persuaded that greater happiness would result from nurses supervising the feeding of thirty geriatric patients by thirty pupils (who had already raced through their own lunch at school), on a one-to-one basis, with all that this entailed in kindness and lack of hurry, than doing it themselves. Shortly afterwards hospitals began to appoint volunteer organisers. Task Force was set up, enabling thousands of pupils to befriend the elderly and housebound. The Schools Council, the Scottish Education Department and eventually the Department of Education and Science were each persuaded separately to produce a report conferring their pedagogic blessing on the concept. A rearguard action had to be waged with those who preferred the words 'voluntary service' to 'community service'. Had they prevailed sceptical head teachers could have argued that of course they were in favour — provided it was undertaken in spare-time or out of school altogether, and did not mean any adjustments to the existing timetable. Conferences were held by Local Education Authorities, from Dumfries to Dorset, from Perth to Plymouth. CSV published kits suggesting new approaches. We strove to convince Heads that collections for charities, no matter how worthy the cause, were not what it was about. Young people, indeed all of us, had entered an era when you could no longer pay others to do your caring for you.

By now it seemed that Community Service in schools had really arrived. True, formidable obstacles remained. To induce a College of Education or a University School of Education to include in their teacher training (or in-service course for experienced educationists) any preparation in the methodology of *how* to develop and adminster more effective programmes for involving pupils in community service proved virtually impossible. One cannot imagine why, but the resistance has proved unsuperable. Yet the question has to be put — *should* teachers be appointed who have had no experience other than that of being taught?

This has led to several profound defects — notably the lack of any provision for growth within programmes. In any academic subject, indeed in any school activity, more is required of a pupil at fifteen than at thirteen years of age. And a seventeen year old should expect to be confronted with more demanding problems than two years earlier. This scarcely ever happens in community service. In effect they all remain at Book One. By continual small doses of the same experience, pupils become immunized or innoculated against the possibility of a major 'take'. For lack of increased challenge — intellectual, emotional or physical — they grow bored. In passing, we underestimated the capacity of the Cadet Forces to score a come-back. With adventurous training on the Outward Bound model in place of the tedious parades and Field Days of former years, with the possibility of diving in submarines of the Royal Navy, or riding in tanks with British troops in Germany, it is hard to compete with more visitations of the old. Virtually only those schools deriving their original inspiration from Kurt Hahn have striven to combine the challenge of rescue work with social concern: in Hahn's words, 'to make the brave gentle and the gentle brave.'

We could, and surely should, have been encouraging young people to tackle some of the problems which most touch upon their own lives — children of one-parent families, drugs amongst their peer group, vandalism, race relations in the school or neighbourhood. Some of these problems are much more likely to be solved by the young themselves, as being the most affected, than by adults. For that matter, have we tried imaginatively enough — or been ready to risk enough — to discover what young people might do positively in Northern Ireland?

Just before the miners' strike ended in 1985, an American high school located on one of their defence installations in East Anglia was negotiating to take their basketball team to some of the colliery communities in the Midlands. It might seem politically naive for American teenagers — from a cruise missile base of all places — to think that their basketball team would have a contribution to make in such a highly charged situation. But what they had, they were ready to give — a gesture of recognition and a willingness to exult in their physical agility. We need to remind ourselves that feelings are enriched if they include sharing joy as well as sorrow, hopes as well as frustrations.

Caring for persons, the more able and the less able serving each other, is what makes a good society. It is not too much to assert that in most countries schooling constitutes a process of systematized selfishness: what matters is how to advance yourself up the academic ladder. Learning to care is frequently left to chance, or it is perceived as a spare time occupation, undertaken after work, at weekends or in the holidays. Community service can play an important role in combatting our innate tendency to self-centredness. Obviously the juxtaposition of challenge with learning to care is not the whole answer. Otherwise every alpinist would be an altruist and every surgeon a saint. Now that massive unemployment means, amongst the collapse of so many other conventions, that new concepts of education and training have to be developed, we have to ask whether this invalidates our stance. Many believe this: it is real jobs we want, not opportunities of service, they declare. 'A boy becomes a man when a man is needed' wrote John Steinbeck — but what if this need is never experienced?

Since it would require a whole book to examine these implications, we have to recognize that we must start to blur the traditional distinctions between work and service, no less than between study and service. In each instance one can merge into the other. The master in charge of Economics at Charterhouse School recently wrote in a letter to *The Times* how he had taken a group of sixth formers, mostly destined for merchant banking, to Merseyside, and he described the educational impact on them of seeing the industrial desolation and talking with young people who now despaired of ever getting a job. An educational impact, yes, but to a certain point only. How much profounder would have been the impact, had they worked together, shared their skills and talents, and joined in some common experience of responding to human needs and tackling conservation tasks. In this context unemployment does not demolish the argument for injecting community service into the curriculum, it immeasurably reinforces it. Otherwise, as the master himself pointed out in his letter, we remain the Two Nations described by Disraeli. Service — or responding to the needs of the community — used to be regarded as the prerogative of young mandarins of gifted sixthformers from prestigious schools. Today, under the MSC, involvement in community programmes has become the last resort of young coolies. Surely it should be for both — a shared experience.

There are occasions when experience should be assessed in terms of its intensity rather than its chronological duration. In *Cancer Ward* Solzhenitsin describes how the calm, clinical cancer specialist realizes for the first time in a flash — when it is *she* who is being examined for a suspected tumour — what an abyss of horror lies in those few seconds before the consultant delivers judgment to the patient. But the kind of endeavour described in the previous paragraph cannot really be fitted into a formal school term or a week's field study trip. It calls for a longer period to achieve results, whether in work undertaken, skills and insights acquired, friendships made, or attitudes changed. Even if we were still in the era of full employment there would be an unanswerable case for interrupting the academic routine of the more socially fortunate and intellectually gifted, enabling them to break away from the classroom and plunge for a year into real-life situations of need. Otherwise, from a dozen years of absorbing cognitive knowledge, without giving out or back anything of themselves to society, they risk mental constipation. Brown University in the States makes a track-record of service given a criterion of admission. In those institutions of higher education in Britain which still interview candidates why do they not ask in what way applicants have applied their talents and energies to community needs? Man does not learn by head alone.

It is important that schools should not assume that community service ends with the termination of secondary education. A movement is also taking shape, in colleges, polytechnics and universities whereby students apply the knowledge and skills they are acquiring, as an integral part of their courses, to human needs and problems of significance to the community. In North America this is sometimes called Experiential Education or Service-Learning. Unesco and our own Department of Education and Science call it Study Service. Obviously more challenging tasks can be undertaken in institutions of higher education. Hong Kong Polytechnic and Coventry (Lanchester) Polytechnic are pioneering in this field.

One further reason for giving greater attention to learning to care is the arrival of the computer. With the fascination that electronic games exercise on children of younger and younger ages, with the installation of computers in virtually every school, and our increasing dependence on high technology in every walk of life, we are faced with two alternatives. One is to *balance* this emphasis with equal stress on experiences which nurture concern. The other is to *apply* the computer and technology generally to the relief of suffering, and the solution of problems that beset humanity.

That intellectual challenge and concern for others are most definitely not incompatible is easy to demonstrate. To secure an 'A' level in Design Technology the candidate has to produce original designs and plans, any one of which could relate to a complex human need or community problem. At a somewhat less rigorous standard, the Schools Concern project in Salford brought hundreds of pupils from secondary schools face to face with disabled people and entailed their inventing some mechanism or device that would help them in their individual disability. Such an explosion of creativity resulted that the programme was expanded to include senior classes in primary schools. It was a nine-year-old girl who remarked: 'Handicap isn't something you can say "I'm sorry" to'. It was a class of primary school pupils who solved the problem of enabling the blind to participate in Bingo on equal terms with the sighted. Technology appears to be ahead of what used to be called the Humanities in its ability to arouse young people's concern for practical social action.

But if the competitiveness of the educational system promotes self-centredness amongst the abler and a sense of rejection amongst the less able, are the approaches I have described so far, or the practical examples described later in this chapter, strong enough antidotes? 'Seldom' must be the regretful answer. The school itself must develop an additional dimension, as a resource centre of help. Institutions can perform more than one role. A teaching hospital provides both for the training of medics and the treatment of patients: indeed the training of doctors-to-be requires the presence of the sick and injured. In California's camps for young offenders, delinquent teenagers are trained to deal with forest fires and to save lives (including one another's) in conflagrations: teams are on constant alert. They do not have to be good in order to do good: rather they become good through doing good. Their rehabilitation is largely dependent on their enjoying a role, recognition, responsibility, yes, and even an element of risk — experiences rarely encountered in the classroom. Even if some skills and many forms of knowledge do not lend themselves to application to community problems, schools should seek, as institutions, ways of responding to needs. And if compete they must, cannot young people compete to help others?

Practical examples

Some practical examples may indicate the rich variety of opportunities for service and the many ways by which teachers and pupils can tackle them.

Alec Dickson

The Newspaper Exercise

Pupils are asked to bring copies of the local newspaper(s) to class — and are shown how to identify reports of incidents or situations to which they themselves might contribute a solution. 'Drowned Child in Flooded Sandpit'. Could pupils fill in, or fence off, the sandpit? Or should they run a campaign to ensure that children in the vicinity can swim or know about water safety? 'Old People's Lunch Club Threatened by Lack of Helpers'. Could pupils step into the gap even though the story may have implied that it was adult helpers in greater number who were needed? 'Protest at Lack of Traffic Lights near Primary School'. If the school is nearby, could secondary school pupils organize a pedestrian crossing patrol for the younger children? 'Ambassador's Wife visits Hospital' may be just the caption on a photograph. But on looking closely at the picture, the face of a boy in bed is seen . . . in a ward otherwise full of adult and even aged patients. Perhaps he is a chronically sick child unable to be nursed at home — but with no one of his own age in the ward to talk to. Could your pupils 'adopt' him?

This approach develops amongst pupils a 'seeing eye', able to detect opportunities for practical intervention where the reporters (and ordinary readers) perceive only a problem or happening. Pupils now begin to read newspapers more critically — yet positively. They have the satisfaction of feeling that they are dealing with a real and topical incident which is making news. If the newspaper is informed, it is likely to publish a follow-up story reflecting credit on the school and its pupils.

Transferring The Location of a School Activity

Most pupils study Art — but need it always be in the Art Department? Suppose that occasionally they did their drawing in an old people's home: what pleasure they would bring to the elderly residents. If they are primary school children, what joy they would give if they sang to people at a centre for the handicapped. One school, once a fortnight — in agreement with the nearby hospital — enables a different class to do their Physical Education down the middle of the ward between the beds: not only do they give delight to the patients (and nursing staff) but they themselves find the experience tremendous fun: most youngsters enjoy an audience.

A 'Living Heroes' Trail

Many schools have developed nature trails. Suppose, instead, they set out to discover people in the neighbourhood who are quietly living a life of real sacrifice or, in the past, have done some unnoticed or forgotten act of courage or compassion. This might mean pupils consulting a pastor or priest, social workers or the archivists at newspaper offices. In this way they might discover a woman who was looking after a paralyzed husband or a Down's Syndrome child: someone who had rescued miners in a pit disaster: or a blinded person who had had to start to master a new job in middle life. The pupils would learn that heroes do not necessarily have to have been dead for over a hundred years or have a statue erected in their honour in the city centre: heroism is within the reach of almost every one of us.

Reciprocity

Many pupils who may be children of immigrant origin are accommodated in circumstances where the family situation makes it very difficult for them to do their school homework, because of cramped living conditions and noise made by other children. Suppose arrangements were made with a nearby hospital that such children should do their school preparation individually at the bedside of patients in an orthopaedic ward. Such patients, recovering from motorcycle or motorcar accidents, can be middle-aged or younger. Because they may come from other parts of the country, it is possible that they may lack local relatives or friends to visit them. So they might welcome, as a relief from boredom, talking with youngsters of immigrant origin and be ready to help them with their school preparation. The pupils would be doing their preparation undisturbed by the hullabaloo in their own families and would be improving their ability to express themselves in English. In this way each meets the need of the other: this is reciprocity.

Co-operation with Other Government Ministries or Agencies

A social worker, invited to address eleven year-olds, chose to tell them of her problem of finding families to accept children-in-care.

She reckoned that no-one would know better than eleven year-olds whether their parents were the kind of Mum and Dad whom any other child would be proud to possess. Nobody would be more likely, too, to know of a bed in their house shortly to fall vacant because of an older sister getting married or an older brother moving to work in another city: moreover, in reaching what is clearly an adult decision, no factor would weigh more heavily with the parents than the probable reaction of their own natural-born child to the presence of a younger foster brother or sister in the home. The social worker's instinct proved correct. That evening several of the pupils who had listened to her pleaded successfully with their parents to consider taking in a foster child. Could there be a better service to the community?

Taking the Police by Surprise — Help From Pupils?!

I wrote some time ago to a number of Chief Constables, asking if they would welcome assistance from school pupils. Several reacted with incredulity: were we seriously suggesting that they, the Merseyside Police, required help from kids? We replied: if young people are not a part of the solution, then they can become part of the problem. As a consequence, some of the Police Forces took the suggestion in earnest, set up 'think tanks' to analyze the whole range of tasks facing them — and proposed twenty very varied ways by which pupils might contribute to the preservation of law and order — all of them genuinely within the capacity of pupils, none of them ethically objectionable, physically dangerous or contrary to young people's natural inclinations. What was significant was the surprised realization of the Police that they are not all-powerful; they, in fact, need the practical goodwill of the public — of whom the young are an important element.

Operation Wheelchair — Part One

A whole class goes to the nearest hospital to collect, by previous arrangement, some thirty wheelchairs, with instructions to return to school, fifteen as 'patients', fifteen as 'escorts'. One is asked to telephone on the return journey from a public kiosk; another to fetch a book from a public library; another to use a public toilet; yet another is given money to enter a cinema. They find in fact that one cannot reach far enough from a wheelchair to dial a number in a kiosk; that it would be suicidally dangerous to descend into a subterranean toilet; that it is not possible to mount the steps of the public library; and the cinema manager, however personally sympathetic, declares that fire-safety regulations forbid the blocking of aisles/exits with any hindrance such as a wheelchair. What pupils have learnt from personal experience is the extent of the *man-made* difficulties which the handicapped have to endure, in addition to their physical disabilities. (NB. When this operation has been conducted in co-operation with genuinely handicapped pupils from a Special School, then the impact has been even greater.)

Operation Wheelchair — Part Two

This is not the end. Two possibilities now face the class. One is to produce a guide book — often at the request of a Ministry or Agency concerned with the handicapped — showing how the disabled can (or cannot) gain access to public amenities and places of entertainment. The other is simply to ask the pupils, now excited by the experience, 'Well, what are you going to do about it?' To this, the normal response is, 'We're only pupils, we can't do anything'. But two or three of them could measure the height of the steps leading to the public library, construct in the school workshop a ramp (perhaps one which telescopes into a small space when unused) and present it to the library, offering at the same time to instal a mirror beside the porter's window. Regarding the cinema, they can telephone to discover the name and address of the editor of the trade journal which almost certainly circulates amongst cinema managements in the region. In the letter which they write to the editor they describe their experience and plead that if one seat is removed in the back row for the benefit of a wheelchair-user, well, the cinema is not likely to be bankrupted. Similarly they can discover the name of the chairman of the committee responsible for public toilets, write to him — perhaps at his private address, thereby ensuring that their letter does reach his eyes! — asking whether he will receive a delegation of two or three pupils to discuss whether the facilities available at airports for handicapped travellers might not be installed in some public toilets in the town.

What pupils have now learnt is even more important than empathy with the handicapped: namely, that — without 'demos', confrontations or boycotts — adult authorities will sometimes listen to the experience of genuinely concerned pupils and may even change their regulations in the light of their recommendations, when based on first-hand research. A similar 'operation' was undertaken by nineteen/twenty year-old girl students at a Teacher Training College in Lancashire. Making friends with Asian immigrant house-wives, the brunettes borrowed Asian dress and went shopping in the local market — where they found how often inflated prices were quoted and short change offered. Some of these student-teachers decided in consequence to teach in multi-racial schools.

Discovering What The Phrase 'Community Care' Really Means

Many mental hospitals are now trying to discharge some of their patients back into the community and encourage them to live in hostels, perhaps being employed in sheltered workshops. This offers two possibilities for schools. We have produced a 'dummy' news-paper reporting the intention to establish just such a hostel for discharged mental patients — a decision which arouses so much controversy in a middle-class neighbourhood that an official enquiry is ordered to hear both sides of the argument. The 'Enquiry' takes place, in effect, in the classroom, each pupil playing the role of an interested member of the local community. In many instances, it is obvious from the background of the individual what his attitude will be: but not always. The pupil who finds himself playing the role of a prominent estate agent, who himself is the parent of a mentally retarded child, begins to comprehend that in real life not all issues can be seen in terms of black and white, or right versus wrong. The conflict between his financial self-interest in seeing rates maintained may be balanced by his concern for his own afflicted child. Pupils in their late teens tend sometimes to see adult indecision as proof of hypocrisy: it is valuable for them to learn that being torn between two loyalties may be the characteristic of an honest man, not of a pharisee.

Pupils Befriend and Train the Mentally Retarded

More definitely practical has been the action of pupils from Solihull, near Birmingham. Influenced by the fact that one pupil's father is distinguished in mental health, psychiatric hospital authorities welcomed the help of pupils in preparing a group of retarded patients for eventual discharge. The pupils began by teaching the retarded trainees the use of simple tools and social skills such as telling the time, handling money, coping with situations in a Post Office and shops, recognizing words such as 'Danger', 'Men' and 'Women'. Then the pupils set up a community help project that brought together local elderly people (none of whom had previously met a retarded person face-to-face); the trainees (who for the first time were giving help rather than receiving it); and the pupils themselves (ranging in age between fourteen and eighteen years). In this 'circle of help' — the pupils' own phrase for this concept — the retarded trainees worked alongside the pupils in assisting the elderly with gardening, housework and decorating — and in so doing learned about the problems of old age; the elderly came to accept the trainees as friends — and began to understand a little about mental retardation. And the pupils extended help to both parties — thereby acquiring experience of what is meant by 'community involvement'. Surely a model example of training in social responsibility.

Utilizing Emergencies

Since the one thing we can be certain of is that crisis situations will face us with increasing frequency — floods, abnormal snow conditions, traffic pile-ups in fog, oil tankers sinking off the coasts, the sudden arrival of refugees (for example, from Vietnam), even acts of terrorism — can we use these to give our pupils (and teachers) a chance to exercise initiative, courage and compassion? When 23,000 Asians suddenly arrived in Britain a few years ago, expelled from Uganda by Idi Amin, they were accommodated at nearby schools in the countryside. 'Geography' and 'Current Affairs' were no longer classroom subjects but human beings in distress, families requiring blankets and warm clothes, children in need of help in accustoming themselves to British schooling and the British way of life; it lay in the power of our pupils to give this kind of practical friendship and they gave it.

Environmental Improvement

The opportunities to better or to beautify one's surroundings are so great that every school should be able to involve their pupils in one way or another. At the University of Strathclyde, students of Architecture and Building Science have been helping in some of Glasgow's schools, at the request of the Local Education Authority, to open the eyes of pupils to what is attractive and what is ugly in their neighbourhood; to see how buildings can embellish or desecrate a landscape; to understand how development and planning can affect opportunities for recreation, increase or discourage vandalism, bring about the displacement of small self-owned shops by branches of multiple-store chains; to prepare their own maps and surveys — and get the children involved in actually improving their environment. The students' contribution is warmly welcomed by the teachers concerned.

What Can Be Done in Rural Areas

But what if pupils (and teachers) in schools situated in rural areas look through the windows and see neither anything that is ugly nor anyone visibly in need of help? Does it follow that community service has no meaning for them? Suppose that they share with others less fortunate than themselves what is uniquely pleasurable in their surroundings. The suggestion is that — in the mid-term break (or even in the first week of the holidays) — they invite a group of immigrant children from an urban area, or children-in-care from a Children's Home, or slightly subnormal children from some Special School, to be their guests, either accommodating them in their families or all of them together 'camping' in sleeping bags in the school's largest classroom. It is not necessary that the school be in the mountains or beside a lake, for the pupils (and staff) to organize a one-week Adventure Training Course, a miniature 'Outward Bound'. In any rural area there will be trees where a 'house' could be erected in the branches à la Swiss Family Robinson — or a canal or river on which an expedition by raft, à la 'Kon Tiki', could be mounted. Experience is that such an arrangement teaches the 'host' pupils much about their own locality which they did not know before — but the ideal is when the visit is returned, with rural pupils, for example, venturing to stay with immigrant families.

Tutoring — Older Pupils Helping Those Younger

When all else fails and neither teacher nor pupils can find suitable projects, perhaps the most obvious opportunity of service is right there under their noses — the chance for older pupils to help those younger or less advanced. We owe it to the Americans that they have re-discovered what is apparent in every family and in every village of the Third World — namely, that younger children learn from older brothers and sisters. In the thousands of schools in the United States — and in those schools in Britain where it is beginning to happen — it is known as tutoring. On a one-to-one basis the older pupil can devote an intensity of personal attention to the individual need of the younger child which even the most experienced teacher in an ordinary classroom situation cannot ever hope to give. When to this intensity of attention is added ordinary comradeship — the older pupils happy to feel that they have something to give and to be genuinely needed, the younger children proud to possess their own senior special friend — then you have the most powerful motivation for learning-and-teaching. In both American and British schools, it is teachers themselves who have introduced, nurtured and supervized this development. It can be between older and younger pupils in the same school — or between pupils in a secondary school and a nearby primary school. It can take place in the library, in a corridor, in any nook or cranny that can be found. Whilst it generally centres on reading difficulties, it can function just as easily in maths or sport.

Recent research indicates that the tutor gains as much as (or more than) the child being helped. This means that tutors do not have to be unusually intelligent or advanced. Provided that there is a gap of a few years between the participants — so that the older pupils feel no fear of 'losing face' in the presence of those whom they are helping — the tutors can themselves be of distinctly modest calibre academically. In the process of helping a younger child to master a subject or skill, he reinforces his own understanding and competence; furthermore, the awareness that he may be acting as a character model for the younger child can give him a deep satisfaction. Where tutoring has been introduced, it seems to encourage a friendlier and more co-operative atmosphere generally throughout the school — as well as an appreciation amongst pupils of the problems which face teachers.

The Curricular Approach

These examples — hundreds more could be quoted from all types of schools — have certain characteristics. First, they imply that 'Community Service' is a subject or activity in the school timetable in its own right. In very many schools it is just that. This is a thousand times better than making no provision at all in the curriculum for pupils to respond to human needs. It may, in many instances, be pedagogically and administratively easier to reserve a place in the timetable for Community Service than to choose in preference a more sophisticated approach.

But, inevitably, voices will be heard saying that the timetable is already overcrowded and that pupils must concentrate on the academic subjects which count towards their grading. Is there, then, another approach which avoids these objections? Fortunately, there is. This approach — the curricular approach — treats Community Service not as a separate activity in its own right, but as an extra dimension of most (indeed, virtually all) existing formal subjects. It has been called — by Chicago University's Professor of Education — *the humane application of knowledge*. In other words, the teacher helps his students apply their skills and understanding to a specific problem of significance to the needs of the community. Here are some examples:

Mathematics at Junior Level

Ten-year-olds, when they visit the elderly, who may be sixty to seventy years older than themselves, may find it difficult to keep the conversation going. A concrete task could be to help the elderly to budget their pensions, asking how much they pay for butter, bread, meat, sugar, coffee, etc. In all probability the old person does all her shopping at the friendly little shop at the corner, being slightly afraid of the Supermarket. Let the youngster run round to the Supermarket, note prices and compare them with what she is paying. He might even escort her to the Supermarket. Results:-

(a) He has exercised simple arithmetic. (NB. This took place at a time when Britain's £.s.d. currency was being converted to decimal coinage — so it constituted a greater mathematical challenge to explain the implications to elderly citizens.)
(b) He had found something concrete and topical to talk about, and where he is not expected to play only a passive, listening role.
(c) He may have genuinely helped the old age pensioner.
(d) He himself has learnt about the cost of living — something

that he never did at home where his mother is responsible for this aspect of life.

English Literature

Talking to sixteen-year olds at a high school in Bombay recently, it emerged that the assigned book in English was *Oliver Twist*. Despite the fact that their command of English was good and although it seemed that some of them knew more about the works of Charles Dickens than many of their British counterparts, the unfamiliarity of the setting — London during the 1830s — made it hard for some of them to grasp the underlying message of the novel. I suggested that the book centred around the relationship between child poverty and delinquency. This relationship they could see for themselves at first hand by visiting the Juvenile Remand Centre barely 1000 yards away. For there, behind its crenellated walls, they would find on any day seldom less than 200 children, some of them already practised in stealing, but many dragged by the police the previous night from beneath some improvised shelter of cardboard packing or a piece of cloth. Within its vast courtyard these children would be just sitting, while hard-pressed staff prepared papers on them for magistrates. The sixteen year-olds jumped at the idea that they should go into the Remand Centre to organize games and tutoring for the children, to befriend them and, upon their discharge or release, to include a few of them at least in their extra-curricular school activities. A few months afterwards, the students sat for their annual examinations and encountered, in the English Literature paper, the question 'Assess the social significance of *Oliver Twist* and evaluate the influence of Dickens as a writer and reformer.' Now suddenly they were expressing their conviction, born of personal experience at the Remand Centre, that the greatness of Charles Dickens lay in that what he wrote was relevant for all times and all places.

Biology

A visit to the Shetland Islands in the North Sea — said to be nearer to Berlin than to London — revealed that the fish-processing ships were throwing overboard the cods' heads, tails, bones, as well as the bits of plastic snipped off the bags in which they were packaged before they went into the ship's deep freezers. The discarded bits and pieces were washed up on shore by the next tide — making the beaches stink and causing offence to summer visitors as well as residents. In addition, there was the risk — now that so many more oil tankers were using the small harbour — of a pipe-connection breaking and spilling oil into the sea — with its rich fishing beds. Result:- a decision by Science teachers in the Shetland Islands to mount a major Marine Biology project the following school year, not only acquainting pupils with the consequences, but acting as a form of adult education for the islands' population.

Classics

The Classics teacher at Eton, asked highly intelligent eighteen year-olds to compare Greek and Roman attitudes to suicide. What had Suetonius and Marcus Aurelius to say about the sanctity of human life compared with Sophocles, Plato and Socrates? Why? Because he knew that many of the senior pupils were taking a responsible part in a local 'crisis' phone-in programme on certain nights of the week, endeavouring to answer pleas for advice or assistance, some of them coming nowadays increasingly from younger teenagers, perhaps contemplating self-destruction. Suddenly, the thinking of great philosophers of 2000 or more years ago snaps into urgent perspective and helps those eighteen/nineteen year-olds to plead more cogently with the anguished young callers not to despair.

Physical Education

Pupils have been told to blindfold themselves first — and then start their Physical Education exercises. After a few moments of chaos and confusion, they are told to uncover their eyes, sit down in small groups, and then, during the remainder of the session, invent two or more games which could be played by sightless children. On another day, a different class is told to tie their legs. Again confusion and chaos. Then they, too, are told to undo their legs and in small groups to devise two or more games which might be played by disabled children. Their ideas are collated and, with simple pictures drawn by a pupil-artist, reproduced on the school's Gestetner. Result:- a handbook of games to enrich the lives of handicapped children attending special schools throughout the whole region.

Handicrafts

At a school in Crewe with low academic attainments, a class of 'difficult' fifteen year-olds (many of them known to the police) is taken by their Handicrafts teacher to the local General Hospital. There they come face to face with nine small children suffering from spina bifida, a congenital deformity of the spine. The boys see for themselves that these children can neither stand nor move. The hospital staff asked: 'Can you design something to make these children mobile?' Back at their school, over a period of six weeks, they devoted every Handicrafts period to experimenting with different materials and different designs. Eventually they return to the hospital, bearing with them nine beautifully polished V-shaped trays, mounted on caster wheels, to cradle the splayed-out legs of each child — who can now move himself in any direction with his finger tips. Result: they have achieved a solution to a human need which had so far baffled the hospital staff.

Science

At Walkden School, in Salford, near Manchester, pupils have designed alarm clocks to waken the deaf, linking old or out-of-date hair dryers with alarm clocks, which blew air on the face of the sleeper at the required hour. They have developed a device which will alert passers-by in the High Street if a baby is snatched from a perambulator. More intriguingly still, they have invented gadgetry which will make neighbours aware, even in winter time (when doors and windows are closed) if an elderly person living alone suffers a collapse: this device involves linking the lavatory chain to a time-switch which operates an alarm if the toilet is not used after eleven hours! At Sevenoaks School in Kent, eighteen-year-old pupils are studying Design in the hope of gaining entrance to universities, developing devices to enable spastic pupils to work more effectively in their school Science laboratories. At Pocklington School in Yorkshire, intelligent seventeen/eighteen-year-old pupils are studying ways of harnessing wind power and solar energy with such competence that two universities are watching their experiments. At Kettering Grammar School in Northamptonshire, pupils have developed electronic mechanisms as delicate as those used by the United Kingdom government: that is to say, they have sometimes been the first to detect the launching of Sputniks before their signals have been picked up by the government's monitoring station at Jodrell Bank. The possibilities for utilizing Handicrafts, Technology, and Science, within our secondary schools to serve the community are endless.

The Great Advantages of the Curricular Approach

To summarize some of the advantages of the curricular approach to community service:

* Not one teacher alone is concerned with enabling students to undertake community service, but a cross-section of the whole staff. Furthermore, each teacher's own interest is more likely to be engaged because the project relates to — or emerges from — his or her field of specialization.
* The vital element of growth — and an intellectual cutting edge — is imparted to community service programme, with seventeen year-old pupils tackling more challenging projects than they did at fifteen, and fifteen year-olds undertaking more demanding tasks than the did at thirteen.
* Not just the socially concerned minority of pupils participate but the whole class — without their being labelled as 'do-gooders'.
* The old conflict — between time spent on community service and time devoted to studies — can be more easily resolved because they are inter-related.

References

BOYER, E. (1983) *High School*, New York, Harper and Row.
BURLEY, D. (1980) *Issues in Community Service*, National Youth Bureau.
COLOMBATTO, E. (1980) *Nation-Wide Social Service: A Proposal for the Nineteen Eighties*, Centre for Labour Economics.
DICKSON, A. (1984) 'Study service, "West German Zivildienst", The California Conservation Corps', *Youth Call.*
DICKSON, A. and M. (1984) *Volunteers*, Furnivall Press, CSV.
DICKSON, A. and M. (1976) *A Chance to Serve*, London, Dobson Press.
GROVES, M. (1980) *Community Service and The Secondary School*, National Youth Bureau.
MARSLAND, D. (1984) 'Work to be done', *Youth Call*

MARSLAND, D. (1982) 'Criticism, prejudice and the interests of young people', *Voluntary Action*, Autumn

POSTMAN, N. and WEINGARTNER, C. (1971) *Teaching As a Subversive Activity*, Harmondsworth, Penguin.

THOMAS, F.A. (1984) *National Service: An Aspect of Youth Development*, New York, Ford Foundation.

Youth Call (1981) 'A debate on youth and service to the community.'

Capitalizing on Youth: Group Work in Education

David Marsland and Michael Day

This chapter was to have been written by Leslie Button. Sadly he died before he could complete the task. His death was a grievous loss not only to his family and many friends, but also to the world of education, to youth work, and to young people. Few have done more valuable work, intellectually and practically, on behalf of young people than Leslie. This book is dedicated to his memory.

Fortunately he has written much and passed on to those who worked with him many of his original approaches and ideas. The authors of this chapter are privileged to be two of those who were deeply influenced by his ideas. We have agreed, with no little anxiety in the face of the impossible task of standing in for him, to give an account of his ideas and methods for the use of group work in education. It is our view that he has been close to unique in Britain in combining an understanding of the nature of young people with the development of ideas and methods which capitalize on the special characteristics of young people to make education more enjoyable and more effective. What we attempt here is to give a clear account of these ideas and methods in order to make them available to others who are endeavouring, as Leslie did, to improve education.

This chapter is not a systematic summary of his many writings, nor a comprehensive evaluation of his ideas.[1] Rather it is an attempt at presenting the essence of his approach to group work as we understand it, and to suggest in practical terms how that approach can be put to use in education. His main published works are: *Discovery and Experience: A New Approach to Training, Group Work, and Teaching*; *Developmental Group Work With Adolescents*; *Group Tutoring For the Form Teacher*; and 'The pastoral curriculum'.[2] We have taken systematic account of all of these.

Over and above his writing, Leslie was very influential as a result of his continuing involvement in training and consultancy with youth workers and with school teachers. Much of what we have learned about group work has come to us through these networks.

In addition, this chapter relies on work undertaken by the Brunel Training Consultative Unit, which has developed from Leslie Button's ideas — in particular the group work curriculum of the Brunel (previously Regional) Basic Training Scheme, and the group work module of the Postgraduate Diploma in Youth and Community Studies.[3] The former is the only university certificated course in Britain for part-time and voluntary youth and community workers. The latter is an advanced in-service training programme for Youth Officers and senior Youth Workers.

The Nature of Group Work

Group work has complex origins in psychotherapy and group dynamics, in Central Europe and in the United States. Since its beginnings it has differentiated into a multiplicity of diverse guises, each emphasizing some particular theoretical or practical dimension. In recent years it has achieved a more coherent and unitary image as a particular type of professional intervention mechanism contrasted with *case work and counselling* on the one side and *community work* on the other.

Even so the nature of group work in the different contexts in which it is used remains distinct in each case and heterogeneous overall. In particular, there are different approaches to and emphases within group work in psychotherapy, social work, youth work, and teaching. It is not our purpose here to examine the origins and development of group work, or to clarify the interconnections between different versions of it. This is in any case undertaken elsewhere.[4] It is important, however, to emphasize that developmental group work (referred to as DGW hereafter), as Leslie Button called his version, is a specific approach with its own unique objectives, theoretical assumptions, and practical techniques. It is on DGW that we focus.

David Marsland and Michael Day

The Rationale For Using Group Work in Education

Leslie Button was unusual in working both with the Youth Service and in the schools. What these two contexts have in common is a shared commitment to social education and a common clientéle of young people. DGW is a method of professional intervention designed to facilitate the social education of young people. The contrast between the characteristic modes of work in these two contexts points up the rationale for using group work in education.

Despite many recent changes, secondary schools in Britain retain certain basic features which limit their effectiveness in accomplishing social education, and indeed others of their objectives as well.[5] For the most part interaction between teachers and pupils takes place in the highly structured situation defined by the classroom, a relatively large number of pupils constituting a class, and a single teacher. The nature of classroom interaction is fundamentally shaped by academic curricular objectives oriented to cognitive learning. The outcomes of pupil-teacher interaction are assessed by one or other formal method of examination of individual curricular learning. Aspects of pupils' personalities, concerns and behaviour other than those directly relevant to cognitive curricular learning are treated for the most part as distractions or interferences. Little account is taken, other than as a source of difficulty for teachers, of group processes within classrooms.

Group work provides an antidote to these weaknesses. It makes individual young people's needs and concerns central. It seeks to incorporate each pupil's whole personality into the learning process. The learning process itself is defined more broadly and deeply than can be encompassed in academic curricular learning. It capitalizes positively on pupil-to-pupil interactions and on group processes. Overall, group work constitutes in the school context a de-formalizing mechanism.

In the Youth Service, by contrast — in youth clubs, youth centres, and the variety of projects established to answer problems of unemployment, ethnic group disadvantage, delinquency, drug abuse, and so on — group work is a formalizing mechanism. Into situations where objectives are, let us say, less than fully explicit, it introduces clarity. Where commonly activity is a mélée of unprogrammed disparate episodes involving groups of young people of various sizes and types in a wide range of voluntary, personal purposes, group work defines goals, tasks and criteria of success. To the general concern in youth work for the needs of young people conceived in a broad and programmatic way, group work adds explicit attention to highly particularized needs and problems — involvement, friendship, identity, autonomy and so on. In terms of this contrast between formal schooling and youth work, group work, as Leslie Button envisaged it and practised it, serves as *a bridge between two polarized spheres* by providing a coherent methodology for social education. The necessity for this linkage is increasingly recognized, for a variety of reasons.

First, youth unemployment is occasioning the return to school of young people who would normally have left at the earliest opportunity. They have special needs which neither traditional teaching methods nor progressive educational ideology can answer adequately. Secondly, unemployment is also having a knock-back effect on younger pupils, for whom the established rationale for schooling has lost its persuasive power to a substantial extent (See the later chapter by Howard Williamson on this). Thirdly, quite apart from unemployment, mounting dissatisfaction with the education our secondary schools are providing has led to widespread demands for 'relevance', 'practicality' and 'learning for life'. And fourthly in some inner city schools their large scale and changing mores have conspired to undermine the type and level of order which genuine education presupposes.

Now, of course, neither social education in general, nor certainly the specific approach to social education which DGW represents, can provide a complete answer to such problems as these. They are massive problems which will require fundamental shifts in educational thinking and policy such as other chapters of this book explore.[6] DGW *does*, however, we are convinced, offer a powerful tool with which to make a significant practical beginning on these tasks. Not the least part of its potential power lies in its unapologetic reliance on young people's own active commitment and involvement. DGW provides a systematic construal of young people's needs and capacities *qua young people*, and a methodology for harnessing their youthfulness to advance their education.

The Objectives of Developmental Group Work

Button defines DGW as:

> A way of offering people opportunities for vital experiences
> with other people, through the membership of supportive

groups who are learning to help one another in personal ways. It is developmental and educative as distinct from problems or crisis based. Our ambition is to help young people to build up their personal resource so that they can cope more adequately with life — and its problems — as it comes along[7].

The aim of the developmental group worker is to use shared experience of participation in a group to provide *structured opportunities for discussion, action, and reflection.* Each of these is designed to draw on the personal and mutual concerns of young people. The resources which are drawn upon are not extrinsic — as in traditional discussion groups — but intrinsic to the current feelings of group members about themselves and others in the group. The method thus requires of developmental group workers considerable expertise, theoretical and practical, about personality and about group dynamics.

The focus is not, however, limited to the subjective world of the group itself, although this has to remain the 'home base' to which there is continuing return. On this basis:

> The support group can operate also as a platform from which to venture into other spheres of life. It can form an arena in which the young person can learn to cope with strangers, to engage in positive communication with adults, to manage his or her own authority feelings, and to make an increasingly creative contribution to family life. In the school context, the supportive group can contribute to each member's confidence in study and participation in the affairs of the school. It can also serve as a vehicle for imparting vital knowledge about health and hygiene, citizenship, the world of work and life in general.[8]

From the beginning Button has stressed that the whole purpose is 'personal education', that is to say transformations of individual skills and understandings required in the normal development of all young people as they move between childhood and adulthood. We have more than enough evidence today that personal education in this sense is not being effectively provided for. Neither our academic 'successes', nor our truanting, delinquent 'failures', nor the larger middling group who move, between the two extremes, rather sceptical and puzzled about the purposes of school *or* life, are being offered save by chance or good fortune an opportunity for the developmental work which personal education requires. Button insists that *it cannot be left to chance:* 'It is not realistic to expect that individual need for developmental experience can be produced in a succession of lessons designed primarily for some other purpose'.[9] DGW provides an arena and a method for providing for personal education reliably.

Arenas For Group Work

The dramatic practical effects of DGW often win over sceptics. People who had assumed it was some kind of mysterious, suspicious nonsense suddenly take a real interest when they see it energize and transform apathetic young people, or help shy youngsters lacking all confidence towards taking a lead in school activities, or shifting aggressively negative youths towards more constructive behaviour. However, even those persuaded of the relevance and power of group work commonly harbour misgivings about regular use of it in normal settings. Youth centre staff, for example, sometimes complain that group work interferes with the normal pattern of organized activities, or alters the relaxed atmosphere they have worked to create. Some school teachers express anxieties about interruptions to the normal momentum of lessons, or presume that attention to small groups is bound to mean neglect of the class as a whole.

It is one of the special marks of Button's approach that he has demonstrated the feasibility of using group work in normal everyday situations and settings. He shows precisely how youth workers and teachers with no more resources than normal can operate DGW effectively. Within even the most challenging youth work contexts, DGW can be undertaken successfully. In ordinary classrooms, at any level of ability and at all ages and stages, effective DGW programmes are entirely feasible. Given commitment, skill, and training, this tool can be used across the whole range of educational contexts — provided only that objectives are fully clarified, planning is comprehensive, and preparation is thorough.

Thus, it is quite feasible to organize programmes of DGW in larger classes in comprehensive schools and in big youth centres. All that is required is confident, authoritative definition of smaller groups of up to twelve within the larger context. The programme itself provides work which others outside the current focal group can continue with individually, in pairs, or in small groups. This work is not extrinsically imposed, and it arises out of attention to pupil's own interest and needs. Moreover, group work legitimates co-operative, autonomous behaviour. Experience suggests that, as a result, absence of direct supervision produces order rather than chaos, and creative involvement rather than destructive disaffiliation.

Certainly this is not a problem which Button can be accused of ignoring, either in analysis or in practice. Here for example is his advice about dealing with a larger group.

The major difficulty in all this is for the worker to make himself available to small groups with sufficient privacy and leisure to develop more intimate conversation. This difficulty can be met by careful planning, and particularly by timetabling the steps to be taken by each small group. In approaching this, a firm appreciation of the elements of the work depicted by Figure 4 (see page 98) can be of special value. Let us assume that three groups each have their own programme. Each group will need to take a good deal of the responsibility for its own planning, and it is possible for the worker to help all three groups meeting simultaneously, though separately, in the same room. At the next stage it may be possible for each group to carry through its activities with only the general encouragement and oversight of the worker. This will necessarily be the case when, for example, individual members or sub-sections of the groups are involved in action research or community service. The element that is more likely to need the individual attention of the worker is at the time for taking stock, when each group may be led into more exploratory and intimate exchanges. If the period when each group meets for its stock-taking is planned to coincide with times when the other groups are engaged in action, it is possible for the worker to give some undivided attention to each group in turn.

In working in this way the worker may have to accept a slower rate of development than if he were to give a small group his whole attention, but his influence does reach many more people. The sophistication of the work may suffer in that the worker will not be able to give the same attention to individual detail, but everybody concerned may nonetheless have a very significant experience. The quality of the experience will be influenced considerably by the preparatory programme, which should induce self-reliance both in individual young people and in the small groups, and a sense of supportiveness in the group as a whole. Greater depth will be added to the experiences if the worker can bring the groups to an acceptance of the need to help one another in a personal way, and help them acquire some skill in doing so.[10]

The Organization of Developmental Group Work

It is sometimes held against Leslie Button in Youth Service circles — where the non-directive is *de rigeur*, participation fashionably re-quisite, and leadership dismissed as old hat — that his approach is unacceptably 'directive'. On the other hand, it is bound to seem to many teachers that group work is hopelessly loose and chaotic.

In the context of these contradictory reactions, the value of DGW, in our view, is precisely its straddling of *the characteristic divide between permissive incoherence and orderly authoritarianism.* Thus:

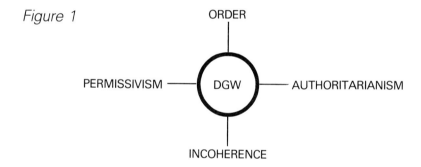

Figure 1

David Marsland and Michael Day

DGW allows, requires, and capitalizes on unpredictable developments arising out of spontaneous interpersonal relationships in the group and beyond it. It refuses to exclude feelings, relevancies, discoveries, and reactions which cannot be fitted into the framework of traditional lessons. On the other hand, it requires and provides for a tough framework of objectives, organization, tasks, and techniques such as non-directive youth work or mere discussion groups lack.

Even in relation to work with natural groups — picked up, as it were, accidentally in the course of youth work in a large youth centre — Button insists that DGW needs to be programmatic, organized, and controlled by a coherent rationale. In school settings the extent of organization DGW demands is demonstrated graphically in *Group Tutoring for the Form Teacher*. Its two volumes, for the lower and upper secondary school, each set out:-

1 The teacher's role.
2 Basic skills and concepts.
3 The teacher's relations with the school.
4 A detailed programme of work for the school year, divided into explicit stages.
5 Working papers providing detailed materials and systematic exercizes for each stage.

The programme for Stage 4 (lower school) and its associated working paper are set out below by way of example.

Figure 2

STAGE 4	*Autumn Term*
PROGRAMME	OBJECTIVES AND COMMENTS

Greetings.

Review caring routine.

Report back outside conversation with adult: Extend practice with outside conversations in readiness for a review of skills and framework in Stage 5.

Leave serious discussions of agendas until Stage 5. Encourage extended practice in outside conversations.

Enquiry into homework programme: Work through small groups with open exchanges (**Working Paper 27**).

  (a) Timetable:

    (i) At what time of the evening or weekend did you do your homework? And was this consistent?

Focus on planning a timetable, and ways of setting targets and sticking to them.

    (ii) How do you decide when to do it? Do you decide or just drift?

Leave the remainder of the enquiry until Stage 5.

    (iii) Did your homework tend to hang over your head for most of the evening?

Encourage firm contracts to carry through a timetable experiment and report back in Stage 5.

  (b) Planning:

    (i) Would it be advisable to plan a timetable so that you can feel free outside those times?

Keep in mind the value of this enquiry to the school as well as to the young people — are there any matters to raise in staff consultation?

    (ii) How can you make sure that you keep to your timetable?

    (iii) Plan a timetable in discussion with your small group.

  (c) Experiment with your timetable this week. We will discuss your experiment and the remainder of the enquiry in Stage 5.

Figure 3

WORKING PAPER 27

Homework — programme and planning

Name .... Form ....

The purpose of this enquiry is to help you to think about the way you plan and approach your homework, and to help your teachers to understand any difficulties that you may face. It is important that you should be honest with yourself in completing the enquiry.

1 Timetable
   Note the exact time that you begin and finish each piece of homework through a single week. If you do it in bits, note the start and finish of each period of time given to it. The table on the next page will help you.

2 Approach
   (a) How easily do you get down to your homework?
       For example, do you get straight into it, do you dither, or does it vary?
       Try to describe your approach.

   (b) Does your homework tend to hang over your head for most of the evening?

   (c) How do you feel when you have finished?

3 Where do you usually do your homework?
   (a) Is the room usually occupied by other people also? How many people?

   (b) Is a television set usually within your vision?

   (c) Is a radio, television set, or amplifier usually within your hearing? With what kind of programmes?

4 Are you sometimes very anxious about your homework? What about?

5 Have you shared this enquiry with your parents?

Figure 3 (continued)

Timetable A week's homework

Day	Subject	Time		*How easy or difficult?					*Did you enjoy it?				
		started	finished	very easy	fairly easy	all right	fairly difficult	very difficult	very much	a little	all right	no	not at all

*Tick appropriate column.

The structuring of the organization of DGW is in terms of three distinct dimensions.

First in terms of *four phases* of group work which Button always insists on:

1 Making contact.
2 Diagnosis.
3 Experience.
4 Evaluation.

Secondly in terms of what he calls *the elements of group work*. In *Developmental Group Work with Adolescents* he has set these out in a diagram showing 'the interlocking parts of group work which reinforce one another'[11]:

Figure 4

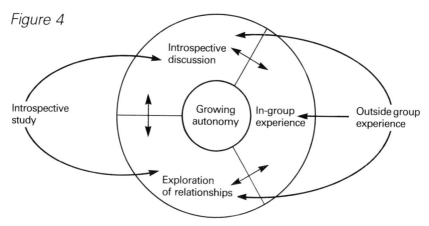

Thirdly, in terms of *a repertoire of techniques* to be used by developmental group workers. These include: group support; physical contact; sociometry; action research; role play; sociodrama; psychodrama; socratic discussion; life-space analysis; friendship studies; and self-description.

Much of Button's influence, in the Youth Service especially, has arisen from others adopting his account of these techniques, and the materials he has developed in association with them. Too often, however, the techniques and materials have been used out of context. Their real value is the role they can play within DGW programmes framed and disciplined by the concepts of objectives, phases, and elements referred to earlier. This tendency to adopt his techniques detached from his concepts and programmatics has often provided ammunition for those in education who are sceptical or critical about group work. It gets to be dismissed as just 'playing games'. Yet no one could be more serious about education than

Leslie Button, or more genuinely concerned that educational experience should reach beyond superficialities to the deepest concerns and needs of young people and of society. The techniques and exercises he developed are merely tools. They are designed to provide group workers with instruments with which to achieve the fundamental objective of personal and social education of individual young people, and with knowledge and skills to underpin the concepts and programmatics of DGW.

In the following sections we examine briefly each of these three dimensions of the organization of DGW — *phases, elements*, and *techniques*. We turn first, however, to three fundamental aspects of knowledge, on which group work relies — adolescent development and needs, personality, and group structure and process. Each of these is attended to less systematically in our secondary schools than is necessary. DGW requires systematic attention to all three.

Needs, Personality and Groups

Currently British secondary education is subject to severe criticism from many quarters, as Alec Dickson's analysis earlier and the later chapters by Beverley Shaw and Dennis O'Keeffe demonstrate. We believe such criticism is well-founded, and that in many respects young people are being short-changed.

Improvement requires a more instrumental approach, more practical relevance in the curriculum, clearer objectives, better trained teachers, and closer attention to the world beyond school for which education is designed to prepare young people. This sort of realism, with its insistence on a sharper, tougher approach by teachers, might seem to militate against either Alec Dickson's recommendation of extending and systematizing community service, or our argument here for substantial incorporation of group work into teachers' repertoire of skills. Serious critics of the schools, such as the businessmen who gave their trenchant views in the Social Affairs Unit's *Trespassing*[12] might reasonably be expected to react by dismissing both community service and group work as just the sort of 'trivial pursuits' they condemn. Are they not exactly the sort of nonsense which stand in the way of the reform of education they demand? Isn't it just such useless rigmarole which teachers are trained in instead of having their subject knowledge strengthened, and their skills in organization, discipline and method improved?

In our view these would be mistaken judgments. On the contrary, improved effectiveness in the secondary schools — such that literacy and numeracy will be strengthened, relevant cognitive and practical skills thoroughly learned, and young people better educated for today's world — requires *more* attention to be given to these apparently soft options. By and large secondary teachers are sketchily and poorly trained in the psychology and sociology of adolescence and youth. They are scarcely trained at all, for the most part, in relation to personality theory and applied psychology, or in group therapy and group work. Yet each of these three areas is of the essence of the practical work they have to do in the classroom.

Traditional schooling largely ignores, except through the minor avenues of extra-curricular activities and pastoral work, the fact that secondary school pupils are adolescent. Little account is taken of the problems this fact poses inavoidably for most young people, or of the needs with which it confronts all of them. Button emphasizes throughout his work the importance of adolescent needs. Developmental group work programmes focus sharply on their impact. *Each of six basic needs provides primary source material for DGW.*

1 For *new experience*. Even in the universities and the upper streams of secondary schools a major blockage to effective learning is simple boredom. Group work provides opportunities for young people to try out new activities and to reflect together about conflicts of interests, long and short term goals, and the relations between purposes and plans, and between decisions and intentions.
2 For *relationships with peers*. A major strength of DGW is the extent to which it acknowledges the importance of peers and friendship. In most schools peer relations and peer group phenomena are construed as negative rather than potentially constructive forces. James Coleman has long ago shown in *The Adolescent Society* how peer groups work powerfully against school objectives if they are not successfully incorporated.[13] Reuven Kahane has provided a persuasive model of how peer groups function and of the inherent difficulties of influencing them.[14] In DGW peer relations are a primary focus, and their role is made explicit and potentially constructive by discussion, action, and reflection in relation to them.
3 For *association with the opposite sex*. Despite co-education, sex education and 'anti-sexist' policy documents, persisting

problems in this area are evident. It is a manifestly basic concern to most young people, as the major themes of youth culture in records, comics, magazines and clothing demonstrate. By and large schools try to imagine it away. DGW makes it a focal concern, to be attended to in the work of groups openly and responsibly.

4 For *significance*. A major task of the period of adolescence and youth is development of the self-concept, self-esteem, and self-confidence. Each of them has to rest on a secure identity and a realistic sense of one's own worth. Adults, including even teachers, seem to fail to a remarkable extent to recognize, let alone accept, young people's anxieties about their own competence and worth. As a result, the scope available to young people to develop towards adulthood in the school context is seriously limited. How common this problem is, is demonstrated by the awesome power which peer groups have simply because they *do* provide for young people meaningful roles and sources of significant identity, and by the escalating influence of the drug culture — which thrives precisely on feelings of futility, aimlessness, and lack of genuine self-assurance.

5 For *a coherent world view*. For perfectly understandable reasons, education in the liberal democracies largely excludes issues of philosophy, religion, politics, and basic values from its purview. Ironically, however, our urge to limit the illegitimate influence of sectarian values in education by a principled focus on knowledge and objectivity tends in practice to increase their effect — since young people's need to explore these issues is powerful and pressing, and we force them to do it on their own in the irresponsible world of peer groups, or under the sway of adults with political or religious axes to grind. Recent attempts at incorporating political education into the curriculum have not been notably successful. This need is going unanswered. DGW takes young people's need to explore deeper purposes and values seriously, and includes it systematically in its programme.

6 To *come to terms with authority*. Youth workers sometimes seem inclined (depending no doubt on when and where they were trained) to dismiss the need for authority altogether. Some teachers have fallen for the same nonsense. For the most part, however, the weakness of teachers is in the opposite direction, with authority unproblematically presumed in

their relations with young people. Young people's need to understand authority and to learn to accept its legitimate use is, especially in a democracy, enormously important. DGW attends to these issues systematically, through discussion and through organized interactions with authority figures, such as policemen. The sense and value of this focus could not be more obvious and indisputable than in the aftermath of our inner city riots.

Thus one major contribution which DGW can make to secondary schooling is to impart, in a sensible, organized way, serious attention to the influences of adolescent development on learning, and to the pressing common needs which young people face in the course of their development.

Scarcely less important is the attention group work gives to personality theory and general psychology. Working with a group in the mode required by group work is impossible without a sound grasp of the key concepts and major approaches. The perspectives of behaviourism, psycho-analysis, and phenomenology are essential if teachers are to be able to make sense practically of relationships in groups. To these matters Button has always given considerable emphasis. The reader's attention is drawn to Chapter 1 above by John Coleman for further analysis.[15] By and large, the grasp that school teachers have of established psychological knowledge is modest, with a dangerous tendency for it to be limited to whichever guru was fashionable — now Piaget, now Maslow, now Rogers — at the time of their training. Group work skills would require of teachers a more systematic and disciplined understanding of psychology, and the capacity to use it in everyday practice.

Group work necessitates even more obviously and fundamentally a sound knowledge of the nature of groups, and of their structure, dynamics, and functioning. In part such knowledge derives from psychology, for example through the work of Lewin and American social psychology.[16] In part it has to come also from sociology and from specialists in group work such as Moreno.[17] Here in general teachers' understanding is even more limited than in relation to psychology — yet group processes are of the essence of all their work. One would not of course deny the intuitive skills of many good teachers in the handling of smaller and larger groups, nor the fact that most teacher training courses will nowadays include some degree of theoretical introduction to group processes. However, neither is adequate and both should be strengthened.

To the extent that DGW is adopted within the schools, a serious upgrading of teachers' understanding of groups will be essential. Button has throughout his writing and thoughout his career emphasized the necessity of group workers developing their theoretical and practical knowledge of groups. Conceptually, his focus on relationships, roles, norms, attitudes, authority and identity provides a useful, if simple, framework for any teacher. On the practical side, his analyses of recording and measurement, of sociometry, and of life histories, among many other topics, provides a group worker and indeed any teacher, with powerful techniques for the difficult business of helping young people to learn.

The Four Phases of Developmental Group Work Programmes

If group work is to be effective there are *four requisite phases* through which the worker must steer the progress of the group: *making contact, diagnosis, experience* and *evaluation*.

It is extraordinary that in most educational practice so little attention is given to the need for participants to know and to trust each other. In British university teaching, where seminars requiring close discussion and argument play a central role, almost nothing is done formally to enable students to get to know each other and to understand their different backgrounds, experiences, and concerns. Even our tutorial system does little to bring staff and students closer together other than in terms of academic and intellectual relations. As a consequence, intellectual work is considerably weakened, with discussion consistently lamed by the intrusion of attitudes and concerns which have not been brought into the open and worked through.

In the secondary schools the situation is not in general much better. Little is done explicitly to incorporate the individual personal aspects of pupils into the business of the classroom. Established friendships between sets of pupils are regularly treated as irrelevant, and quite commonly as negative influences. Antagonisms between pupils are usually blocked off rather than worked through. In consequence, many young people treat classroom interaction as dealing with superficialities, and reserve their deepest feelings and concerns for the unguided arena of the peer group. As a result teachers lose an enormously powerful resource for encouraging motivation and involvement, and find their academic work with pupils hampered by the effects of all kinds of sub-fusc processes.

The process of informalisation in secondary schools — use of christian names, replacement of 'lectures' by handouts and discussions, practical projects, group visits, and so on — has probably gone much less far than is commonly believed — and in any case it is inadequate as an answer to these problems. It may even be counter-productive, since these approaches stop short of making mutual understanding and trust a formal part of school work, and leave the teacher with much less control than he or she needs in order to lead effectively.

In group work explicit attention to the need for participants to know each other well, and to work towards mutual respect and trust is in all situations the first step on which all the rest depends. Group members must be given opportunities to talk together in a variety of pairings and in the group as a whole about themselves, their feelings, and their purposes in the group and more broadly. Exercises of many sorts can be used to encourage, through physical contact and shared activity, the lowering of inter-personal barriers and the development of mutual trust. The group leader must of course be a part of this process, relinquishing the teacher's usual defensive, self-protective shell. At the same time he/she must be a skilled interpreter of what is happening and what it means. Phase 1 is *the essential prerequisite to genuinely developmental group work*.

It is however merely the first phase. It is designed to be used instrumentally as a basis for the next phases. In some versions of group work — but certainly not in Button's work — contact and trust have come to be seen as ends in themselves. Nothing has done more to get group work a bad name. If the result of DGW programmes is merely the creation of little groups of young people with gratifying feelings of mutual belonging, nothing useful has been achieved. The whole point is to use the powerful resource this provides in order to effect significant positive transformations in knowledge, skill and understanding and to facilitate maturity. Movement in these directions requires next a second phase aimed deliberately at helping group members to discover and understand who they all are individually and in relation to each other, the needs and problems they face, and the resources and limitations there are available in the group for useful work. *This is the phase of diagnosis.*

Button has argued for the use of a wide range of techniques for diagnosis, in particular social enquiry, sociometry and friendship studies. The purpose of any and all of these techniques in the diagnostic phase is to make available to the group knowledge and understanding about its individual members and their relations. There is obviously the danger here of infringement of privacy, and *confidentiality* between the worker and individuals and within the group as a whole is a crucial aspect of group work. On this, however, Button says, speaking from considerable experience:

> We may be held back from prying out of a respect for the privacy of the youngster, but is it not rather a question of opening to young people opportunities to use the worker as a confidant should they wish to do so? By keeping the situation 'safe', by not approaching areas that may be charged emotionally, we may in practice be signalling that we are not prepared to share their anxieties and burdens. Many youngsters, who have obviously gained considerably from intimate conversations of this kind, have indicated to us that they would have liked a similar opportunity long before, but the youth workers or teachers with whom they were in contact had not led them into suitable conversations and thus opened the way for their confidences.'[18]

Moreover, the initiative and responsibility must be clearly and confidently taken by the worker:

> Here we face what seems to be quite a basic principle of communication. It would seem necessary that the person who is senior in a partnership must open up the channels of communication before the junior partner will take the initiative. It is as if he must demonstrate that a particular area of conversation is legitimate. It is not enough to say that he is open to receive confidences: he must actually begin conversation that will have accustomed them both to exchanges in specific areas of intimacy. Examples of this can often be seen in family life. It is unusual for children in the family to open up new areas of intimate conversation — about sex, say — and the kinds of topics discussed will usually depend upon the conversation initiated by the parents. It also points to the uncertain position of, for example, youth workers who say that their club members know that they may bring any problems to them. Making ourselves available as a confidant is an active rather than a waiting game.[19]

The result of the diagnostic phase should be a fully interpreted understanding, available to all members of the group, of precisely who each of them is, how they relate to one another, and how the normative and interactional structure of the group works.

Out of this begins to develop Phase 3 — *the phase of experience*. The content of this central phase is essentially defined by the 'elements of group work', with which we deal in detail below. Button argues that it should include both experience inside the group and activities outside. He illustrates the limitations of exclusively in-group conversation as follows:

> For example, one of our collaborators brought together a group of apprentices as an experiment in group work in industry. Although the conversation in the group overflowed into their normal time at work, there was little in the programme beyond the contact and conversation with one another. The boys gained a great deal from their experience, and the manager was so impressed by their obvious development that he suggested that it might be helpful if the group could make themselves responsible for receiving the new annual intake of apprentices. But when the occasion arrived the boys sheepishly gathered into a corner, and showed themselves quite incapable of receiving the newcomers: one of the things they had not been able to learn in their closed group was how to meet strangers.
>
> This is a very simple illustration of the limitations of the closed conversation group. It is usually necessary to seek certain activity that takes the members beyond the confines of the group in order to offer them opportunities for vital experience, and to feed new impetus into the relationships within the group.[20]

Thus the experience has to include an ordered programme of discussion, action, and reflection, all worked through in further discussion within the group, and as a result providing opportunities for further activity and reflection. In *Developmental Group Work with Adolescents*, and particularly in *Group Tutoring for the Form Teacher*, Button has provided an enormous amount of tested material appropriate for use in such programmes. As an illustration we reproduce the Planning Schedule for the first half of the Summer Term of Year 2; see Figure 5.[21]

Figure 5

PLANNING SCHEDULE: YEAR TWO

THEME	STAGE 25	STAGE 26	STAGE 27	STAGE 28	STAGE 29	STAGE 30
The pupil's place in the school	Plan assembly.*	Rehearse assembly.*				
Caring community	Revise caring, Group's programme for this term.**					
Relationships, the self and social skills	Planning empathy.***	Cooperation with teachers and school.				
		Role-play and role-reversal.***	Consultation. Teacher as a visitor.***			
Communication skills			Prepare for action research.**	Our community — other people's lives and interests. Begin action research.**	Conclude action research — report.**	Visitors (leading to responsibility and authority).***
School work and study skills		Being inventive and imaginative.*				
Academic guidance and careers education						
Health and hygiene						
Personal interests	Know our district. Personal investigation during Easter holiday.*			(a) Personal statements. (b) Prepare for a visitor.***	Our interests and enthusiasms. Visitor.***	Activities I would like to take up.**

In 'The pastoral curriculum' Button argues that 'a number of major themes need to be sustained throughout the whole of a five years pastoral programme'. These are: the pupil's place in the school; the pastoral group as a small caring community; relationships, the self and social skills; communication skills; school-work and study skills; careers education; health and hygiene; and personal interests.

Any DGW programme ought to be completed by *a phase of evaluation*. The worker must facilitate group members' systematic reflection on all they have experienced together, what each of them has contributed and gained, the value of the exercise as a whole, and where it all leads next. For this purpose detailed record keeping by the worker is of course essential, and this is something Button has consistently emphasized. It is not an easy task, since the group work experience is a much deeper and more complex process than traditional teaching and learning. Compared even with record keeping in counselling there is the added complexity of the inter-individual level. To answer this difficulty, and also as part of group members' own learning, they should themselves keep records throughout, and be able to use them actively in discussion. The evaluation phase is not merely a way of ending the programme. It is itself a crucial part of the developmental process. It needs to be done thoroughly, sensitively and well.

These four phases are necessary parts of any and every DGW programme. The worker should plan and control them and the flow from one to another very carefully. The structuring they provide is necessary if group work is to maintain its coherence and momentum.

The Elements of Group Work

To outsiders, what actually happens in group work often seems a complete mystery. Sometimes it even seems as if the insiders, the initiates of group work's rituals, as it were, are intent on preserving a boundary of mystification in order to guard its special, secret nature. Button was never of this persuasion. He put great effort into clarifying the nature of what is admittedly a complex process, and into making an understanding of it available to anyone willing and able to use it in helping young people.

The diagram in Figure 4 on page 98 above, reproduced from *Developmental Group Work with Adolescents*, represents in simplified form what he saw as the core of DGW. His comments on it are as follows:

> In the diagram I have attempted to bring together in a coherent framework the elements of group work that I have described. The growing autonomy of the group and of the individual is shown as being central to the whole purpose. The in-group experience, the benefit that arises from being a member of an intimate, supportive and objective group, changes in quality as the group develops. The outside experience to which the group expose themselves will feed immediately into the quality of the in-group experience as well as into the personal experiences of each individual. If the outside experience is wisely chosen, it is likely to stir the members of the group and will therefore help to stimulate the exploration of relationships and introspective discussion. These two elements will feed into one another, and enhance further the quality of the experience involved in being a member of the group. If the group can be encouraged to undertake some kind of introspective study, this will immediately stimulate their introspective discussion and probably the exploration of relationships as well.
>
> It is possible to recognise these elements as steps that may be influenced by the worker. When the worker sees the process analytically in this way, he is in a far stronger position, for he is better placed to recognise opportunities that are offered to him. The elements are interlocking and reinforce one another, and this adds to the possibility of accelerating the process.[22]

The relationships between the six elements, the way they support and feed each other, in complex patterns defined by the nature of group structure and process, and shaped by the patient skill of the developmental group worker, are extremely important. Button's programmes and materials, together with his analysis of the nature of group processes and of the worker's role, are indispensible to an adequate understanding of these relationships. It is also essential to comprehend fully the nature of each of the six elements separately.

Autonomy — of the individual members and of the group as a whole — is the object to which the process in its totality is directed. However, Button is always clear that autonomy should not be allowed to provide an excuse for irresponsible permissivism on the part of teachers and youth workers, or for immature, selfish behaviour by young people. The whole point of the group context is that participants have to take realistic account, as in real life, of other people and of their relationships with them. Thus:

> We are in an age of increasing choice, of individual morality, and of a democratic life in the sense that we are each of us freer to decide how we should behave. This adds greatly to the need for a capacity for personal judgement and action, and the pressures that emanate from powerful commercial interests add urgency to this need. Part of the deliberate purpose of the worker will be to help the youngsters build a basis for that independent action. In this context it may be well to remind ourselves that personal autonomy means that we must also be in control of our own impulses.
>
> It is possible for the group worker and social worker to take the respect for the personal autonomy of the client to absurd lengths, sometimes under the banner of being 'non-judgemental'. Does this mean also that we must be 'non-influencing'? If we take any hand in people's lives we must necessarily be influencing them; our position is one of inescapable leadership, which we shall exercise as surely by our inactivity as by our positive intervention. Are we to be so neutral that, for example, we shall not attempt to steer young people away from anti-social activity which bears directly on their neighbours? And when we see that a youngster's unhappiness arises from an inability to get along with his peers, are we not to act upon this insight which may have been denied to the youngster himself?[23]

In group/outside group experience. Button's approach stresses the value and importance over and above all that goes on inside the group of outside activities to which group experience can meaningfully give rise. He instances in his analysis of this element a project involving interviewing strangers in the street:

> I shall call this 'outside experience' as distinct from 'in-group experience' arising from the interchange between the members of the group. We are then faced immediately by the question: what kind of experience based on what kind of activity? The intrinsic experience inherent in the activity will need to be appropriate to the needs of the individual members of the group, and the activity should also stir the group as a whole in ways that are helpful to its members.

For illustration I will revert to the example of interviewing a stranger in the street as part of a longer on-going project. The personal experiences reaching the group member as a result of this will include: daring to tackle the stranger who is preoccupied with his own concerns and does not expect to be approached in this way; marshalling the necessary explanation and putting the other person at his ease; conducting himself in an acceptable and attractive way; ordering his procedure and maintaining the flow of the exchanges; expressing appreciation and making the other person feel the encounter was rewarding. The experience accruing to the group, working as a team, will depend upon how the project is being approached, and may include: envisaging and debating the project; formulating an enquiry (with all the discussion, sifting of suggestion, and the allocation of the work entailed); rehearsing the approach to interviewing, each facing his own fears of rejection and encouraging colleagues in their efforts; leaving the other members of the group in order each to undertake his personal share of interviewing (which may be a major step with a tight group who always hang around together); and processing the material. The corporate experience of the group so much depends upon the approach of the worker; some youth workers and teachers seem under an inner compulsion to assume all the organising roles themselves.[24]

Exploration of relationships should by now be clear enough. Where Button's approach in this area is most valuable is his elaboration of techniques and exercises, especially role-play, to 'stir the group and the equilibrium of their relationships.' 'A certain element of stress', he suggests,

> would seem to be a prerequisite of personal movement and development. If, therefore, we can encourage the group to undertake some activity that demands new roles and interpersonal relationships, and stirs emotionally the individual members, it is possible that we may be able to accelerate the process of development and therapy.

Introspective discussion is about 'internal emotional states that underlie behaviour, including our feelings about ourselves.' Here is one of Button's examples:

Janet, feeling the support of the group and having been stirred by the discussion, described in a moving though faltering statement the depth of her shyness, which at times brought her a feeling of nausea at the prospect of meeting new people. Already by reason of her statement her position had changed. With great sensitivity the group discussed her feelings with her, and considered with her what they could do to help.[25]

Leading introspective discussion is patently a fine art which requires training, experience and skill. We suspect it may well be because of its difficulty as much as for any other reason, that youth workers and teachers shy away from it. But the need for it in young people's development is manifest, and it can be greatly facilitated within the framework of DGW programmes. This is not least because the sixth element — *introspective studies* — will be in regular systematic use.

These provide, by contrast with usual academic school work or everyday youth work, material directly relevant to such discussion. For example, a friendship study or a sociometric study or a personal enquiry — simple exercizes providing a shared record of personal information — usually serve immediately to stimulate discussion, which DGW can then encourage, deepen and guide. Together, the six elements of group work provide simultaneously a framework for understanding its nature, and a programmatic guide for undertaking it successfully.

Techniques and Materials

Of course teaching has gone much beyond the traditional, minuscule repertoire of 'chalk and talk' — even in higher education, the most conservative sector of the profession. This is largely potential, however, rather than actual. The everyday reality, even in many primary schools and certainly in most secondary schools, includes large tracts of talk, boardwork and note taking. Nor, of course, can teaching of any sort dispense with teacher talk — preferably clear, intelligent, knowledgeable talk, modulated to particular purposes and to particular young people's capacities and needs.

However, neither such traditional fare, nor the more recent adoption of open discussion, project work, and activity, can sufficiently answer the difficult tasks posed by personal and social education, or the objectives set for itself by DGW. For this we require a much wider range of techniques, and a large array of varied materials. Here Button serves those who are persuaded to work along his lines very well. In *Discovery and Experience* and *Developmental Group Work with Adolescents* he provides a useful introduction to many different sorts of techniques, and offers a wide variety of tested materials. For example the appendices to the latter include a Group Enquiry to explore processes in and feelings about groups, and a range of measures for use in self-description. The body of the text explains sociometry, friendship analysis, contact exercizes, socio-drama, and life-space analysis. *Discovery and Experience* provides frameworks for training in group work, materials for personal enquiries, group observation and friendship study, and forms for recording group work.

Group Tutoring for the Form Teacher elucidates the nature of 'Socratic group discussion', describes 'support exercises to be used in developing group trust', and examines role play and action research. In its two volumes this recent book also provides a detailed stage by stage programme of group work over the five years of secondary education. It also offers *more than one hundred* working papers for planned stage by stage use. Each of them includes objectives, rationale and methods. Further material stimulated by Button's approach, and developments of his techniques, have been produced by the Brunel Training Consultative Unit as part of the Basic Training Scheme for youth and community workers and the group work module of the Postgraduate Diploma.

All of these techniques and materials can strengthen the effectiveness of teachers and youth workers in their task of personal and social education of young people. If they are used within a coherent DGW programme, their effects can be even more constructive and powerful.

Conclusion

Our primary purpose here is to tempt more teachers in schools, colleges and universities, more youth workers, more probation officers — more of all those professionally committed to helping young people with their personal and social eduction — to read Leslie Button's work for themselves and to equip themselves to try out DGW. We are convinced it is indispensible. Certainly the evidence suggests it is enormously helpful.

Everyone involved in education is willy-nilly a group worker; it is simply an unavoidable part of the job. If we acknowledge the fact explicitly, and systematize and strengthen this aspect of our work — perhaps by adopting the overall philosophy and method of DGW — we shall be better able to help the young men and young women of the eighties and nineties. They will need all the help we can give them.

We reproduce below in Figure 6 the evaluation schedule from *Group Tutoring For The Form Teacher*. It indicates graphically the sort of transformations DGW seeks to effect[26].

Figure 6

Appendix

Evaluation — The Progress of Individual Young People

The Schedule

This evaluation schedule should be seen as an opportunity to review the development of the group members' social skills, their self-feelings and their attitudes to school. The schedule is designed to provide opportunities for an examination of individual progress, and to note even small movements in the many facets of life.

Most of the headings lead to a *continuum* from one extreme to another. Typical descriptions are given of the two extremes and a central point, but judgment should be made within the general spirit of the themes rather than being tied to the specific descriptions. Placing along any line will be a matter of some subtlety, so intermediate positions will be needed on many of the *continua*.

Original Position

It is important that there should be an early statement of the member's position as the work begins. It may be possible to seek the advice of other people who have been regularly in touch with the person concerned so that their views can be taken into account when determining the member's original positions on the continua.

However, it has been our experience that it is difficult for the outside observer to penetrate sufficiently deeply into the individual's personal position to be able to offer a really sensitive judgment. So it is therefore possible that some retrospective adjustment to the original placing may be needed as the on-going discussion involved in the work reveals the true original position.

Figure 6 (continued)

The Group Member's Self-Assessment

Perhaps the most reliable guide available to us is the group member's own assessment as he becomes increasingly articulate about his own personal position and feels himself encouraged by a supportive group. It is also an important part of the group member's experience to evaluate his own position and progress. For this reason this evaluation paper should be used deliberately and creatively as part of the experience.

The specific sections of the schedule could be dealt with step-by-step as the emphasis of the programme touches the issues raised by each part of the schedule.

Evaluation Schedule

Meeting and Greeting People

	Shy/abrupt. Avoiding if possible. Embarrassed by approaches. Passes off.	Can respond with reasonable ease, as long as the other person makes a move.	Can make the running. Puts the other person at ease. Can negotiate in tricky situations.
Known peers			

Any comments:

Meeting and Greeting People

	Shy/abrupt. Avoiding if possible. Embarrassed by approaches. Passes off.	Can respond with reasonable ease, as long as the other person makes a move.	Can make the running. Puts the other person at ease. Can negotiate in tricky situations.
Strange peers			

Any comments:

Opposite sex

Any comments:

Known adults

Any comments:

Strange adults

Any comments:

Figure 6 (continued)

Eye Contact

Acute embarrassment. Always looks down or away.	Can manage momentary eye contact, but tends to avoid.	Easy and unconcerned.

Any comments:

Conversation
Fluency

Abrupt. Monosyllabic.	Operates through brief bursts. Can respond to the other person's prompting	Sustained conversation.

Comments:

Depth

Narrow. Concrete.	Can describe events and interests.	Wide. Personal. Abstract.

Comments:

Listening

Intolerant of the other's statement. Full of his own statement/of himself.	Tolerates the other person's statement. Will usually stay with him long enough to hear him out.	Deep and encouraging interest in the other person.

Comments:

Figure 6 (continued)

Speaking in Public (e.g. the classroom)

Will avoid if possible. Embarrassed/ confused if required to respond in public	Can respond without embarrassment, but rarely takes the initiative.	Can make a balanced and sensitive contribution in public without embarrassment.

Comments:

Persistence/Consistency

Fickle and changeable. Gives up when slightest effort required. Cannot give attention for many minutes.	Will attempt a task, but interest wanes after some time.	Sticks to even a difficult undertaking, in an effort to see it through.

Comments:

Resilience to Uncertainty

Cannot stand uncertainty. Contracts out or causes trouble.	Uneasy with uncertainty, but can be contained.	Copes easily and without anxiety with uncertainty.

Comments:

Resilience to Opposition and Hostility

Meets oppositon or hostility with immediate anger or submission.	Meets like with like. Escapes rather than copes.	Is not easily embarrassed or stirred up by hostility. Meets hostility with reasoned response.

Comments:

David Marsland and Michael Day

Figure 6 (continued)

Coping with Obstacles

| Immediately frustrated, angry, defeated. | Persists to a point, and then becomes frustrated. | Looks around the problem and considers alternatives. Can relax when progress is not possible. |

Comments:

Response to Authority

| Confused, submissive rebellious, angry. | Tends to respond strongly to authority-sometimes unreasonably. Easily cowed by authority behaviour. | Engages with ease. Copes with even unreasonable authority behaviour. |

Comments:

Self-confidence

| Timid. Very easily deterred from action requiring any personal risk. | Needs encouragement and support in engaging in any action that involves new people or situations. | Will take on challenging situations without stress. |

Comments:

Figure 6 (continued)

Self-esteem

Strong self-doubts. Sense of being a failure. Sense of being unworthy.	Unsure of his own value, but not unduly inhibited by it.	Relaxed in accepting other people's regard.

Comments:

Attitude to School Work

Antagonistic, apathetic, resistant, passive.	Works as required without giving much trouble.	Cooperative, enthusiastic, consistent effort.

Comments:

Attendance at School

Frequent unjustified absences.	Attends regularly, but absents himself whenever reasonable excuse offers itself.	Faultless in regular attendance and on time.

Comments:

In 'The pastoral curriculum' Leslie Button begins his analysis as follows:

> It has been part of the tradition of British education that school is concerned with all round development, and this is a tradition that Britain has exported to a number of other countries. It is sometimes argued that a healthy daily routine is all that is required: that the spirit of the school will rub off on the pupils, and this is all the social training that is necessary. The argument often harks back to the small personal school, in which mutual knowledge and respect could form the basis for a healthy development of attitudes.
>
> Times have changed, and there are grounds for the widespread anxiety about the relationships that exist in the larger school of today. It is not only a matter of size: there is a growing depersonalization in our society, and there has been a world wide challenge to authority that has inevitably influenced attitudes and relationships in school. But it is still true that everything that goes on in school, every activity and every hour of the day carries with it a social and emotional message, which will have its impact on the experience and attitudes of all concerned.[27]

DGW explicitly addresses the 'social and emotional messages' adults with professional authority convey to young people. We believe it can improve them and enable them to be conveyed much more effectively.

Notes

1 DAVIES, B. (1975) *The Use of Groups in Social Work Practice*, London, Routledge and Kegan Paul.
2 BUTTON, L. (1971) *Discovery and Experience*, Oxford, Oxford University Press; (1974) *Development Group Work with Adolescents*, (7th Impression, 1985) London, Hodder and Stoughton; (1981) *Group Tutoring for the Form Teacher*, (4th Impression, 1984) 2 volumes, London, Hodder and Stoughton; (1982) 'The pastoral curriculum', in NIXON, J. (Ed.) *Drama and The Whole School Curriculum*, London Hutchinson.
3 Available from Brunel Training Consultative Unit, Brunel University.
4 BERNSTEIN, S. (Ed.) (1972) *Further Explorations in Group Work*, Bookstall; BION, W.R. (1961) *Experiences in Groups*, Tavistock; BROWN, A. (1979) *Groupwork*, Heinemann; BLUMBERG, A. and GOLEMNIEWSKI, R.T. (1976) 'Learning and Change in Groups, Pen-

guin; DOUGLAS, T. (1976) *Group Work Practice*, Tavistock; FOULKES, S.H. and ANTHONY, E.J. (1965) *Group Psychotherapy: The Psychoanalytic Approach*, Penguin; GLASSER, P. *et al* (1974) *Individual Change Through Small Groups*, Free Press; JOHNSON, D.W. and F.P. (1975) *Joining Together; Group Theory and Group Skills*, Prentice Hall; KONOPKA, G. (1972) *Social Groupwork*, Prentice Hall; McCAUGHAN, N. (Ed.) *Group Work: Learning and Practice*, Allen and Unwin; OTTAWAY, A.K.C. (1968) *Learning Through Group Experience*, Routledge and Kegan Paul; ROBERTS, R.W. and NORTHEN, H. (Eds.) (1976) *Theories of Social Work with Groups*, Columbia; YALOM, I.D. (1975) *The Theory and Practice of Group Psychotherapy*, Basic Books.

5 REYNOLDS, D. (Ed.) (1985) *Studying School Effectiveness*, Lewes, Falmer Press; RUTTER, M. *et al* (1979) *15,000 Hours: Secondary Schools and Their Effects on Children*, Open Books.

6 MARSLAND, D. (1981) 'Vast horizons, meagre visions,' in ANDERSON, D.C. *et al Breaking The Spell of The Welfare State*, Social Affairs Unit, and (1985) 'Sidestepping de-nationalisation,' *British Journal of the Sociology of Education*, Vol. 6, No. 1.

7 *Group Tutoring*, Volume 1, p. 2.

8 *Ibid.*, p. 2.

9 *Ibid.*, p. 2.

10 *Developmental Group Work*, p. 168; see also *ibid*, Chapter 9 as a whole and 'Discovery and experience', Chapter 8.

11 *Developmental Group Work*, p. 75.

12 ANDERSON, D.C. (Ed.) (1984) *Trespassing? Businessmen's Views on the Education System*, Social Affairs Unit.

13 COLEMAN, J.S. (1961) *The Adolescent Society*, Free Press.

14 KAHANE, R. (1975) 'Informal youth organisations: a general model', *Sociological Inquiry*, 45, 4.

15 COLEMAN, J.C. (1980) *The Nature of Adolescence*, Methuen.

16 LEWIN, K. (1951) *Field theory in Social Science*, Harper and Row, and (1935) *A Dynamic Theory of Personality*, McGraw Hill; CARTWRIGHT, D. and ZANDER, A. *Group Dynamics: Research and Theory*; KELLY, H.H. and THIBAUT, J.W. (1978) *Interpersonal Relations*, Wiley; NEWCOMBE, T. (1961) *The Acquaintance Process*, Holt Rinehart Winston; SHERIF, M. and C.W. (1965) *Social Psychology*, Harper and Row.

17 MORENO, J. (1953) *Who Shall Survive?* Beacon House, and (1964) *Psychodrama*, Beacon House; ANDRIESSEN, E.J.H. and DRENTH, P.J.D. (1984) 'Leadership: theories and models', in DRENTH, P.J.D. *et al. Handbook of Work and Organisational Psychology*, Wiley; DOUGLAS, T. (1970) *A Decade of Small Group Theory*, Bookstall; HARE, A.P. (1962) *Handbook of Small Group Research*, Free Press; HARE, A.P. *et al.* (1965) *Small Groups: Studies in Social Interaction*; HEAP, K. (1977) *Group Theory for Social Workers*, Pergamon; HOMANS, G.C. (1951) *The Human Group*, Routledge and Kegan Paul; KLEIN, J. (1956) *The Study of Groups*, Routledge and Kegan Paul; RIJSMAN, J.B. (1984) 'Group characteristics and individual behaviour', in DRENTH, P.J.D. *et al. op. cit.*; SPROTT, W.J.H. (1958) *Human Groups*, Penguin; OLMSTED, M. (1959) *The Small Group*, Random House.

18 *Developmental Group Work with Adolescents*, p. 46.
19 *Ibid.*, 47.
20 *Ibid.*, 69.
21 *Group Tutoring For The Form Teacher*, Vol. 1, p. 134.
22 *Developmental Group Work*, p. 74.
23 *Ibid*, p. 68.
24 *Ibid*, p. 70.
25 *Ibid*, p. 78.
26 *Group Tutoring*, p. 179ff.
27 In Nixon, J. (Ed.) (1982) *Drama and The Whole School Curriculum*, Hutchinson.

Young People and Values: The Case of The Youth Service

Errol Mathura

One of the major derelictions of duty by educationists in recent history is their neglect of and contempt for values. Values matter of course in the life of every man and woman. But they matter absolutely crucially in education, and in the life and development of young people. Where adults responsible for the care and training of young people forget this fact, or deny it, we can be sure that mischief is afoot for society as a whole.

In this chapter I examine what seem to me to be gross weaknesses in its approach to values in the Youth Service. The Youth Service is a very important part of our education system, but it is only a small part. I venture to suggest that much of what I argue in relation to the Youth Service applies at least as much to our schools and colleges, indeed to every sphere in which adults are allowed a professional role and responsibility in relation to young people. The recent influential official analysis of the Youth Service known as the Thomson Report baldly asserts that 'It is no part of the Youth Service, as we see it, to be simply an instrument of cultural reproduction.'[1]

Yet the purpose of the Youth Service must at least include the induction of young people in a culture, a language of discourse, an inheritance of procedures, rituals and skills: the inculcation of past practices. There are two pasts. One, the sequence of events, of actions performed, ideas elaborated, moving through a complex series of processes until the present is reached. This is the past of institutions: the school, the family, theological doctrine, military strategies, a Highland lament composed and played to reconcile a bereaved and unhappy people to a contingent misfortune. This is the true past which has happened and has deposited its residues with a ready promiscuity; and which now forms the recalcitrant facts of our current existence. The other past is the perceived past, malleable, provisional and susceptible to retrospective reconstruction by those alive. It is the past which is recorded in memory, written down and are the results of encounters bred of reluctant and energetic engagements. This past is heterogeneous, it includes the injunction: 'Thou shalt not kill' and with a hint of modernity: 'School, drive slowly.' Although the past is 'there', its consequences can, to some extent be got around or frustrated; departures for it are possible, frequent and enduring, due in large measure to mimesis rather than creation.[2]

In the history of a particular science one can come to a point where problems which were subsequently soluble, were insoluble because what was 'given' in the history of that science or the procedures of investigation at the moment did not provide the means of a new understanding. Those who laboured on such problems therefore, did so in vain until they or someone else solved the anterior problem or until the invention of the requisite observational instruments. Thus even in the most rational of human enterprises, one is dependent for one's effectiveness on the 'appropriateness' of the available tradition. Scientists are inducted into the past as it gradually unfolds before the reasoning mind can go forward on it. Understanding is an exertion and an engagement, sometimes deliberate, sometimes unsought, simply because we are resolved to inhabit an even more intelligible, or an even less mysterious world.

In the field of Literature where departures from the past are superabundant, there is a muscular corpus of literary works combined with a state of current literary opinion, which are made available to aspiring writers.[3] This literary 'given' is constantly being modified and amended by new interpretations; circumvented or revised by writers of robust and imaginative minds. But they all must start at different points in the available stock of existing works; they must be inducted into a literary tradition. T.S. Eliot could not have written as he did, if he was innocent of the many authors who had forcibly criticized the agnosticism of modern society in the past. The same is true in Music: Mozart was inducted in the musical corpus of Bach and Haydn; Wagner, for all his 'revolutionary departures' ransacked the past for material for the Ring Cycle and he found Lohengrin in an ancient and anonymous epic.[4] In Art, Modigliani stood on the shoulders of Picasso, whose modification of previous representation of the human head and body was made possible, because he, too, was inducted into the artistic past of European art.[5]

In sport, one is inducted into the rules of cricket, a complex of great names, various and vivid innings, anecdotes, field settings and the roles of umpires. In football, tennis and boxing too, their traditions are absorbed and invoked by participants and spectators alike; their past is the provision of the constraining device of precedent. In language too, the very currency of our intelligence, the only facility known to man with which to keep ideas clear and emotions memorable — induction into its usage and tradition is a prior necessity to modification and the current fad of novelty hunting.[6] 'If everybody were to start where Adam started, he would get no further than Adam did.[7] Induction into a culture, therefore, means an intimate engagement with beliefs and patterns discovered in the past and shared with contemporaries, ancestors and predecessors alike. It is a provision from the past to the future, mediated with amendments in the present. The corpus of culture and traditions which descends to the adolescent like a family heirloom does not come entirely from within the family; much of it comes from an external pool of beliefs and procedures, widely shared in society, like: the importance of substituting argument for violence, the efficacy of the principle of queueing, and the enduring catalogue of civilities which so quietly lubricates social relationships.

A Youth Service which incorporates into itself little of the past, or worse still, disdains it, stunts its members; they are thus left with a negligible set of minor categories, beliefs and distinctions which are not easily extended, modified or elaborated. They will lack the 'orientations', the fundamental, prosaic, original attitudes which enable them to function.[8]

The statement therefore, 'that it is no part of The Youth Service, as we see it, to be simply an instrument of cultural reproduction,' is at once irrational and consolatory, uniting as it does the blundering economy of a narrow understanding with a rough contempt for the underlying and ubiquitous continuities of social life. As there are no discontinuities in experience, there are none in life as there are none in History.[9]

The authors, themselves, possessing a scanty culture, have brought a sterile exhuberance to a complex issue. For it is in the very act of 'cultural reproduction' that the adolescent, pushed and jostled as he is by temperament, time and temerity, which hurry past in a steady stream, like children leaving school, that his individuality is shaped and developed; that his brain and muscle are joined like the smooth sweep of a scythe into a single movement towards some cultural modification and perhaps, creativity. After all, where could the totally few come from? If it originated nowhere but in the private imagination set wholly free, it would lack all communal aspects and utility and no one would know how to live under it. It would be like the invention of a new word: rootless, mobile and obscure of meaning — an offensive irregularity. However, no imagination is so free and unfettered as to be able to construct something wholly new, comprehensive, detailed and efficacious. The very idea is absurd. The authors have confused participation with creation, a vigorous error, vigorously pursued.

> We see the Youth Service as deeply educational, in the sense that it should be helping young people to become whatever it is in them to be. The experience of reflection must follow a line freely chosen by the young participants themselves.[10]

This statement provides for a philanthrophy which is so universal that it destroys any virtue which it may have. The enduring tension between education and freedom is severed at a stroke. All educators/ youth workers know that some basic rules are of crucial importance, not only for routine and stability in relationships, but also in the sphere of social education. Are youth workers to permit young people entering youth centres to determine for 'themselves' whether they will depart from such fundamental principles as fairness, freedom and consideration for others? Will they determine for 'themselves' whether promises are to be kept, the property of others is to be respected or to breach the rules on fraud, theft or lying? The authors of the Thompson Report have themselves given up the exertions of argument for the relaxation of assertions: they tend to think of *all* morality in terms of individual decisions and choices; that like a volcano, it is spontaneous, and like spontaneity, it is ephemeral; and like dust, it can never cohere. No one could sensibly be said to freely 'choose' between alternatives unless they are in possession of some principle which makes alternatives morally relevant. Individual choice is indispensable to character development, but it cannot be infinitely elastic over the whole field of moral behaviour. How many of us have ever 'freely chosen' to decide whether lying is wrong or have 'chosen' not to set fire to our neighbour's barn?[11]

> Youth Workers have, of course, a certain kind of authority but their authority has to be of a different kind from that of teachers and parents and other caring adults. His/Her relationship with young people must be non-directive.[12]

There has been a healthy rejection of the traditional forms of authority which bestowed unlimited prerogatives to men over women and to parents over children, and which though it was initially, meant to be protective, entailed frequent brutalities. This misuse of authority has misled many into believing that there is no place for authority at all, except in the sphere of Statute and state action. This is both a progressive and promiscuous all-or-none type of reaction. In schools, home and youth centres, there is an obvious need for authority, provided it is rationalized and provided it is carefully related to the task in hand and made appropriate to the relevant differences between persons. There is an inner compulsion to confuse being *in* authority with being authoritarian. The failure of a referee's authority in a football match will not lead to an era of cooperation and harmony, but to the instant emergence of twenty-two referees, each with varying criteria.

Authority is crucial in the Youth Service. It is authority which mediates the gap between the generations. Without it, knowledge can only be handed down by bribery or coercion. Progressives in revolt against all forms of authority have invested their idiosyncracies on their appeal to the needs and interests of young people; consumer preference has become the order of the day: the ethos of the Youth Service and Tesco merged; and therapy, taxes and consumption converged — errors in triplicate. It is only by submission to, and in the exercise of authority, that it is possible to get on the inside of a rule and to see its operation for oneself. The proper and sustained exercise of authority and the development amongst young people of a rational attitude to authority, is one of the most important functions of the youth worker.

The need, therefore, for 'non-directive relationship between workers and young people'[13] is the vignette of a doomed prescription. It is to confuse source with direction. Plato, refusing to throw his coat over such a progressive puddle, wrote:

> Then in a Democracy there is no compulsion to exercise authority if you are capable of it, or to submit to authority if you don't want to; you needn't fight if there is a war — it's a wonderfully pleasant way of carrying-on in the short run, isn't it?[14]

After realizing that we seldom make prudential allowances for the infirmities of man, he scathingly continues:

> The father and son change places; the father standing in awe

of his son, and the son neither respecting nor fearing his parents in order to assert his independence ... the teacher fears and panders to his pupils who in turn despise their teachers and attendants; and the young as a whole imitate their elders, argue with them and set themselves up against them, while their elders try to avoid the reputation of being disagreeable or strict by aping the young and mixing with them in terms of easy good fellowship.[15]

It is the vanity of every age to believe that theirs is the most crisis ridden. 'We are living through a period of rapid transformation in many of the ideas and characteristics which make our society what it is'.[16] The antiquity of the abuse is no reason not to recall it:

First men like Anaxagoras came with their physics and metaphysics, casting aside the timeless myths; then the Sophists, and with them Socrates, started to challenge the traditional ways of behaviour and even law and political arrangements as nothing better than arbitrary, and often badly chosen conventions. In the old days, sages like Solon had been revered because in their sayings and their lives they expressed hopes and ideals widely shared in the community. The new sages seem to be doing quite the opposite, trying to tear down accepted beliefs and values, especially in religion and morals.[17]

Coming a trifle nearer to our own time, similar 'transformations' were taking place:

But the spirits of men had fled from the old religion; it still commanded their service, but no longer their hearts and beliefs. With its indeterminate gods and colourless myths, were fables concocted from details suggested by Latin topography or pale reflections of the adventures which had overtaken the Olympians of Greek epic, with its prayers formulated in the style of legal contracts and as dry as the procedure of lawsuit, with its lack of metaphysical curiosity and indifference to moral values, with narrow-minded banality in the field of action.[18]

Let us step back into the world of paganism for a silhouette of Social Education:

Then I must surely be right in saying that we are not to be properly educated until we can recognise the qualities of discipline, courage, generosity, greatness of mind and others akin to them, as well as their opposites, in all their many manifestations.[19]

But Social Education is subject to the laws of inverse relevance: the more you talk about something, the less you are prepared to do anything about it. But such is the dogmatic certainty of those with an arid blindness to the deeper, more impulsive and nobler springs of human behaviour, that they show a failure to grasp the complexities of moral and political problems, and consequently do possess a facile optimism about the degree or possibility of human improvement: in summary, a confidence combined with sterility of imagination. When the Youth Service Development Council could write: 'We are not so much concerned to-day ... with the communication or an agreed belief or value system....'[20] Rather than be favoured by an argument, justifying such trenchant unconcern, we are patronized by an assertion; the statement is made ex-cathedra, a kind of secular Papal Bull. But without 'an agreed value or belief system' how is one to participate in a cricket match? Is the role of the umpires to be the subject of negotiations? Are his decisions on the LBW rule to be referred to an appellate body, and is that body's decision to be final or made the subject of further enquiry? In the Youth Service and elsewhere:

the worshippers of innocence have laid on the future the task of repairing all their mistakes. But forgetting that innocence petted and prolonged, can only make dupes and cynics, they have produced conditions in which strength other than physical cannot grow. The notion that 'free growth' and 'integrity' in the young, require the absence of formal manners — no thanks and no subordination, no regard for time or fitness, no patience with difficulty or distaste, no feelings of reverence or pride, and in many 'excellent' households, no respect for objects and no constraints of cleanliness — that anarchical notion seems curious only till we see it as the first step in liberation from power and its attendant responsibility. Those who are reared in this permissive atmosphere, seem embarrassed by, almost afraid of, human respect. They try hard to earn the opposite by affecting a slovenliness of dress and a lack of reliability which are so outre as to prove casualness a branch of study. Their behaviour at least, shows thoroughness: having nothing, claiming nothing, he knows nothing, can be required or reproved. What is odd is the

expectation that such a mode of life should produce individuals, that is, persons distinguishable from one another.
... What is left for private or social purposes is a kind of
moral vagrant, who projects upon his surroundings, the
menace of his own indiscipline.[21]

The idea that for over four hundred years, hundreds of thousands of
men could be press-ganged into the Royal Navy and yet come to
like the sea for itself, is quite beyond the minor minds of many of
those who are 'deeply concerned' about the Youth Service.

Notes

1 (1982) *Experience and Participation*, Report of the Review Group on
  the Youth Service in England. CMND 8686.
2 SHILS, E. (1981) *Tradition*, University of Chicago Press.
3 KERMODE, F. (1975) *The Classic: Literary Images of Performance and
  Change*, Faber and Faber.
4 GUTMAN, R.W. (1968) *Richard Wagner, the Man, his Mind, and his
  Music.*
5 GOMBRICH, SIR E. (1972) *The State of Art*, 12th Edition, Phaidon
  Press.
6 SMITH, L.P. (1928) *Words and Idioms: Studies in the English Language*, Routledge and Kegan Paul.
7 POPPER, K. (1973) *Objective Knowledge: An Evolutionary Approach*,
  Oxford, pp. 106–90.
8 PARSONS, T. (1954) *Essays in Sociological Theory, Pure and Applied*,
  The Free Press, pp. 89–103.
9 CARR, E.H. (1964) *What is History?* Penguin Books.
10 *Experience and Participation, op. cit.*, p. 15.
11 PETERS, R.S. (1966) *Ethics and Education*, Allen and Unwin.
12 *Experience and Participation, op. cit.*, p. 34.
13 *Ibid.*
14 PLATO (1955) *The Republic*, Penguin Classic p. 330.
15 *Ibid.*, p. 336.
16 *Experience and Participation, op. cit.*, p. 3.
17 FINLEY, M. (1975) *The Ancient Greeks*, Chatto and Windus, p. 138.
18 CARCOPINO, J. (1941) *Daily Life in Ancient Rome*, Penguin, p. 138.
19 PLATO (1953) *The Republic, op. cit.*, p. 143.
20 (1969) *Youth and Community Work in the Seventies*, HMSO, p. 5.
21 BARZUN, J. (1959) *The House of Intellect*, Secker and Warburg, p. 79.

Uncharted Youth: Adolescence and the Secondary School Curriculum

Dennis O'Keeffe

Introduction

This essay is written in the deep and anxious conviction that the education system in England and Wales, especially at secondary level, is in a condition of confusion and drift. I do not say that the case is uniquely ours; I have even worse impressions of the maintained systems in some other liberal societies. Clearly the condition of many high schools in the United States is parlous. Nor have the teachers' unions and educational experts in this country succeeded in imposing on the whole system that extraordinary hostility to external examinations which obtains in Australian education.

Nor should it be taken that the situation is irrecoverable. Lord Young claims that both spontaneous forces and government measures are gradually, indeed rapidly, shifting our educational resources in a direction appropriate to an advanced economy.[1] Let us remember that one characteristic of a decentralized education network like ours is that what is true in context X may not be so in context Y. That a publicly financed system could ever work in the absence of centrally legislated prescription and proscription, demanded of its practitioners a powerful intellectual and moral consensus. It is this consensus which I allege now to be broken down, not, I would suggest, in terms of its being replaced by an alternative 'radical' or subversive consensus; but in terms of its loss of cohesiveness and self-assurance. Fragmentation and confusion are the appropriate names for our school curriculum now. We are fractured and divided, not ruled, by cheap fashionable nostrums and spiteful Marxisant crusades.

The old consensus survives in its general political version *outside* the world of school. To re-establish the educational equivalent, however, we must either impose it bit by bit through government as the expression of public will, or filter it back into the curriculum piecemeal by the only device history has yet revealed to us as sensitively effective for the large-scale expression of private preferences — direct money expenditures. All the signs are that the present administration favours the first course of action, indeed that it is determined to effect irreversible changes in this regard.

Though I would prefer the second course, I am not proposing an unconstrained consumerism. We do not advocate, or at least rather few of us do, the unfettered sale of heroin, to name only one undesirable line of production. A fifteen year-old schoolgirl may find pop music endlessly 'relevant'. We do not accede to her demands. The 'purpose' of some of the boys in her class may be to pursue professional football every waking hour. Again, we will at the very least modify and contain these interests in some educationally appropriate way.

This said, it is difficult not to view the way we treat many of our teenagers with the gravest alarm. We sadly neglect them educationally, and the saddest index of this neglect is how little we *know* about them. The educational syndicalist who springs up to deny this charge might ponder the fact that we do not even have systematic data, more than a hundred years after compulsory universal education was introduced, and forty years after the 1944 Education Act, as to standards of literacy and numeracy. If that is not neglect, then what is? There is, I believe, a systematic connection between the absence of data and the neglect of persons. The suppression of evidence is typical of the world's tyrannies.[2] Although the citizens of free societies may at times be appalled at the information about them gleaned by third parties, it is hard not to see this as a smallish minus against the great range of benefits which derives from the presence of information and evidence.

School dominates much of our early lives. It is intolerable that the uncertainty which attends the economic as well as other aspects of human life should be compounded in the educational case by a perverse denial of information. Alongside this lack of data goes a widespread political reflex to the effect that education must be mainly in the social wage in order to protect the poor and the weak. It is notable that no one has ever produced the slightest evidence that the educational social wage works like this.[3]

The inconsistency in treating lower-ability pupils as devoid of any worthwhile curricular opinion, that is in effect as unimportant when they are at school, lies in the fact that outside school adolescents simply *are* important. It is not possible to understand modern liberal-capitalist society without undertaking a careful economics and sociology of its adolescent population. Millions of young people are caught in the ambiguous nets which our arrangements have created for them. They are important in the economic system; their preferences have dramatically altered the pattern of resource allocation and the composition of economic output. Millions of other human beings are directly dependent on their money expenditures. For this reason their preferences are painstakingly examined. Yet we confine these young people till the age of sixteen in a compulsory institution. We have now despaired — if we ever wanted to interfere — of telling them what entertainment they should like, how to dress in their free time or what style of food they should eat. Indeed in this last matter we have yielded the Platonic pass even in school, for the most part. Even our doubts about adolescent decisions in the adult world are softened by our sense of the energy and inventiveness they often display. We should at least remember that our weekend retail system would break down without them.

Yet in school we mostly ignore their preferences unless they coincide with our own. We impose on them a mainly producer-shaped curriculum where active decision-making in the spirit of the institution is largely confined to those students who share the preferences of the producers.[4] Those politicians and educationalists who in the last ten years have increasingly questioned this state of affairs have been moving in the right direction. The central, and in my view unsustainable, fault in our arrangements, is that they simultaneously reduce the influence of extrinsic considerations in the framing of curriculum and reduce the effectiveness of school as an agency of social control. The Marxists have often said that school is a reproductive agency of the bourgeoisie;[5] it is much closer to the truth that school delivers the working classes into the hands of middle class intellectuals who can decide at will what sort of education and training they receive. Marxists have also been to the fore in identifying education as a source of 'social control'.[6] It would be nearer to the mark to say that education has become a progressively weaker agency of control and that (curricular) steps should be taken to restore its crucial functions in a civilized order.

It is important to be clear as to what allegations are being made. It is *not* proposed that there are very large numbers of dedicated Marxian revolutionaries amongst our teachers, though the minority who are of this persuasion may have a disproportionate influence. Not all teachers wish to hack away at standards of work and behaviour. Nor do all teachers seek to align themselves with 'anti-racist', 'anti-sexist' and 'multi-cultural' crusades. Nor, indeed, are racial and sexual prejudice fictions. They are reprehensible evils which, however, are unlikely to be effectively combatted by the stylized and hysterical campaigns-cum-witch-hunts which are being levelled against them.[7]

What I am saying is that the whole curriculum is *drifting* and therefore vulnerable and up-for-grabs. No one has a full picture of what is happening. No one fully understands the processes whereby curricular or pedagogic innovations occur, either bogus or genuine ones. The system is under-charted, under-supervized. What we can now introduce, however tentatively, is a socio-economic anatomy of the problem.

The Sociology of Nationalized Learning

Our education system is a publicly financed one, a decentralized liberal structure which has emerged from the good intentions of educationalists and governments. Its character cannot be understood outside its peculiar political economy. Just as liberalism is a specifically 'western' phenomenon, so public-sectoral liberalism is very western too. Such liberalism is paradoxical in that it frequently generates ideas which are hostile to the market economy which alone can sustain the liberal polity on which in turn the liberal curriculum depends. It may be that there is about intellectual activity something inherently misanthropic. At any rate the liberal curriculum in its Marxisant manifestations may come intemperately to bite the hands that feed it.[8]

I personally have no doubt, for example, that were the whole society to be administered according to the principles which seem to guide the Inner London Education Authority, then we should soon be living in a socialistic despotism. At present we are protected by the wider phenomenon — a liberal society — on which a runaway liberal-radicalism is parasitic. However, if there were no market economy, then, as all modern history confirms, there would also be *no liberal polity* and in turn *no liberal curriculum*.

The usual name for nationalized production of goods and services is socialism. What we have is a *socialist* education system in a capitalist economy. Its origins in nineteenth century paternalistic legislation, whether prompted by terror, moral panic or philanthropy, are outside the scope of this chapter. The syndicalism our fathers have left us is not. Our socialist education system is not, as occurs in the fully fledged version, controlled by a despotic state. A majority of teachers doubtless recoil from the very idea. But it is controlled by a loose aggregation of activists, teachers' union bosses and educationalists.

Who was behind the campaign against spelling and grammar? Who pressed for the raising of the school leaving age in 1972? Who favoured the child-centred and loose-structured pedagogy which for years obtained in our primary schools, and who now promotes the idea in our secondary schools that learning is for learning's sake or that education is a moral crusade? Who was behind the sociological afflatus?

I doubt if anyone favoured *all* these policies and attitudes, and taken individually they mostly have things to recommend them as *views*, though as a package they are disastrous. The point, however, is that we cannot pin-point exactly how these movements occur, or precisely how their attendant decisions are made. Certainly it is not *most* teachers who make them any more than most parents and citizens are consulted about them. As to the Marxist charge that they are the machinations of a capitalist 'power-structure' — it is too ludicrous for words. Just as a putative ruling-class which could not come up with some better instrument for its perpetuation than the Inner London Education Authority would not deserve to survive, so one worth its salt would scarcely allow the backdoor Marxism of the hate-relations industries to spread its evil influence in our schools as manifestly it is spreading.

Let us remember that the same unaccountable team which gave us anti-racism and anti-sexism and other comparably sonorous neologisms, is now busy preparing 'peace-studies'. At least it seems to be the same team. It is actually characteristic of a syndicalist system that observers find it difficult to penetrate the inner recesses of decision-making. This, however, is precisely what is wrong. Education is both very expensive and very important. That part of it which we require by law our young citizens to undergo cannot be left to chance or minority fiat, even when the minority is enlightened, which in this instance is not self-evidently so.

A strong *prima facie* case can be made for the view that education in liberal societies is increasingly dysfunctional.[9] There are, of course, international variations. France with its proud and deliberately absorptive intellectual culture strikes me as in far better educational shape than England and Wales. We can infer the depth of our malady from what might be called 'the occasions of curricular offence'. Undoubtedly some nonsense is taught but it is the wide-spread failure to teach basics which is so worrying. And the unease amongst teachers is widespread too. This explains their nervous reaction to criticism. Allege that large numbers of teachers are racial bigots or wittingly or unwittingly given to the denigration of the female population, and few teachers' hackles rise. Argue that teachers are the agents of monopoly capitalism or of ethnocentric fixations and no nerves of professional pride are much jarred. But say that *academic standards* are not what they should be and peda-gogic tempers flare instantly.

It is the same with behaviour. The educationalist protocol permits loutish and criminal activity to be associated with un-employment or the iniquity of government policies. We even have Dr Hargreaves' word for it that petrol-bomb throwing football fans have been 'failed' by the community.[10] Why should teachers feel so insulted at the suggestion that the schools might be partly to blame?

I think it is because both teachers and public know that much of the talk of anti-racism and anti-sexism and so on is so much hot air. Not many people are interested in the absurd thesis that education 'reproduces' capitalism, though if this tired fantasy were explained to them they would probably wish it were true. The campaigns against racism and sexism are extravagant minority cults, the last despairing knockings of the burnt-out Marxist enterprise. Few teachers and very few members of the public would carry a flag for anti-ethnocentrism whatever precisely this hideous phrase means. *But public and teachers alike do care about the real purposes of education: the transmission of knowledge, skill and acceptable standards of behaviour.*

For years Mark Blaug has been telling us that the system is in economic disequilibrium.[11] The gross distortion in the economic structure directly attributable to the inadequacy of our arrangements for educating and training our young people has now gone on for decades. The teaching force itself, despite the presence of many excellent staff, is not good enough. The political economy of the profession favours an irrationally narrow salary structure with quite inadequate pay for the highly qualified, long-experienced career teacher. The largest union, the National Union of Teachers, has persistently sought to narrow differentials. It is absurd that half our teachers are still non-graduates. Now that the grammar school is gone it may even prove difficult to maintain Great Britain's once quite extraordinary intellectual pre-eminence for the privileged few. The shortages of skills persist, side by side with the dole queues.

Only a system which frustrates market signals as relentlessly as our maintained system could manage to churn out, year after year, the excess flow of social scientists and historians we achieve, whilst at the same time we are short of production engineers, plumbers and electricians.

I said before that the educational consensus, the compact of practitioners that is, has lost its cohesion. This means that one governing principle of public sector administration in liberal societies has lost its efficacy in the educational case: the principle of competence. An occupational group must be united if it is to be left to its own devices. I submit that this is simply no longer the case with the teachers. They have always constituted a somewhat uneasy ideological coalition. Not all countries, for example, would see the logic of combining primary and secondary teachers with their radically different philosophies and styles, in one administrative net. But in general some painfully visible gaps have opened between different groups of teachers.[12] The only real unity comes from the organized syndicalism of the NUT and the in-house experts of the tame educational press. The government should keep its nose out of the curricular garden, in which everything is rosy except classes that are too large, rampant sex and race prejudice and underpaid teachers. If there are any problems they will go away if only enough money is thrown at them![13]

Costs are disguised so that successful pupils and students ride a consumerist merry-go-round of arts and social sciences and, increasingly one fears, may be drawn into the shrill excesses of the various 'antis', the theoretical core of which, where they have one, turns out to be a Marxism which its practitioners cannot sell on a full-frontal basis, and whose emotional roots are a pathological rejection of capitalism, the rule of law, the tradition of tolerance, and, above all, of all things British.[14] The forces of technologically induced change cannot, of course, be stopped in the long run, but they can be, and have been, delayed. The huge army of 'experts' in the various areas of agitation, part scoundrels and part debased priesthood, will prove difficult to dislodge. I personally doubt if the children will believe most of the rubbish they are taught. But it does waste their time whilst the essentials of education and training are neglected.

Meanwhile only recently have our less able students begun to receive anything remotely appropriate to their intellectual aptitudes. Here too the experts have been allowed in on the act, threatening its very essence with a horrible sub-behaviourist jargon which is

enough in itself to alienate any sensitive teacher.[15] Many secondary
students are still at the same time needlessly tormented by a pseudo-
liberal curriculum that is widly remote from their interests and
capacities. The lack of a nuts and bolts curriculum conspires with
poor teaching method to generate the huge truancy which, so long
ignored and covered up, is now emerging as a major social problem.

There seems no end to the madness which some would impose
on our unfortunate less able children. To the sum of 'French' or
'German' and social studies, there have been added of late the new
hate relations curriculum and even, seemingly straight from the
columns of Peter Simple, 'anti-racist maths'.[16] Combine this with
the lack of monitoring of their levels of competence in mathematics,
English and craft and you get an easy understanding of why so
many children truant.

The anti-practical bias of the system is simultaneously pervasive
and contradictory. The older aristocratic-gentry disdain for business
and trade is now matched up with sub-Marxist ideas of strangely
similar anti-instrumental bias. The movement towards Pre-
Vocational education may prove fruitful, especially for below average ability students. But it will have to compete with the many
determined contrary tendencies. Indeed the neo-behaviouristic terminology the movement is dressed up in is perhaps intended to
obfuscate, to divert potential hostility from what is obviously a real
nuts and bolts movement.

It is widely recognized that a curriculum cannot be tailored to
fit the occupational structure directly. However, the twenty years
since the modern economics of education got into its stride have
increased our awareness of the economic importance of education.
We know that the future structure and composition of the labour
force cannot be predicted accurately and that this rules out of court
old-fashioned man-power planning. But we also know that, however complex and incompletely understood the connections, there
is a vital link between a society's skill and knowledge order and its
general economic performance. Though cynics might say that Mark
Blaug's recent summation leaves the question of curricular content
in much the same condition as the one we came in to find twenty
years ago (the liberal curriculum is a good idea now as then) it is not
too much to hope that economists of education may turn their
attention onto the curriculum, especially, as I for one would argue,
given the intellectual cul-de-sac that the sociologists have made of
it.[17]

Certainly thanks to writings like those of Blaug we do now

have a major change in intellectual perception. Education systems *are* now widely recognized as provider-dominated, syndicalized, highly insensitive and inefficient users of the citizens' resources. Education systems and their personnel are now in part subject to that widespread recoil from most socialist forms of production which has been manifest in most advanced liberal societies in the last five or so years. More than this, there is at last some growing recognition that education, whatever its non-economic aspects may be, *is* part of the economy, *is* part of that range of activities whose demands on scarce resources must be constantly scrutinized in the interests of efficiency and equity. There is developing a growing sense that one curriculum may be more appropriate than another for an advanced economy. There is already a welcome shift towards science and technology and business studies. Though a 'planned' curriculum is no more feasible than an economy planned in its entirety, it is almost certainly the case that the version of certification-screening for job-placement which we use is unsatisfactory. Even if the central principle of the curriculum remains the liberal one that intellectual activity is inherently worthwhile, it would not follow that any one liberal curriculum is as good as another. Business studies, liberally taught, might be a better background than a liberally transmitted anthropology!

It is clear that there is a frustrated demand for private education and there are common complaints about maintained education. The low academic standards and slack discipline of the system are widely perceived, though popular resentment is disguised by the extremely expensive character of the private remedy. Let it not be forgotten what a disincentive to the expression of educational verdicts derives from the fact that anyone who wishes to make one has to pay twice.

For many of our students the curriculum on offer does not seem of a character appropriate and relevant to the needs of citizens in an advanced, complex economy. To the rejoinder — what evidence is there for this charge? — the answer must be: whatever general arguments may be adduced the absence of good evidence one way or another is itself a symptom of the problem. Indirectly we can observe the failure of the curriculum in the now undeniable flood of truancy. A school experience in which the gifted are allowed to pursue free-wheeling intellectual activity as a discursive right, in which art-for-art's sake and lightly assumed missionary mantles are encouraged, turns out on inspection to be one where the less gifted majority are increasingly discouraged, increasingly coerced and increasingly absent.

Rumours of Change

There are two main ways out for a nationalized system which runs into popular disfavour. One is some version or other of *internal* reform. If Sir Keith Joseph is regarded by history as an innovator it will be because his policies aimed at improving the curricular lot of children not cut out for the liberal experience. If he and Mrs Thatcher have felt that public opinion is simply not ready for outright educational denationalization, then they may well have read the signs aright. It is in any case easy to square our administrative changes at the present with questions such as: what curriculum would parents and children of the 'non-academic' type choose if they could? The move towards Pre-Vocational Education is, in my view, tending the way its beneficiaries would go if they were consulted.

But the more drastic course is, I hold, irremovably on the agenda. The theoretical perception may have run ahead of the political will; but powerful arguments may well force themselves on the popular imagination simply through the turn of events. All the signs of public unease at what is being done (or not done) in the name of education and at the taxpayer's expense are clear to see. I incline to Arthur Seldon's view that in the long-run citizens will simply refuse, as their real incomes grow, to see their children confined within a strait-jacket of syndicalist devising.[19] The question of increasing private financial pressure on the curriculum — given the survival of a free society — is not as to *whether* but as to *when* the level of popular discontent will prove uncontainable within the present pattern of arrangements. Private money will simply sweep away the impediments to the expression of citizens' educational preferences sooner or later.

There may have been a case for a nationalized education system in the early stages of an industrial order, given the need for the rapid imposition of raw social control and for the inculcation of a few basic skills. This is special pleading akin to that for protective tariffs for infant industries. Some of us are inclined to doubt the educational case even in these limited terms. What justification is there *today* for treating most of the population as if it were some mindless *lumpen proletariat*? There is an obvious inconsistency in saying that citizens are competent, on the whole, to choose their own food, clothing, housing, entertainment and transport, but not the education and training of their children. Can we really be said to need state compulsion and provision for the many on the grounds of the helplessness of the few?

Those perspicacious spirits who understand very well the wrongness, the inappropriate character of much of our educational practice, but insist nevertheless on the utmost caution, who counsel the intractability of the case, may be given a harsh verdict by history — the charge that they played at softly, softly when the proposals they deemed over-ambitious and premature were already being secured by perceptions and preferences arising in a spontaneous yet calculated way. Bit by bit, sometimes painfully, our society is getting richer. The technological transformation we are now witnessing will, in my view, take us to levels of affluence of which we have so far had no more than a glimpse. Given that school is a huge intrusion into adolescent life, shall we make the mistake of constituting the official curriculum as the poorest of the experiences our children have, not freely and rationally pondered like other purchases, but a withered and closed imposition? Indeed, to speak in these latter terms is to speak too mildly. The genteel secret garden is now a howling wilderness where all too many of our young must wander aimlessly, fortunate enough if they escape the disfiguring attentions of pitiless beasts of intellectual prey.

Notes

1 YOUNG, D. (1985) 'A nation learning to change' in *The Times*, 26 March.
2 O'KEEFFE, D.J. (1981) 'Curricular Yogis and Cost-Benefit Commissars', in *Journal of Curriculum Studies*, September.
3 And neo-classical welfare analysis would surely suggest, *a priori*, quite the opposite conclusion, certainly if it were conducted with half an eye to the empirics of socialism.
4 The curriculum in liberal societies is supply led in the general sense. However, because such societies lack (by definition) a centralizing despotic state, a curious reversal sometimes occurs such that a *privileged* consumption comes to be the curricular dynamic. The growth of school sociology, for example, is a case of pampered and misanthropic insider-trading.
5 The literature is vast, tendentious and puerile. A typical enough case, however, is: DALE, R., ESLAND, G. and MACDONALD, M. (Eds.) (1976) *Capitalism and Schooling*, Routledge and Kegan Paul.
6 SHARP, R. and GREEN, A. (1975) *Education and Social Control*, Routledge and Kegan Paul.
7 My own view, outside the scope of this paper, is that advanced liberal

society is increasingly functionally indifferent to the sex, race and other ascriptive aspects of its economic agents.

8 I believe that Marxism is a classic case of a degenerating intellectual paradigm, absorbing wave after wave of modification without ever defining the grounds of refutation. Now that it is dying in France it is more than likely to die here too. However at present its damaging course still has some way to run.

9 I owe to Geoffrey Partington of the Flinders University of South Australia this neat way of putting it, so obvious seeming — once it has been voiced!

10 HARGREAVES, D. (1982) *The Challenge for the Comprehensive School*, Routledge and Kegan Paul.

11 BLAUG, M. (1970) *An Introduction to the Economics of Education*, Allen Lane.

12 The largest teaching union, the National Union of Teachers (NUT) is losing its dominance in my view, clear testimony to the impossibility of combining, in the long run, an increasing heterogeneity of function with a homogeneity of remuneration.

13 FLEW, A. *et al* (1981) *The Pied Pipers of Education*, The Social Affairs Unit.

14 The antinomian literature adorning the walls of many Inner London Education Authority institutions, for example, is on an appalling scale.

15 I draw the reader's attention to the promiscuous use of the word 'skill' for example 'life-skills'.

16 I saw one of these lessons in a South London school recently. I will supply details to interested readers.

17 BLAUG, M. (1982) *Where Are We Now in the Economics of Education?* University of London Institute of Education.

18 It is not known, admittedly, whether the truant's recoil is from subject matter or the way it is presented.

19 SELDON, A. (1980) *Corrigible Capitalism, Incorrigible Socialism*, Institute of Economic Affairs.

Tripartism Re-Visited: Young People, Education, and Work in the 1980s

Howard Williamson

The area of young people, education and work is such a broad one, imbued as it is with a range of theoretical perspectives as well as practical issues. These are mediated inevitably by fundamental questions concerning class, race and gender divisions amongst young people, as well as the plethora of questions which pertain to the purpose and role of education in contemporary Britain, and the relation of youth to the labour market and an economy in crisis. Moreover, any analysis which takes *young people* as its starting point — rather than, for example, the structure of education or the demands of industry — should ideally address questions concerning the relationship of education and work to other issues which are of central importance in the lives of young people: for instance, leisure, housing and mobility. A basic consideration must therefore be the extent to which changes in educational and occupational opportunity reduce or enhance the access of young people to resources which may be used to avail themselves of wider opportunities. Many young people today, their choices increasingly constrained from all sides, are moving through the acute anxieties of adolescence to a chronic crisis of young adulthood (Williamson, 1985).

It needs to be emphasized, however, that different categories of youth will always experience differential opportunities and will engage in different types of 'trade-off' within those opportunities (Williamson, 1983a; Jones *et al*, 1983). Thus the 'choices' made by individual young people at any particular moment remain as unpredictable as their outcomes, though they rest within the constraints of particular circumstances: nonetheless, not all working-class lads become like Willis' 'lads' (Willis, 1978); similarly, youth training schemes are viewed in an extremely good light by *some* young people, though often for very different reasons (Jones *et al*, 1983, Williamson, 1981).

Given the very real uncertainty about the future of both work and leisure (and the relationship between them), it seems to me that those charged with making provision for young people in education and training and in work have a responsibility to live up to their constant assertion of the need for 'flexibility' and 'adaptability' and thereby to ensure that young people, whatever their aptitudes, gender, class or ethnic background, can retain a level of choice for as long as possible. My reading of the contemporary structure of opportunity within education, training and work suggests that this is becoming increasingly *less* the case. Indeed, it smacks of a warped reworking of the kind of tripartism developed in 1944 and laid to rest — in theory at least in most areas — after 1965.

This essay does not pretend to be a comprehensive or definitive statement on this matter: it is designed to explore — in general terms — *some* of the significant themes concerning young people, education and work in the 1980s. My hope would be to provoke the reader into condemning my arguments as unpersuasive or into supplementing my contentions with material from personal knowledge and experience.

Preliminaries

In a speech to the Society of Education Officers on 25th January 1985, Lord Young, then Minister Without Portfolio and former Chairman of the Manpower Services Commission, reiterated the view popularly held in many quarters that too many young people were emerging from eleven years of compulsory schooling without a single qualification that employers would accept. Too often they were de-motivated and lacked the personal qualities required. He added: 'I believe our failure to gear education and training sufficiently towards the requirements of employment is a major obstacle in the path of enterprise' (*The Guardian*, 26th January 1985) Yet twenty years ago — indeed forty years ago — employers had no qualms about recruiting unqualified young people whom schools had 'failed'. The economic crisis which has developed since the mid–1970s has generated new forms of crisis in education and for young people. It is not, despite common assertions to the contrary, the other way around.

Much of the educational response to its own and the wider

crisis has been to try to become more 'relevant' to the needs of industry, though there is still little clarity about what such needs actually are (Finn, 1982). Education may allow itself to be moulded by what it perceives to be the demands of industry and develop curricula which are simultaneously both real and false responses. They are real because employers may only consider those young people who have experienced such curricula; they are false because the knowledge acquired may still have limited application or 'relevance' in the world of work. Work experience, for example, gained 'properly' through the school curriculum may mean little but count for a lot. For, whatever the real causes of the economic crisis (and they are no doubt complex and obscure [Stonier, 1980]), responsibility for the 'problem' has been thrust increasingly on the failings of education, and it is young people who have borne the brunt.

The danger of education making any attempt to 'meet the needs of industry' is that it is likely to exacerbate the rigidities within education along traditional lines. The traditional inequalities in opportunity — in terms of class, race, gender and region — will be strengthened. As the state imposes a disproportionate burden of the economic crisis on certain groups of the population — one of which is young people — so the education system is likely to impose, explicitly or implicitly, a disproportionate burden of the new 'educational' problems on certain groups of young people. Where jobs are few and far between, decisions will have to be made as to which students may also have to be 'prepared' for other things (though this may still take place under the guise of 'relevance'). Those in receipt of different curricula, in school and post-school, may find their futures more determined than ever before (in that alternative pathways will become closed to them), though categorization and differentiation will be justified as an 'appropriate' response to the 'needs of industry'.

Yet the relationship between education and the labour market is a complex and unclear one. For sure, British education has historically reflected the wider cultural under-valuation of manufacturing specifically and industry more generally (Weiner, 1982). Indeed, historically, 'education' has been *dissociated* from any direct relation to industrial demands — it has been seen as preparation for life; preparation for work has been the domain of vocational training. Increasingly, though, elements of the educational (school) curriculum have taken on a vocational appearance and such developments have become all the more prevalent as the recession deepens with effects both for the 'youth labour market' and for the resourcing of education. The Manpower Services Commission (MSC) has started to make inroads into schools, offering large financial carrots to those schools willing to increase the scale of their vocational provision.

Historically, changes in the content and structure of education have been 'sold' at least partially on the grounds of responding more appropriately to the needs of young people; more often than not, they have in fact borne a stronger, though not total, relation to wider social, economic and political considerations. My argument here will be that we are perhaps witnessing the establishment of a new kind of insidious tripartism within education and training provision for young people in the 1980s. It resembles in principle, though not in structure or form, the hierarchical system of education established forty years ago by the 1944 Education Act, though today there are not even the misleading claims of 'parity of esteem' which attached to that earlier provision.

A Brief Historical Background

'By the mid-1970s the inter-relationships between youth unemployment, education and training, dormant for decades, reached the centre stage of British political life' (Varlaam, 1984, p. 3). Dramatic changes in the labour market were raising significant questions about how to develop appropriate responses to the growing problem of youth unemployment (Rees and Atkinson, 1982) and, increasingly, about the content and purpose of educational (and training) provision.

The 1944 Education Act sought, theoretically, to procure an end to social inequalities in education: education was considered to be the starting point for engineering a more just and fair society. The tripartite system of grammar, technical and modern schools in theory 'matched' the academic, technical and practical aptitudes of young people through the allocatory mechanism of the eleven-plus examination. The three types of school were argued to have 'parity of esteem', simply reflecting the different types of ability within the population. However, the rhetoric of equality of opportunity hardly squared with the reality whereby discrediting definitions were applied to some eighty per cent of the school population in the shape of 'failure' at eleven-plus and subsequent education in secondary modern schools (few areas actually had technical schools). Indeed, the sense of 'individualized failure' was heightened since the ideology of equality of educational opportunity prevented the externalization of blame for failure on the wider social and educational structure (Karabel and Halsey, 1977).

This tripartite system provided the workforce for different levels of the economy but, given the liberal ideology which prevailed at the time, was subjected to intense criticism on social and academic as well as economic grounds. The system was argued to be socially divisive, wasteful of academic talent (criticism of the value and efficacy of assessing children at eleven intensified) and in fact ill-equipped to respond to the *changing* demands of the economy. As a result, the growth of comprehensive education during the 1960s allowed for the deferrment of formal selection and theoretically permitted more scope for individual potential to be identified and fulfilled, though 'children still went to school with others who were likely to end up on a nearby rung of the social ladder' (Ford, 1970; Jackson, 1964).

Whatever education offered, or did not offer, to young people in terms of the requirements of the economy, the transition from school remained relatively unproblematic. Further and higher educational opportunities were expanding and so there was not discontent arising from 'blind alleys'; the labour market was buoyant. Young people moved relatively smoothly from adolescent dependency on school to the status of young workers (Veness, 1962; Carter, 1966; Maizels, 1970; Ashton and Field, 1976). There were few dissenting voices about the content of education as it related *to the economy*, though there was considerable criticism of the abject failure of education to counteract traditional social inequalities (Halsey, Heath and Ridge, 1980). It may, however, be of interest to note the strong parallel between observations by Fyvel in the early 1960s and latter-day pronouncements by industry and the MSC which should be familiar enough to the reader:

> there is a fair measure of agreement amongst teachers that the secondary modern school system with its present-day curriculum is inadequate as a 'bridge' to working life.... What is needed is education much more purposefully designed to produce not only technological adaptability but also social adaptability — to prepare young people both for their working life and their social life in the new affluent society that lies ahead of them (Fyvel, 1963, p. 239 and p. 247).

The language is much the same, despite a radically altered economic context.

As early as 1969, the first of a series of Black Papers on the 'fight for education' maintained that the 'free play' in education, particularly at the comprehensive school level, had led to the decline of educational standards, doing no service to either young people or to economic requirements as they pursued a misguided egalitarianism:

> comprehensive schools, because many of them have no recognisable academic goal, have a distorted picture of enrichment/compensatory programmes and much of our education over the past decade has been steered away from the able towards the average and the less than average. We are ... exchanging excellence for mediocrity ... the flight from the recognised maintained sector ... is becoming a flood.... The root causes are a profound disquiet about academic and social standards; about learning and discipline; about culture and anarchy.... The revolutionary ethic will not work in education because it engenders just those things we can least afford as a society — instability, insecurity, mediocrity and, ultimately, repressive conformity (Green 1975, pp. 25–6).

The questions whether there was actually 'free play' in comprehensives and whether educational standards were genuinely in decline have remained controversial ones, which have been vehemently challenged. Nonetheless, the watershed in the debate about the relationship between education and the economy was signalled by Prime Minister Callaghan's Ruskin speech in October 1976, placing this debate at the highest level on the political agenda: 'Callaghan opened up to public discussion the apparent disparity between current educational values and the need to provide young people with the skills knowledge and understanding necessary to cope with modern industrial society and to lead to full life' (Varlaam, 1984, p. 3). The ensuing debate and subsequent Green Paper (DES, 1977) made it clear that future educational policy was to be more directly subordinated to 'what were perceived to be the "needs" of the economy and the then government's industrial strategy' (Finn, 1982, p. 45). It was an almost inevitable consequence of the previous decade's criticisms of educational irrelevance to the world of work, suddenly made politically and publicly attractive by the impending crisis of youth unemployment, for which education was a convenient scapegoat. What is significant above all else for this paper is that even the rhetoric of 'equality of opportunity', which had been a central, if elusive, goal of educational provision for thirty years, evaporated in the face of the new objective of 'educational *relevance*'.

Throughout this post-war period, whatever the specific structure and content of educational provision, traditional hierarchies of disadvantage and opportunity had persisted. Children from the middle classes had gained most from educational change and expansion (Halsey, Heath and Ridge, 1980); this is no longer particularly surprising, as it has become increasingly clear that welfare policies constructed to compensate for or positively discriminate in favour of the more socially disadvantaged are unlikely to make significant inroads into the structure of class inequality in Britain (Reid 1981). It is one thing, however, to recognize that education may be an ineffective tool for social engineering, quite another to assert that education should collude in the *compounding* of social disadvantage. Until the mid–1970s, education bore only an indirect relation to the preparation of young people for work. Despite pressures to reconstruct education along more 'relevant' lines, the DES faced acute problems in attempting to develop a national response in view of the financial and political autonomy of local education authorities. And while education 'argued about the nature of the problem' (Varlaam, 1984, p. 7) the MSC, unconstrained by tradition or precedent and with almost absolute political support and licence, moved in to define the 'problem' and to implement solutions. Its influence, initially restricted to the post–16 education and training sector, has steadily permeated — directly and indirectly — into schools themselves.

Tightening the Links: The New Vocationalism

Much has been written in recent years about the rationale for and the effects of the 'new vocationalism' (*cf.* Gleeson, 1983, Bates *et al*, 1984). Despite the fact that within schools themselves there was already a partially established trend in curriculum design to include 'work-related' issues, there was a sustained characterization by politicians and industrialists alike of 'unaccountable teachers teaching an irrelevant curriculum to young workers who were poorly motivated, "over-aspirated", illiterate and innumerate' (Finn, 1982, p. 46). During the 1980s, as a result, a 'new realism' has impinged upon more traditional educational considerations, guided actively or implicitly by the MSC and the resources it commands. The world of work has intruded increasingly into the school curriculum in the form of work experience, so-called social education (but see Davies, 1979), vocational guidance and preparation, and social and life skills training. The problem has become defined on the basis of the *deficiencies* of young people in terms of their aptitudes for and attitudes towards the world of work, which demand 'compensatory' strategies before they are 'ready' or 'suitable' for employment. Initially, the MSC intervened directly in the post-school sector — i.e. via the Youth Opportunities Programme — to provide young people with a 'bridge to work'; today it is the schools which bear the responsibility for tackling the basic 'deficiencies' of youth while the MSC complements their work in 'training up' young people in the more specific skills and attitudes deemed necessary to find and keep employment. This is the rhetoric. Indeed it is a reality for many young people, except insofar as both the *assumptions* underlying such strategies are misguided (Atkinson *et al*, 1982) and the *outcomes* are unpredictable — where are the jobs after 'relevant' schooling and 'quality' training? Despite the tightening of the links between education and work, the problems of transition become more acute, not less, suggesting that the real cause of the problem clearly lies elsewhere.

Broken Transitions and Training Schemes — Filling the Gap

If the inability of young people to find work reflects their personal deficiencies, then an increasing proportion of youth is becoming 'deficient'! Those who were the first victims of the recession were those most educationally and socially disadvantaged — the less able, the bottom forty per cent, etc. It was, in the late 1970s, still partially persuasive to assert that this group was 'unemployable', at least in the sense that they lacked the skills which would give them any competitive edge in the labour market, though most had faced few problems when that market was more buoyant (*cf*. Parker, 1974, Willmott, 1969). Training schemes were designed, differentially admittedly, to equip these young people with the skills which would restore their competitiveness (though at whose expense?) in the labour market (MSC, 1977). By the 1980s, however, the *scale* of the fracture in transition meant that a majority of minimum age school leavers were unable to find work; forecasts for 1985 leavers suggest that sixty-eight per cent of sixteen-year-old leavers would be unemployed or on the Youth Training Scheme in December 1985 (Youthaid, 1985). The plausibility of the 'deficiency' and 'unemployable' thesis is thereby steadily undermined. The extent to which training schemes can be argued to be 'compensatory' has limits to its credibility. Consequently, recent developments in post-school training initiatives have made more *rigid* the divisions between scheme types *within* YTS than ever existed in YOP. I am not suggesting that YOP had no hierarchy — it did, but there was some flexibility between levels which, according to some research, was a positive feature of the programme which should have been retained (Jones *et al*, 1983). YTS, on the other hand, operates with clearly defined levels which cater for the different 'needs' of different 'calibre' youth. Some parallels with the old structure of education may already be detected.

The broad rationale for most training schemes (whatever their 'quality') is, however, much the same as the rationale for changes within the school curriculum: to provide young people with the skills, qualifications and attitudes 'relevant' for future adult and working life. The mythology upon which such a rationale is constructed is worthy of a brief mention. I have discussed already the issue of 'unemployability' — within this broad, and misleading, concept are five distinct, though related, contributory themes: unrealistic aspirations, lack of work experience, lack of the correct attitudes, lack of 'stickability' and lack of social skills. Though it is difficult to tease out what constitutes a lack of realism about aspirations (since, as Jenkins [1983] has suggested, all things were possible given the 'right breaks', just that few would ever get them), most evidence suggests that young people's aspirations are in fact fairly accurate anticipations of their likely achievements and destinations (Roberts, 1968, Gray *et al*, 1983). Aspirations may be 'unrealistic' only insofar as the labour market constricts and as employers seek higher qualifications for lower-status jobs. On the matter of work experience, it has been shown that many young people have in fact had quite extensive experience of part-time work while at school (Finn, 1984, Low Pay Unit, 1985) and, if they do not have the 'correct' attitudes to work, this is because they are only too familiar ... with the exploitative, low-paid and humdrum world which they are seeking to enter. (Furthermore, there is little clarity about exactly what are the 'right' attitudes.) Likewise, job-changing has traditionally been seen in terms of an individual problem (lack of 'stickability') when it might equally be interpreted as a rational response to poorly-paid and dead-end employment; indeed it is relevant to 'ask why some young people who obtain what are generally accepted as poor or low status jobs actually stay in them' (Jones *et al*, 1983, p. 43). Finally, the view that many young people lack the appropriate social skills is not only to adopt a culturally arrogant perspective but also to divert attention away from the structural sources of young people's employment problems. I am not suggesting that all young people are wholly prepared for work and life — there will inevitably be aspects with which they require familiarization — but the 'deficit model' which informs the content of 'social and life skills' training is to miss more critical issues (see Atkinson *et al*, 1982).

It is, anyway, patently fallacious that *all* young people, or even a majority, have such depths of deficiency. As I have said already, the flimsiness of the whole argument would become transparent if it was asserted that this was the case. When one in six school leavers entered YOP at the end of the 1970s, such arguments remained just about credible. When two in three go on YTS, they are no longer tenable. And while there are significant and crucial differences in terms of regional labour market characteristics, nationally one in three minimum age school leavers still find work or go into further education (see Youthaid, 1985). The critical issue is, therefore, which young people take which tracks, why and how. Though the structure of both schooling and post–school provision is complex and subject to continual revision and change, it appears to me that a similar kind of tripartism to that of the 1950s, and an extension of the kind of tripartism within FE identified much more recently by Gleeson (1983), is being constructed. It is being constructed not only following school but increasingly within school itself, which puts different groups of young people on course for *only* certain post-school 'opportunities'. The situation is confusing because it *cross-cuts* provision like the Youth Training Scheme, all the more so as YTS caters for an ever-growing proportion of the school leaving population. Whether or not the provision made for these different groups is *actually* relevant to their occupational futures is, in some respects, to miss the point; it still has a powerful *symbolic* function in that the type of 'matching' processes which allocate young people to one position or another within the hierarchy have the effect of conveying crucial messages concerning assumptions *which have already been made* about their 'calibre' and their 'suitability' for subsequent educational and occupational pathways.

Educating and Training Young People:
A New Tripartism?

As the distinction between the education and training of young people has become more blurred, the forms of provision and methods of certification and assessment have become varied and complex: 'the danger is that young people will be lost amongst the empire-building of competing interests' (*New Society*, 17th January 1985). My view is that in fact, despite the sustained claims for the comprehensiveness of this provision, there is an ever more likely, and invidious, possibility of a return to a tripartism even more rigid than that obtaining during the 1950s. Instead of the 'academic', 'technical' and 'modern' distinctions made following 1944, we are experiencing a new three-tier distinction between the 'academic' (as traditionally conceived), the 'technological' (concerned with the information technology field) and the 'technical and social' (focused on basic practical and life skills). There is still some sliding between the categories particularly as the institutional forms which make such educational and training provision (schools, colleges, training schemes) do not simply provide just one of these types of 'education', as grammar, technical and modern schools did in the past. For example, within most schools and colleges there is academic, technological and technical and social provision; YTS provides both technological and technical and social training. Simultaneously, however, the new tripartism is also more rigid, in view of the decline in 'second-chance' type alternatives for those who have been 'wrongly allocated'.

Young people are categorized and allocated to different levels within this tripartism. Those identified as suitable for the 'academic' curriculum[1] remain relatively untouched by considerations about the world of work: 'commonly the more able students are simply steered away from practical subjects, those which are given low value by institutes of higher education and the professions, into a totally academic curriculum' (*The Guardian*, 19th February 1985). At the other end of the scale, 'the less able find themselves guided, often unwillingly, into the more practical and vocational options' (*ibid.*). In the middle, characterized most powerfully today by the MSC-initiated Technical and Vocational Education Initiative (TVEI), are those deemed suitable to receive education and training in the new technologies. In the post-school arena a similar process is at work: some young people pursue their academic pathways in schools and colleges; another group avail themselves of the 'technological' training within the best of YTS, in colleges on BTEC courses (and within TVEI once it is properly established); at the bottom end a substantial number of young people are offered a more staple diet of basic technical and social education and training in the lower echelons of YTS (on Mode B and small-employer Mode A schemes).

Why should we be concerned about such developments? For surely it can be argued that such differential provision is a response to the different capabilities and needs of young people (the argument of 1944) and we might also contend that such divisions have in fact always existed within education and training provision — it is just that they are now being rendered more explicit. Moreover, we should welcome the fact that there are today substantial resources available to make provision for a group of young people who have traditionally been neglected in education and training policy. All these points are fair to a degree, though vulnerable to challenge. But it is the *effects* of this alleged tripartism which are unwelcome since this differential categorization of youth may not only be based on contentious grounds and on speculative conceptions of the future but may also serve to *exacerbate*, compound and confirm traditional structures of disadvantage and opportunity, not just on the basis of class, race and gender, but also of region. These will be discussed below, following some more immediate concerns about the effects of this new tripartism.

Firstly, within schools, it has been argued that the investment in and emphasis on new technological studies is stripping other curricular areas of much needed resources (Waddilove, 1985). TVEI, albeit still in its infancy, offers new technological opportunities to about ten per cent of pupils of the appropriate age (fourteen-plus) in sixty-one local authorities but, although viewed by many as a crucial element of every secondary school curriculum, it has to date lavished disproportionate resources in the form of teachers and equipment on a relatively small group of pupils, possibly at the expense of the rest (Nash, Allsop and Woolnough, 1984; O'Connor, 1985).

Secondly, those receiving technological training within the best Mode A schemes on YTS are likely to constitute the pool from which employers recruit new workers — given that there are so many young people seeking work, selection will as always, have to be on the basis of ever-more subtle 'indicators' and 'filters' (Ashton, Maguire and Garland, 1982). The technological pathway, through school and college or YTS, will enable its privileged participants to cross some extra hurdles in this process. Whether or not their experience and expertise is directly relevant to the employer's needs matters less than the fact that their presence on such a pathway signifies to potential employers their 'employability' and that they are of a reasonable 'calibre'.

In contrast, thirdly, those who have not followed this route, who are not computer literate, are — implicitly — 'illiterate', signifying questionable employability and a lack of 'calibre'. For these young people will have moved along a kind of technical and social pathway, first within school with a diet of education for life and, following school, with mundane work experience and social and life skills training on the lower levels of YTS. Hargreaves has pointed to the self-fulfilling prophecy which can be created when schools may be considering 'suitable' pupils to be involved in 'leisure studies'. His argument holds for the theoretically broader Preparation for Life courses offered in schools (Wilcox and Lavercombe, 1984) and on some training schemes:

> But who would take such courses? If leisure studies are designed for those who are most vulnerable to unemployment (the most likely trend), then teachers would have to select or 'guide' the appropriate pupils; inevitably they would be the 'less able' who are considered unsuitable for public examinations in academic subjects. In making such predictions teachers might well create a self-fulfilling prophecy whereby those expected to be unemployed (and so kitted out with leisure skills) would in fact become unemployable' (Hargreaves 1981, p. 201).

We should note that similar anxieties were expressed about the 'labelling' of eleven-plus failures in the earlier tripartism.

The post-school experience of this group would be generally located within the bottom end of YTS. Though not necessarily totally ineffective (we should always remember that participants may define the purpose of schemes and their reasons for participation in terms different from official ones), this experience would have a value only in the short-term and would essentially constitute the kind of 'blind alley' claimed, misguidedly, for the whole spectrum of recent government youth training measures (Cole and Skelton, 1980, Scofield *et al*, 1983).

Further education colleges are currently the most clear embodiment of this new tripartism (see Gleeson, 1983, though his classifications are somewhat different from mine). They provide education for those on status 'academic' pathways, education and training for those on technological pathways (computer studies, etc.) and a technical and social education and training for YTS trainees. The different groups of students may well have attended the same schools but, within FE, they are often subjected to physical and organizational separation and thus *symbolic and ideological* differentiation (see Moos, 1983).

The pertinent question which remains, however, is who has access to the different tiers of contemporary education and training provision. We are all too aware that post-war educational opportunities have — for quite diverse reasons — manifestly failed to counteract inequalities in opportunity based on class, race and gender. Research on YOP suggested that such inequalities were sustained (Jones *et al*, 1982) despite the explicit intention of YOP to give most help to the 'least qualified and the least able' (MSC, 1977, p. 28). YTS, unlike YOP, makes no such claims. It would appear that the tighter links between education and training (between fourteen and eighteen will reduce even further any *potential* for the 'less able' and less privileged to break out of their disadvantaged position (despite claims that training schemes allow individuals a fresh start to demonstrate their worth). Rather, the existing structure of unequal opportunity for different groups of young people will be reinforced. If anything, more able young people from disadvantaged groups will be *pushed down* the hierarchy on transition from school, though few will get any chance to climb up. YTS is catering for an increasing proportion of school leavers. It needs more and more places to accommodate them and is dependent for most of these places (Mode A) on the goodwill of employers. Employers utilize the same recruitment strategies for YTS as they would for real work. The 'best' YTS employers can therefore select those they perceive as the 'best' YTS candidates. This is self-evident. But the consequence is likely to be that even the more able young people from socially disadvantaged groups (young women, young blacks) — *even those who may have started out on 'technological' pathways* — may find they are unable to cross the hurdles imposed by what are often, even if not deliberately, discriminatory recruitment practices on the part of such employers. (The compounding of social inequality on YOP is discussed by Williamson 1983b; the problems faced by ethnic minority youth in their search for apprenticeships by Lee and Wrench 1983; and issues concerning more general racial disadvantage in the labour market by Troyna and Smith 1983.) My contention is therefore that the traditional hierarchy of opportunity constructed on the basis of combinations of social class, gender and ethnic origin is likely to become more rigid since both the actual content *and* the symbolic characterization of each tier within education and training is not only likely to respond to this hierarchy in the first place (allocatory processes are strongly influenced by *socially*-derived assumptions about ability) but will also reduce even further any potential for 'upward mobility'.

Moreover, *regional* inequalities are also likely to be exacerbated. Without 'technological' employers, technological pathways become dead-ends. The areas where youth unemployment is most acute are precisely those areas where, obviously, (a) there are fewer employment opportunities, particularly in the 'new' industries and (b) the most YTS places are needed to soak up the young unemployed. And YTS relies heavily on employers to provide places. In these areas, then, a far greater proportion of young people will be the 'beneficiaries' of blind-alley technical training and work experience perhaps in the very jobs that are on their way out. The worrying consequence of all this is that *disproportionate* numbers of young people from job-starved localities will be effectively imprisoned within those areas since they will have been denied the opportunities which might (a big 'might' with four million unemployed) have encouraged and permitted geographical mobility to more affluent regions.[2]

The new tripartism is not yet fully formed. There remain blurs, overlaps and some confusion as to whether allocatory decisions should be made *firmly* within school or left until school leaving. TVEI heralds the possibility that such decisions may be made increasingly at 14. Yet even the present system of post-sixteen allocation, guided strongly, we must recognize, on the basis of experience of different school curricula, has already been depicted as a vicious sixteen-plus, more divisive than the eleven-plus ever was (Roberts, 1984). The 'less able' are no longer being prepared for the more menial positions in the labour market but for futures of extended unemployment, punctuated by occasional work. The 'most able', in contrast, can for the most part still by-pass the depressed youth labour markets and avoid the depressing experience of unemployment and the constant, demoralizing struggle to find work — any work. The middle band, like their technical school predecessors, currently rest in an uneasy limbo: their destinations and the job opportunities available to them are not yet properly known.[3]

The criticisms of the earlier tripartism are, however, as pertinent today. We are witnessing a climate of social division not experienced since the 1950s, a pervasive sense of unfulfilled potential in many young people, and a feeling that despite the sacrifices which have been made in the name of 'relevance' contemporary education and training measures are *still* not as closely geared to economic needs at they might be, since the latter remain inadequately articulated. Moreover, although we do not really know what the future economic and social world requires of contemporary youth (hence the language of 'flexibility' and 'adaptability'), we are ever more ready to identify and classify and label different groups of young people. This is justified explicitly on the grounds that differential responses reflect *their* different needs; it has the effect of propelling them along pathways which appear to 'confirm' these suppositions and on which there is in fact little room for manoeuvre or opportunity to demonstrate the flexibility which is apparently desired of them. Finally, therefore, I wish to turn to a brief consideration of alternative strategies.

Choice and Flexibility

> If manure be suffered to lie in idle heaps, it breeds stink and vermin. If properly diffused, it vivifies and fertilizes. The same is true of capital and knowledge. A monopoly of either breeds filth and abomination. A proper diffusion of them fills a country with joy and abundance (quoted in Johnson, 1979, p. 85).

> Let's face it, it's a rat race. It's nothing but a rat race, so apart from anything else you've got to learn 'em to be ... rats, to get a living (YOP scheme supervisor in Jones *et al*, 1982, p. 57).

But should *education* 'learn 'em to be rats'? We must recognize the distinction between the contemporary *problems* faced by, and the *needs* of, young people. Too often the former are transformed into the latter and, though there is clearly a strong relationship between them, this is not necessarily the case. At the same time, ideological opposition to recent developments which assert a more 'relevant' response to the contemporary 'needs' of youth is at risk of throwing the baby out with the bathwater. In highly constrained circumstances, young people still attempt to exercise choices which may be based on ill-founded knowledge. For example acquiescence to youth training provision may be grounded in aspirations to skilled work and perceptions that such training may offer the necessary certification (Williamson, 1982). However, whatever the flaws in those perceptions, the initial *aspirations* are based not so much on any genuine desire for skilled work *per se* but because skilled work has *in the past* been associated with high pay and secure employment. This may no longer be the case. My point is that young people's hopes, aspirations, expectations and 'choices' may well be based, partially at least, on an understanding of circumstances which no longer prevail. For young people are no more able than anyone else to predict the structure of future social and occupational opportunities. But given this uncertain future they do need to be equipped not simply in terms of literacy and numeracy but with a whole battery of skills in, for example, managing relationships, assertiveness, self-organization of time during periods of unemployment. Without them, they will be even more heavily disadvantaged (see Bates, 1984).

This climate of uncertainty and unpredictability of social and occupational futures (*for all of us*) has the potential to generate new forms of educational provision along a continuum from repressive, divisive and directive strategies to participative, democratic and progressive strategies: 'By shifting social learning to a more central position, work experience opened up both progressive and conservative possibilities: on the one hand, open schools and experiential learning; on the other, the subordination of educational goals to employer needs' (Stronach, 1984, p. 49). Wilcox and Lavercombe, discussing the growth in Preparation for Life (PFL) courses, point to their potential in encouraging pupils to adopt a critical approach to the social world and their relationship with it but recognize the danger that they may in fact be 'facilitating an *uncritical* acceptance of conventional wisdom' (1984, p. 21, my emphasis). But presumably, in view of the tensions which do exist between the different levels and interests responsible for making educational provision, it would be possible — given a concerted effort by various parties — to drive a wedge between these interests, thereby achieving a creative penetration of the system which would allow more democratic/participative/progressive forms of provision to be constructed. I recognize the enormous difficulties of doing so, not least the financial and ideological whip-hand of the MSC. Nonetheless, the ever more insidious tendency for the curriculum to be imposed and evaluated unilaterally by not only teachers but also increasingly by 'trainers', rather than chosen or organized or judged by, or even debated with, the pupils themselves (Hargreaves, 1981), must be checked.

The essence of education for young people in the 1980s should be founded on the *interaction* between their felt needs and experiences and the wider knowledge of the social world possessed by those who teach them, *not* on various, often spurious and patronizing, judgments about needs and capabilities which effectively confer privileged pathways on some and condemn many to straitjacketed educationally and occupationally impoverished futures. As Dunn has argued, 'the present socio-economic system would seem to demand that if we are not to lose our young people altogether into the drains of neutralised despair, we need to stir their imaginations' (1984, p. 76). The world of work should not be ignored but there is a crucial difference between learning for work and learning *about* work, particularly if such an education builds 'as a priority, on the young people's past experience, knowledge and skills which are relevant to the immediate present' (Atkins, 1985, p. 38).

In many respects, all this is to re-assert the purpose of *education* (not necessarily schooling). Education needs to have the potential for developing a consciousness which is independent of the needs of the labour process (Gleeson and Mardle, 1980), in which learners are active participants and not passive recipients, through which learners become more 'aware of, competent within, able to change, the definite social relations of a particular society' (CCCS, 1979, p. 258). Surely the purpose of education must be to extend the potential for young people to exercise choice rationally and responsibly, to equip them with the capacity for greater self-determination, *not* to define them and decide for them. The practical implementation of such 'social education' methods as alluded to above is, for sure, problematic, especially in view of the powerful competing re-definitions of the nature and purpose of education and appropriate curricula. But neither is it merely rhetoric from liberal and radical critics of contemporary educational provision (a Social Education Project in Birmingham with which I am associated bears witness to its potential). Two final points therefore need to be made here. First, there is the familiar question of 'whose side are we on?'. Are 'educators' passively going to allow themselves to collude with MSC-inspired definitions of the differential 'calibres' of young people and operate in effect as the handmaidens of industry? Are they to willingly engage in the rigid systematic categorization of young people? Secondly, once the fallacy of the 'deficit model' of some youth has been effectively exposed, 'new methods' can no longer be justified as 'relevant' only to the so-called disadvantaged. The future, I will say yet again, remains unpredictable — admittedly to differing degrees — for all young people. *All* young people need to be participants in the educational process of developing a more critical understanding of the social, economic and political world in which they live.

Conclusion

The 1980s have witnessed the demise of any pretensions within education to act as a vehicle for social engineering a more just and equitable society through attempts to construct greater equality of opportunity for the more socially disadvantaged. The old transitions between school and work have, for an increasing number of young people, collapsed. We can view this with yearning and regret. Yet we must avoid being sidetracked by a desire to re-establish a 'golden age' of educational provision which never in fact existed. It was a time when the majority of young people reaped few benefits from education and in whom education invested *no* resources after the age of sixteen. The breaking of educational traditions has provided space for both optimism and pessimism. The first few years of the 'new vocationalism', inspired — if that is the right word — by MSC dogma and finance, should suggest to those concerned about young people today that pessimism was perhaps the more accurate perspective. Nonetheless, those with such concerns — teachers, youth workers, FE staff, some careers staff — should continue to press for forms of education and training and of curriculum development to be based on principles of partnership, participation and understanding rather than irrelevance, imposition and ignorance. Even Joey in Willis' study enjoyed his English classes; we never really found out why (Cousin, 1984). The form and organization of education and training as well as its content need to be radically re-assessed if young people are going to benefit from the resources currently available to them — whether their futures are in or out of work. The critical question, of course, is whether such resourcing would be curtailed if there were significant re-orientations in curriculum design in a more 'liberal' direction: 'he who pays the piper....'

The advocates of 'relevance' currently exert most influence on the structure and content of education and training initiatives, though it still remains important to inquire 'relevant to what?' and 'relevant to whom?'. There has been a reluctance (inability?) to move beyond general statements about the 'need for relevance' towards specifying precisely those features which together would allow 'relevant' provision to be made. This is hardly surprising since realistic conceptions of 'relevance' must ebb and flow with the changing social and economic tide. Where such attempts have been made (i.e. through the blinkered focus on deficient and undersocialized youth), ensuing assertions have been constructed on patently shaky foundations. Yet the 'case for relevance' has led to ever tightening links between education and training and to the dominance of individualistic definitions of the 'problem' and coercive strategies to resolve it. Its consequence has been to strengthen the processes by which young people are categorized — at age fourteen or sixteen — and prepared, academically, technologically, or technically and socially, for the future. What concerns me, and no doubt others, is that the pathways to which such different categories of youth are consigned, while extremely firmly bedded, do not and cannot have predictable outcomes in terms of 'relevance' to future social and economic needs. They can, however, inhibit the possibilities for readjustment by young people to changing circumstances. Yet though the future is *so* unpredictable, this 'does not deter our many sociological and economic seers who are adept at presenting plausible sketches of future possibilities in the guise of highly probable predictions' (Hargreaves, 1981, p. 197). The apparently neutral/objective allocatory procedures of the eleven-plus conferred on a significant proportion of young people a heightened sense of *personal failure* — my contention is that such a sense of individual failure is a consequence of a new fourteen to sixteen-plus and is being revisited, unnecessarily and quite unjustifiably, on a similar proportion of youth today.

The distinction between education and training needs to be re-stated and re-affirmed. Education must be concerned with heightening potential, with self-realization; the social components of education have the responsibility of enabling all young people to become 'the best possible versions of themselves' (Marsland, 1985, p. 3). Education should not be about constraint and directiveness. As Steinberg has maintained, the education system has to be 'split open and many more allowed through, if the *Angst* of the eighties is not to turn to something much worse by the nineties' (1985, p. 403). But our considerations of what counts as appropriate educational forms need not — indeed, should not — be based upon fears about the riotous potential of youth. As Mungham has argued, the cry of young people is for incorporation: 'their concern is not to subvert a social order, but to join it' (1982, p. 38).

All young people are today entering an increasingly complex social and occupational world. Not only do they require a basic education but they also require an increasingly important social and political education together with 'work-related' and vocational training. Without all these components, they will be unable to participate to their full potential in that social world. The means by which such education should be delivered should be through their *experience* — whatever their background — not on speculative prognoses of their 'place' in the social order. We must not be sidetracked by false trails about, for example, personal deficiencies, a lack of readiness for the world of work, or a lack of social competence. The majority of young people are only *too ready* to join an occupational order which has been closed off to many of them. And although young people continue to attempt to exercise some choice and control within this problematic social and occupational world, their situation is being increasingly straitjacketed and constrained by external and ill-defined, but symbolically crucial, forces and expectations, particularly from government and industry. Those charged with the broad remit to 'educate' young people have a responsibility to offer them a space within which they can 'decode' what is going on around them (Dunn, 1984), not to act as the lap-dog of these external forces. They have a duty to make provision based on a real not rhetorical flexibility in curriculum design in order to encourage and develop a similar flexibility in young people themselves. They do, of course, have some responsibility to familiarize young people with industrial and economic needs, but not to condemn a significant proportion of their charges to 'blind alley' futures while pretending to offer them 'relevant' technical and social education. That is the most insidious consequence of the new tripartism.

Notes

1 Students in theory make choices, but such choices are firmly guided by teachers, careers teachers and careers officers and heavily constrained by class sizes and (perceptions and self-perceptions of) ability.
2 It has, however, been argued that *irrespective* of regional labour mar-

kets some private managing agents of YTS are deciding to offer 'cheaper' YTS courses (i.e. retailing rather than clerical). The question this raises is: are courses deemed to be 'too expensive' those which do offer some real skill training while 'cheap' courses are for jobs which, in better times, young people have traditionally entered without any training? (Buswell, 1985). My argument still applies but rather less forcefully if this is the case.

3 All the current emphasis on the need for 'new technological' training *may* be something of a red herring. It has been suggested that the number of new technology jobs available to young people in any particular year is relatively small in view of the numbers of young people who are being guided towards such work (Waddilove, 1985, Harris, 1985). If this is the case, it is likely to have the effect of 'squeezing out' technical and social students even further.

References

ASHTON, D. and FIELD, D. (1976) *Young Workers: From School to Work*, London, Hutchinson.

ASHTON, D., MAGUIRE, M. and GARLAND, V. (1982) *Youth in the Labour Market*, London, Department of Employment Research Paper No. 34.

ATKINS, M. (1985) 'The pre-employment curriculum: a right of passage', *Youth and Policy* No 11, pp. 37–40.

ATKINSON, P., REES, T., SHONE, D. and WILLIAMSON, H. (1982) 'Social and life skills: the latest case of compensatory education', in REES, T. and ATKINSON, P. (Eds.), *Youth Unemployment and State Intervention*, London, Routledge and Kegal Paul.

BATES, I., CLARKE, J., COHEN, P., FINN, D., MOORE, R. and WILLIS, P. (1984) *Schooling for the Dole*, London, MacMillan.

BATES, I. (1984) 'From vocational guidance to life skills: historical perspectives on careers education', in BATES, I. *et al., op. cit.*

BUSWELL, C. (1985) *Employment Processes and Youth Training*, paper presented to International Sociology of Education Conference Westhill College, Birmingham, January.

CARTER, M. (1966) *Into Work*, Harmondsworth, Penguin.

CCCS (1979) *Unpopular Education*, London, Hutchinson.

COLE, M. and SKELTON, B. (Eds.) (1980) *Blind Alley*, Ormskirk, G.W. and A. Hesketh.

COUSIN, G. (1984) 'Failure through resistance: critique of *Learning to Labour*', *Youth and Policy* No 10, pp. 37–40.

DAVIES, B. (1979) *In Whose Interests: From Social Education to Social and Life Skills*, Leicester, National Youth Bureau.

DES (1977) *Education in Schools: A Consultative Document*, London, HMSO.

DUNN, J. (1984) '"Staying in bed": young people, transition and the role of political education' in VARLAAM, C. (Ed.), *Rethinking Transition: Educational Innovation and the Transition to Adult Life*, Lewes, Falmer Press.

FINN, D. (1982) 'Whose needs? Schooling and the "needs" of industry', in REES, T. and ATKINSON, P. *op. cit.*

FINN, D. (1984) 'Leaving school and growing up: work experience in the juvenile labour market' in BATES, I. *op. cit.*

FORD, J. (1970) 'Comprehensive schools as social dividers', *New Society*, 26 Feb.

FYVEL, T. (1963) *The Insecure Offenders*, Harmondsworth, Penguin.

GLEESON, D. (Ed.) (1983) *Youth Training and the Search for Work*, London, Routledge and Kegan Paul.

GLEESON, D. (1983) 'Further education, tripartism and the labour market', in GLEESON, D. *op. cit.*

GLEESON, D. and MARDLE, G. (1980) *Further Education or Training?*, London, Routledge and Kegan Paul.

GRAY, J., McPHERSON, A. and RAFFE, D. (1983) *Reconstructions of Secondary Education: Theory, Myth and Practice since the War*, London, Routledge and Kegan Paul.

GREEN, G. (1975) 'Why comprehensives fail', in COX, C. and BOYSON, R. (Eds.), *Black Paper 1975*, London, Dent.

HALSEY, A., HEATH, A. and RIDGE, J. (1980) *Origins and Destinations: Family, Class and Education in Modern Britain*, Oxford, Clarendon.

HARGREAVES, D. (1981) 'Unemployment, leisure and education', *Oxford Review of Education* Vol. 7 No. 3, pp. 197–210.

HARRIS, M. (1985) 'Invasion of the tape-apes', *New Society*, 7 March.

JACKSON, B. (1964) *Streaming: An Education System in Miniature*, London, Routledge and Kegan Paul.

JENKINS, R. (1983) *Lads, Citizens and Ordinary Kids: Working-Class Youth Life-Styles in Belfast*, London, Routledge and Kegan Paul.

JOHNSON, R. (1979) '"Really useful knowledge": radical education and working-class culture, 1970–1848', in CLARKE, J. CRITCHER, C. and JOHNSON, R. (Eds.), *Working Class Culture*, London, Hutchinson.

JONES, P., WILLIAMSON, H., PAYNE, J., and SMITH, G. (1983) *Out of School: A Case Study of the Role of Government Schemes at a Time of Growing Unemployment*, London, Manpower Services Commission, Special Programmes Occasional Paper No. 4.

KARABEL, J. and HALSEY, A. (Eds.) (1977) *Power and Ideology in Education*, New York, Oxford University Press.

LEE, G. and WRENCH, J. (1983) *Skill Seekers — Black Youth, Apprenticeships and Disadvantage*, Leicester, National Youth Bureau.

LOW PAY UNIT (1985) *Working Children*, London, Low Pay Unit.

MAIZELS, J. (1970) *Adolescent Needs and the Transition from School to Work*, London, Athlone.

MARSLAND, D. (1985) *Youth Workers and Unemployment: Talk or Action*, paper presented to International Sociology of Education Conference, Westhill College, Birmingham, January.

MOORE, R. (1984) 'Schooling and the world of work', in BATES, I. *et al, op. cit.*

MOOS, M. (1983) 'The training myth: a critique of the government's response to youth unemployment and its impact on further education', in GLEESON, D. (Ed.) *op. cit.*

MSC (1977) *Young People and Work*, London, Manpower Services Commission.

MUNGHAM, G. (1982) 'Workless youth as a moral panic', in REES, T. and ATKINSON, P, (Eds.) *op. cit.*

NASH, M., ALLSOP, T., and WOOLNOUGH, B. (1984) *Factors Affecting the Uptake of Technology in Schools*, Oxford, Department of Educational Studies.

O'CONNOR, M. (1985) 'A technical hitch in the system', *The Guardian* 15 Feb.

PARKER, H. (1974) *View from the Boys*, Newton Abbot, David and Charles.

REES, T. and ATKINSON, P. (Eds.) (1982) *Youth Unemployment and State Intervention*, London, Routledge and Kegan Paul.

REID, I. (1981) *Social Class Differences in Britain*, London, Grant McIntyre.

ROBERTS, K. (1968) 'The entry into employment: an approach towards a general theory', *Sociological Review* Vol 16 No 2, pp. 165–84.

SCOFIELD, P., PRESTON, E., and JACQUES, E. (1983) *Youth Training: The Tories' Poisoned Apple*, Leeds, Independent Labour Publications.

STEINBERG, J. (1985) 'Eighties Angst', *New Society*, 14 March.

STONIER, T. (1980) 'Technological change and the future', in CHERRY, G. and TRAVIS, T. (Eds.), *Leisure in the 1980s: Alternative Futures*, London, Leisure Studies Association.

STRONACH, I. (1984) 'Work experience: the sacred anvil', in VARLAAM, C. (Ed.) *op. cit.*

TROYNA, B. and SMITH, D. (Eds.) (1983) *Racism, School and the Labour Market*, Leicester, National Youth Bureau.

VARLAAM, C. (1984) 'Introduction: rethinking transition', in VARLAAM, C. (Ed.) *op. cit.*

VENESS, T. (1962) *School Leavers*, London, Methuen.

WADDILOVE, K. (1985) 'Let the micros rot!', *The Guardian*, 19 Feb.

WEINER, M. (1982) *English Culture and The Decline of the Industrial Spirit*, Cambridge, Cambridge University Press.

WILCOX, B. and LAVERCOMBE, S. (1984) 'Preparation for life: curriculum issues', in VARLAAM, C. (Ed.) *op. cit.*

WILLIAMSON, H. (1981) *Chance Would Be a Fine Thing*, Leicester, National Youth Bureau.

WILLIAMSON, H. (1982) 'Client responses to the youth opportunities programme', in REES, T. and ATKINSON, P. (Eds.) *op. cit.*

WILLIAMSON, H. (1983a) 'A duty to explain', *Youth in Society*, November.

WILLIAMSON, H. (1983b) 'WEEP: exploitation or advantage?' in FIDDY, R. *In Place of Work: Policy and Provision for the Young Unemployed*, Lewes, Falmer Press.

WILLIAMSON, H. (1985) 'Struggling beyond youth', *Youth in Society*, January.

WILLIS, P. (1978) *Learning to Labour*, Teakfield, Saxon House.

WILLMOTT, P. (1969) *Adolescent Boys of East London*, Harmondsworth, Penguin.

YOUTHAID (1985) *Bulletin*, Issue No. 20, February.

Comprehensive Schooling and Procrustes

Beverley Shaw

Pupils who reject secondary schooling do not reject it only because they find it boring. Perhaps most, if not all, pupils find school boring at least some of the time, but are prepared to put up with it because of its occasional rewards, and the promise and prospects that success at school holds out. Young people who reject schooling do so because it is boring, holds out few prospects for the future, and is without any intrinsic interest as well.

This is not an original claim, and certainly does not bear on comprehensive schools alone. At the head of the motto quotations for Chapter 1 of the Newsom Report (1963), *Half Our Future*, a report on the education of what Newsom described as the average and below average pupils of secondary modern schools, there is this story: 'A boy who had just left school was asked by his former headmaster what he thought of the new buildings. "It could all be marble, sir," he replied, "but it would still be a bloody school"' (p. 2).

It is my contention in this chapter, however, that going comprehensive has exacerbated in this respect the condition of schooling in Britain. Very largely, comprehensive schooling came about as a result of the activities of a handful of excessively energetic Procrustean educationalists and evangelists (see Flew, A., 1981 for a penetrating analysis of Procrustes at work in modern Britain). Procrustes, it will be remembered, was the hotel owner of Ancient Greece who offered his guests the hospitality of the Procrustean bed, for which all guests could be fitted by the expedient of stretching the limbs of guests too short, and chopping down to size those too large. The Procrustean educator believes above all in equality, interpreted all too often as a literal equality of treatment and outcome.

An example of just such Procrustean thinking is to be found in an article by R.J. Royce, a lecturer in the Faculty of Educational Studies of Brighton Polytechnic. In an attempt to rebut arguments scandalously in favour of private schooling, Royce asserts in the triumphal manner of a disputant with an irrefutable knock-down argument: 'In so far as particular schools or classes of schools favour or disadvantage pupils in general a case can be made in the name of equality against such schools' (1982, p. 107). Thus if schools fail to be equal, what more can then be said? Perhaps it might be whispered that if state schools are not as good as those schools which are private, and to some degree therefore independent of the state, local or national, then perhaps equality can be achieved if state schools are improved. Royce, the economic realist, points out, however, that there are limits to public expenditure; and: 'It may well be that the United Kingdom cannot afford the cost of providing all with educational standards given to the few' (1982, p. 106). Therefore, for the Procrustean educational equalizer: 'The remaining alternative is to lower the standards of the best to that of par with all others, or to close them down if they refuse to comply with this directive' (*ibid.*, p. 107). (For an extended discussion of these arguments from equality, see Shaw (1983), Colbeck (1984), and Shaw (1984).)

The Procrustean grip over comprehensive schools is revealed in the demand that all pupils are to be treated equally, despite manifest differences in ability, aptitude and interest among pupils. We do not have to look far for evidence of this. Consider a report of a committee on the curriculum and organization of secondary schools chaired by Dr David Hargreaves, still at the time Reader in Education, University of Oxford; his translation, to the position of Chief Inspector of the Inner London Education Authority (ILEA), followed hard on the publication of this report by that authority. The report, *Improving Secondary Schools* (1984), is willing to note the limitations of such schools, at least in the ILEA. A good deal of the blame is put on the public system of examinations. Such examinations press teachers, parents and pupils 'to acquire knowledge, skills and practical abilities, and the will to use them' (pp. 33–34). No bad thing one might think; but then the authors of this report claim that such an achievement is gained at the expense of '. . . an understanding of the social, economic and political order, and a reasoned set of attitudes, values and beliefs'; and also results in a failure of pupils 'to prepare for their adult lives at home, at work, at leisure, and at large, as consumers and citizens'; and 'to develop a sense of self-respect, the capacity to live as independent, self-motivated adults and the ability to function as contributing members of co-operative groups' (pp. 34–35).

All these are aims that appeared earlier in one of the now defunct Schools Council's publications, *The Practical Curriculum* (1981). It may be noted that the aims quoted above include those traditional to schooling ('to acquire knowledge, skills and practical abilities ...'); and those more general aims that one might wish simply to subsume under the notion of upbringing. For example, the capacity to live as an independent, self-motivated adult is open to us all, despite sometimes rather than because of our school days. In short, one may not need schooling to become an independent self-motivated adult, whilst acquiring knowledge, and learning skills may necessitate it. Furthermore these categories overlap; for 'acquiring knowledge' is precisely what is involved in developing 'an understanding of the social, economic and political order'. *Improving Secondary Schools* goes on to argue that the 'present system of public examinations *guarantees* underachievement ... by excluding some pupils from all public examinations' (italics original, p. 34); and by excluding pupils from the achievement of such aims as are quoted above, and listed and enumerated in *The Practical Curriculum* — other than the acquiring of knowledge, skills and practical abilities.

We can agree that for those who do not enter a public examination it is *guaranteed* that they will fail to gain whatever success the examination offers. Where does this obvious truth take us? Only if it could be demonstrated that pupils are wrongly excluded from sitting an examination, that is for reasons other than total incapacity to answer whatever questions are set, is there any case to answer. Exclusion from one set of exams, of course, may suggest that if examination success, at whatever level, is synonymous with school achievement — and this may well be true (see Flew, 1976) — then the answer is not to abolish public examinations, but to widen their scope, so that there are examinations at a variety of levels, and employing many modes, to test that whatever has been taught in schools has been properly learned.

As for the failure of public examinations to test whether their pupils have, for instance, become 'an independent self-motivated adult' this again cannot be disputed. Perhaps it could be said that success in public examinations, if this truly revealed genuine learning and the acquisition of skills, would at least provide the preconditions for independence, and perhaps, also reveal a degree of 'self-motivation', by which some capacity for initiative and freedom may be meant. This is no more than a suggestion; the capacity of any one of us to be an independent self-motivating adult may well rest upon the conditions of the society in which we live. This has to be a society offering opportunities for independent action, and for freedom of thought and expression; all of which may be opportunities wasted on young people who lack knowledge, skills and practical abilities, and the will to use them. Does this perhaps describe too many of the ex-pupils of our inner-city comprehensive schools? For example those ex-pupils, described by Dr Robert Burgess in his *Experiencing Comprehensive Education* (1983). He recounts how, in his pseudonymous Bishop McGregor School, the pupils on the non-examined course in the fourth and fifth years (a course named or 'labelled' pejoratively, the Newsom course) negotiated a truce between the teachers and the taught whereby the teachers would be given a relatively easy ride if their notional pupils were allowed to 'mess about' and 'to have a laugh'. Yet, in a moment of insight on this course one pupil remarked: 'We can do what we like and when I can do just what I like, I don't like it' (quoted in Burgess, 1983, p. 227).

Discussion of what is on offer in our comprehensive schools often acknowledges that much of it is not valued by pupils. *Improving Secondary Schools* quotes from comments supplied as evidence to the committee; one such, from a divisional education welfare officer (EWO), argues that:

> ... the comprehensive secondary school appears to be largely based on the needs of the smaller proportion of the more able, mature and home-supported pupils, whose educational needs are primarily cognitive and exam-orientated, rather than on the needs of the larger proportion of less able, often less mature and sometimes less home-supported pupils whose needs are not just cognitive and are often not exam-orientated, but are also emotional and social (p. 34).

This bi-partite division of the school population is perhaps a little crude insofar as it suggests that there are two, and perhaps only two, distinguishable groups: the exam-orientated and more able intellectually, and the less mature, less able, less home-supported pupils, not exam-orientated pupils. Yet it is certainly an improvement on the belief that inequalities between children arise only from the misperceptions of teachers only too eager to categorize and to differentiate. The education welfare officer's remarks suggest that what is required is more variety in schools, or preferably that some schools should provide for one general category of pupils and other schools for a different grouping. Yet to the Procrustean equalizer, the evidence of the EWO will not deter him from mono-curriculum planning. In the equalizer's eyes, if comprehensive schools cater for a minority of able children, leaving the rest to flounder, and to become disaffected and mutinous, then the curriculum must be transformed, indeed such that all, including the minority of able and exam-motivated pupils, will follow courses reconstructed to satisfy the supposed emotional, social, and non-cognitive needs of the majority.

Sources of the Problem

How has this sorry state of affairs come about? To answer this question we must consider the theory and practice of comprehensive schooling, and the history of this ramshackle system. In a chapter of this length attention to these issues must necessarily be limited and selective (for a more extended treatment, see Shaw, 1983). A start at least can be made by examining the thought and action of the politican who was more than most responsible for the creation of comprehensive schooling in Britain: Anthony Crosland (1918–1977).

In a chapter of his influential *The Future of Socialism* (1956), writing as an intellectual and theorist of the Labour Party, Crosland attempted to provide a justification for the destruction of the grammar and secondary modern schools, and their replacement by a system of common or comprehensive schools. It would be wrong to believe that at its time of writing the views on schools expressed in the *Future of Socialism* were widely accepted in the Labour Party. On the contrary, the notion of the comprehensive school was regarded with some suspicion, and both Labour politicians and ordinary party members were more concerned with making the bi-partite (or in some LEAs the tri-partite) system work in a post–war world where resources for education were obviously limited (Parkinson, 1970).

In the 1950s the Labour Party was out of office. Typically political parties in Western democracies use time out-of-office to consider what new directions to strike out for. On *The Future of Socialism*, Susan Crosland was to comment as her husband's biographer: 'The book appeared at a time when there was an ideological vacuum within the Labour Party which had just suffered a second consecutive defeat at the polls' (Crosland, S., 1982 p. 67). There are aspects of *The Future of Socialism* which may have marked a step forward in Labour thinking. In particular perhaps, Crosland's views expressed in section IV of his book's 'Conclusion', headed intriguingly enough: *Liberty and Gaiety in Private Life; the Need for a Reaction against the Fabian Tradition* (p. 521, italics original). Crosland remarks here: 'Total abstinence and a good filing system are not now the right sign-posts to the socialist Utopia: or at least, if they are, some of us will fall by the wayside' (p. 524).

One right sign-post to the socialist Utopia was apparently pointing towards comprehensive schooling, for Crosland in his chapter 'The influence of education', reaches the somewhat tentative conclusion that 'we must surely incline, as socialists, towards a "comprehensive" system of education, under which all children would ideally share the same broad experience at least up to the official school-leaving age' (p. 267). However tentative, here is the egalitarian and Procrustean equalizer speaking: *all* children — ideally let us note — must 'share the same broad experience'. There is the proviso of course that this is up to the school leaving age, at Crosland's time of writing then fixed at fifteen. There is the expression 'same broad experience': is this a canny politician playing with words so that a 'same broad experience' can be of indeterminate width?

We may never now know; but certainly his grounds for this belief in a common schooling are curious. They were not, as later become increasingly fashionable, based upon the belief that the eleven-plus tests of the day were iniquitous, monstrously unjust and unfair. Indeed his comments on eleven-plus testing could well have been made by some unregenerate defender of élitist grammar schools such as Sir Eric James, High Master of a highly esteemed and selective direct grant school, Manchester Grammar. But it is Crosland who wrote:

> It was thought that a child's whole future was decided on a single day's test. No doubt much of the dislike of such tests was based on ignorance or exaggeration. Their results in fact were never decided on a single day's test. Immense care was commonly taken over borderline cases. There was always provision (though often imperfect) for re-testing and transferring 'late developers'. And the better secondary modern schools began increasingly to provide advanced courses and thus a route to the higher occupations (p. 267).

Following that it is difficult to see what case the bi- or tri-partite system had to answer. Crosland, however, believed that the system, despite its merits, was bitterly disliked and resented. He provides no evidence for this belief, and polls taken in the 1950s and 1960s provide no corroboration, see Shaw (1983). Indeed Crosland argues that: 'the seeming justice of the process of selection ... may have actually exacerbated the resentments' (p. 267). Crosland appeared to believe, falsely, that there was widespread resentment of the selection system, and that different schools increased the amount of envy in society. Envy is an evil; therefore to reduce the evil of envy, the system, despite or because of its being as fair and just as it could be in an imperfect world, must be destroyed.

Crosland asserted that: 'The object of Comprehensive Schools is not to abolish all competition and all envy ...' (p. 272). Perhaps this was not possible even in a Socialist utopia — it 'might be rather a hopeless task, but the object is to avoid the extreme social division caused by physical segregation into schools of widely divergent status, and the extreme social resentment caused by failure to win a grammar (or, in future, public) school place, when this is thought to be the only avenue to a "middle-class" occupation' (p. 272). The grammar schools were to be abolished to reduce some envy, social resentment, and competition, it appears. Yet Crosland provides no evidence for this extreme social resentment; and Michael Parkinson an educational historian, in his *The Labour Party and the Organisation of Secondary Education, 1918–1965* records that a Labour Party commissioned public opinion poll in 1957 suggested in general: 'the vast majority of the public were ignorant of the issues involved in comprehensive reorganisation', and, on the issue of selection, that 'only ten per cent of the sample, anyway, felt that segregated education was socially undesirable ...' (Parkinson, 1970, p. 81).

But even if envy was more widespread than these polls suggested, or indeed was as widespread as Crosland mistakenly believed it to be, to what extent can such envy be reduced by attempting to blur differences and distinctions? It is of interest here that, in a brief comment on the organization of comprehensive schools, Crosland wrote: 'Division into streams, according to ability remains essential'. (p. 272). Thus whilst the bi-partite system will go, the grammar, the technical and the secondary moderns will be abolished, in the new schools the old distinctions will remain — albeit under one roof. Whatever the good sense in Crosland's brief comment, it undermines altogether the notion of sharing the same broad experience. It suggests rather a politican attempting to placate the furies of envy believed, falsely, to have been at work in the land.

Nor were other supporters of comprehensive schooling so ready to accede to the notion that selection would be retained within schools whilst allegedly abolished between them. Professor Robin Pedley, in his 1978 third edition of *The Comprehensive School*, first published in 1963 and reprinted nearly every year since, argued that: 'to transfer selection from outside the school to inside the school still entails rejection for the great majority of children and the thwarting of many parental hopes' (p. 104). Headmaster Maurice Holt puts the same point more picturesquely: 'it is difficult to think of the streamed or banded comprehensive as any less incongruous than a Nash terrace with a thatched roof' (1978, p. 163). These supporters of comprehensive schooling were simply pushing the logic of such schooling further than Crosland. If comprehensive schooling is, as Crosland claimed it to be, a schooling in which 'all children would ideally share the same broad experience' (see Crosland above), then *any* kind of distinction or difference of treatment or teaching becomes seen as invidious: as a failure to match up to the comprehensive ideal.

Thus comprehensive schooling leads irrevocably to the mixed ability class. Whether there is *educational* virtue in the mixed ability class is a large topic in itself. Certainly one headmaster, has thought it has a social value, for he is quoted, in one study of mixed ability teaching (Reid *et al*, 1981, p. 25), as saying: 'Unstreaming is socially desirable, you shouldn't have all the kids with dirty vests in one form'. This egalitarian headmaster did admit however, that 'the able (pupils) would get on faster if they were streamed'. It is of interest on this very point that Reid, *et al*, quoted an experienced remedial teacher, who, whilst repeating the conventional wisdom that segregation was in many respects reprehensible, admitted 'it did cater for the less able academically' (Reid, 1981, p. 86).

Crosland, in a footnote to a sentence stating that LEAs ought to be encouraged to go comprehensive, presciently commented: 'But with the important proviso, in large cities which are divided into rather clearly-marked one-class neighbourhoods, that the catchment areas are so drawn as to straddle neighbourhoods of different social standing' (p. 275). It is to Crosland's credit that, when as Secretary of State for Education in 1965, he issued Circular 10/65, it urged 'authorities to ensure, when determining catchment areas, that schools are as socially and intellectually comprehensive as is practicable' (para. 36). In the event of course this turned out not to be practicable in many areas. Within the ILEA, Professor Michael Rutter in *Fifteen Thousand Hours: Secondary Schools and their*

Effects on Children (1979), comments that, with respect to his research: 'Despite administrative efforts to ensure that ability group-ings should be reasonably comparable across all London schools, there were fairly major variations within our sample' (p. 154). Three of the twelve schools sampled had less than five per cent of children deemed 'top ability'. Only in one school did such pupils make up a quarter. Ethnic minority proportions varied from four per cent to fifty-four per cent.

There are good reasons for this state of affairs. As Crosland suggested in 1956, and this is probably truer today, large cities are 'divided into rather clearly-marked one-class neighbourhoods'. But it has proved difficult indeed to draw up catchment areas so as to ensure that social and intellectual mix without which a comprehen-sive school is comprehensive in name only. Parents and pupils have resented bussing; many prefer a school for their child to be reason-ably near — as do LEAs aware of the financial costs of school transport. Comprehensive schools have become neighbourhood schools, and are influenced, to a degree, by the character of their neighbourhood. For some parents, paradoxically, the coming of comprehensive schooling has introduced parental choice through the backdoor. If choice of school depends upon proximity to school what could be easier than for well-to-do owner-occupiers to move to a catchment area with a favoured school. And where does this leave the occupant of a council house, or those without the means to pay over the odds for a house in a favoured area?

Crosland was also aware that the public schools, to a degree independent of the state and maintained out of fees rather than rates or taxes, were a threat to a truly comprehensive system of educa-tion. Despite, or because of, being a public school man himself, Crosland claimed, in a reference to private schooling: 'that these schools are superior, and notably the "public schools", is beyond dispute' (p. 261). He also understood the logic of comprehensive schooling well enough to see that it would 'be absurd from a socialist point of view to close down the grammar schools, while leaving the public schools still holding their present commanding position' (p. 275).

No strongminded believer in comprehensive schooling can countenance the existence of private schools. Such schools permit parents to exercise freedom of choice and allow them to place their children in schools other than comprehensive. For example, a postal survey conducted in 1982, on behalf of *The Sunday Times*, collected 600 replies from MPs, top civil servants, company directors, Oxbridge dons, QCs, and comprehensive school headteachers. Of this latter group, *The Sunday Times* (28th February, 1982) revealed that a significant minority sent their own children to private schools. *The Sunday Times* gave an example of just such a headmaster:

'The head of a London boy's comprehensive, whose own two boys, aged twelve and fourteen attend independent day schools. He feels that public schools offer more chance of examination passes "because of their (a) academic environment and (b) social environment". He would have chosen a state school instead if there had been "a higher percentage of well-adjusted, well-motivated children of good academic calibre in the state schools — but they are not around in such numbers any more in inner London"'.

The logic of comprehensive schooling demands that no other type of school must be permitted to exist. So long as there are grammar, direct grant and private schools, parents can and do opt out of the comprehensive system, thus it is claimed weakening comprehensive schools and making them less comprehensive and non-selective. The fact that the parents who freely choose a grammar or private school for their children are, in general, the better informed on educational matters — and may well be, as noted, comprehensive school headteachers — only worsens the position of comprehensive schools. In these circumstances it comes as no surprise to find that supporters of comprehensive schooling are strongly opposed to private schooling. For such private schools, to a degree independent of state control, violate what Caroline Benn (wife of Tony) ennunciated as the Law of Co-existence: 'The selective school gets more selective, the comprehensives get less selective. That is the law of co-existence' (Benn, 1976, p. 41).

Paradoxically, the development of comprehensive schooling, has given a boost to the private schools. Despite the ever increasing cost of private education, demand has never been stronger. In these circumstances one can understand why the Labour Party, strongly committed to maintaining and extending comprehensive schooling, is now equally committed to the destruction of private schooling. The 1981 Labour Party Conference approved the proposal, by seven million votes to seven thousand, to abolish private schools within a period of 'no more than ten years' (for a discussion of the possible consequences of this proposal, see *Choice in Education. An Analysis of the Political Economy of State and Private Education*, by S.R. Dennison, 1984).

Crosland, writing in the mid-1950s and a member of a Labour Party far more liberal and tolerant of diversity than today's Labour Party, expressed his own doubts about the abolition of private schools, despite his recognition that their continued existence could not be endured if grammar schools were to be abolished.

He rejected the notion of abolition, partly on the grounds that such abolition would be unpopular amongst the electorate: 'It (abolition) is out of tune with the temper of the country, and is therefore not likely in any event to be politically practicable' (Crosland, 1956, p. 262). The continuing popularity of private schools is shown in the many opinion polls that have been held since Crosland wrote those words. For example a National Opinion Poll, commissioned by *The Observer* in 1981, showed that abolition still remains 'out of tune with the temper of the country'. And the same poll revealed that seventy-two per cent of the respondents, if money was no problem, would choose an independent fee-paying school for their children if they were unable to get a state school of their choice (*The Observer* 8th February, 1981).

Crosland also believed that abolition was ruled out because such abolition would be an infringement of personal liberty:

flat proscription is undesirable on libertarian grounds ... the interference with private liberty would be intolerable; the closing of all independent schools would naturally encourage a strong demand both for private tutors and, places in schools abroad; and the resulting inequalities would compel the extension of the ban to these facilities also (p. 262).

Strange sentiments from one who when in office as the Secretary of State for Education (1965–7) launched Circular 10/65, the government instrument that led to the destruction of most of the maintained grammar schools in Britain. Indeed Susan Crosland recalls, in her biography of her late husband, that on retiring from a meeting with grammar school headmasters understandably concerned about the abolition of their schools, he remarked 'If it's the last thing I do, I'm going to destroy every fucking grammar school in England'. Crosland added 'And Wales, And Northern Ireland.' Not Scotland, for as he explained, schools there come under the purview of the Secretary of State for Scotland (quoted in Crosland, S. 1982, p. 148).

Crosland, in office, showed no such clear determination about private schooling. His expressed libertarian views led him to stop short of abolition. Instead, he argued that 'the most sensible

approach is to work for a gradual integration of these schools into
the State system of education' (1956, p. 263). Yet is the distinction
between abolition and integration a distinction without difference?
As Brenda Cohen remarks in her *Education and the Individual*, 'in
effect and in outcome it is impossible to distinguish the object of full
integration from that of abolition. The distinction between the two
aims is purely semantic' (1981, p. 18).

Crosland set up, against the advice of senior officials at the
DES, the Public School Commission. This was given the logically
impossible task of integrating, without abolition, the Public schools
with LEA schools. Understandably the Commission, whilst produc-
ing a number of reports and recommendations, failed in its task.
Crosland later confessed that the scepticism of his civil servants was
justified (see Kogan, 1971, p. 177). The Direct Grant schools proved
a softer target. The Donnison Report recommended their abolition
on the grounds that their existence was incompatible with comprehensive reorganization — they presumably violated Caroline Benn's
Law of Co-existence. Shirley Williams, as Labour Secretary of State
for Education, 1976–79, followed this recommendation and with-
drew direct grant status from these schools. Most of them promptly
went private, thus increasing the size of the independent sector and
improving its quality.

Comprehensive Practice

As Secretary of State for Education (1965–7), Crosland was given
the opportunity to put his theories into practice. Susan Crosland
quotes Sir Toby Weaver, then a top civil servant at the DES, as
remarking of her husband: 'He was the first person to stop talking
about comprehensive reorganisation and take a decisive step towards
it' (p. 144).

This decisive step was to issue Circular 10/65. Although already
in draft form before Crosland took office, his biographer wife
reports that he 'took the draft out, polished it, and began negotiations with the multitude of local authority, teacher and other pressure groups that surround Education' (p. 144). The circular, after this
re-drafting, was issued, 12th July, 1965, to LEAs and the Governors
of Direct Grant, Voluntary Aided and Special Agreement Schools.
All these bodies were informed it was the government's declared
objective 'to end selection at eleven-plus and to eliminate separation
in secondary education' by preserving 'all that is valuable in gram-

mar school education for those children who now receive it and to make it available to more children'.

In *The Future of Socialism* Crosland had written that 'there can be no question of suddenly closing down the grammar schools and converting the secondary moderns into comprehensive schools.' It is to Crosland's credit that when in office he did not attempt immediately to legislate for comprehensive schooling. LEAs were invited to submit plans for going comprehensive along six different lines suggested in Circular 10/65. No resources were to be provided for going comprehensive, although from 1966 the DES sanctioned loans to LEAs for capital expenditure (for building or extending schools) on secondary schools only so long as they were comprehensives. Nevertheless it was difficult for the LEAs, particularly those under Labour control, to refuse to go comprehensive so long as Labour Governments were in power. Some, however, did refuse and County Durham, the first local authority to be Labour controlled in Britain, did not become fully comprehensivised until 1981.

It is not within the scope of this chapter to outline or discuss in detail the manner by which Britain (excluding Northern Ireland) went comprehensive. Collections of case studies on this major reform (Batley *et al*, 1970, Saran, 1973, James, 1980) reveal that it was the work of a handful of energetic local politicians and educational administrators. Public opinion on this fundamental change was rarely sought, and generally ignored if expressed. Batley, *et al*, in one case study of *Going Comprehensive* (1970) in Gateshead, and in Darlington, wrote: 'The machinery of consultation seems, in both towns, to have been valuable as a pill sweetner. But it is hard to detect any point where the plans finally adopted were modified by the advice given' (p. 98).

Crosland made little or no reference to what was to be taught to whom in the comprehensive schools — except that all children in such schools 'would ideally share the same broad experience' (p. 267), albeit in schools divided into streams according to ability. Circular 10/65, re-drafted by Crosland, asserts that such schools will preserve 'all that is valuable in grammar schools' and make it more widely available. In a phrase made famous by Hugh Gaitskell, comprehensive schools would provide 'a grammar school education for all', and that is how such schooling was sold to the electorate in the 1960s. Yet how can an education created to answer the needs of approximately the most able twenty-five per cent of pupils in secondary schools be made available for all? Except, at the cost of diluting it radically, or forcing reluctant pupils to study subjects at a level beyond their intellectual capacities and willingness to learn? Surveys of secondary schools since comprehensivisation rather suggest that this is indeed the consequence. The survey carried out by HM Inspectors of Schools, *Aspects of Secondary Education in England* (1979) point out that 'the establishment of comprehensive schools has not led to any radical reshaping of the curriculum, which essentially continues the practice of the selective schools with some added features from the modern schools' (p. 260).

Thus the creation of comprehensive schools has not led to the destruction of the grammar school tradition. Rather this tradition has survived within the comprehensive schools — no doubt watered down and attenuated (for evidence of such decline, see Stevens, A., 1980). Nevertheless enough remains of the grammar school tradition for it to come under fire from those writers who, whilst supporters in theory of comprehensive schooling, are frequently dismissive and hostile about what has been achieved in practice. One such critic is Dr. David Hargreaves, who provides a most pertinent critique of comprehensive schooling in his *The Challenge for the Comprehensive School* (1982).

One of Hargreaves' major hostile criticisms of comprehensive schools is that 'what can fairly be called the grammar-school curriculum continued to hold its central and dominating position in the secondary-school curriculum, despite comprehensive reorganisation' (p. 51). It might have been more perceptive of Hargreaves to have seen that such a development was *because* of comprehensive reorganization rather than despite it — given that comprehensive schools had as their declared objective 'grammar school education for all'. However, he is surely correct in arguing that such a curriculum is unsuitable for *all* children. And it is the strength of the ILEA document *Improving Secondary Schools*, perhaps in part following the thinking of its chairperson, Dr Hargreaves, that it similarly pointed to the unsuitability of much current examination work for many pupils in ILEA schools. For along with grammar school curriculum go GCE examinations, since expectations were raised by comprehensivisation that it would offer GCE examination successes for all. Whether this has been the actual outcome of going comprehensive is a matter of considerable current debate.

Nevertheless, Hargreaves draws the wrong conclusion. Rather than accepting that pupils differ, that there are horses for courses, everyone must still follow the same curriculum, albeit one designed with a majority in mind — a 'central, core curriculum, for pupils between the ages of eleven and fourteen and fifteen, which should be organized around community studies and the expressive arts' (p. 128). This removes what Hargreaves calls the 'cognitive-intellectual' element from the curriculum; but what is the cost? Formal study of intellectually demanding studies — the accursed 'cognitive-intellectual' — will be delayed for the intellectually able until fourteen or fifteen it seems. Yet for these children, learning in depth such subjects as mathematics, science, music and languages, can begin fruitfully much earlier. As Auriol Stevens remarks in her book on that neglected minority *Clever Children in Comprehensive Schools* (1980): 'Holding children back "because all can't none shall" — is an unwarranted oppression' (p. 30).

In the context of this volume what can we learn from the story of going comprehensive? The most general message is to beware the Procrustean equalizer in education, the theorist who believes that equality is the supreme good. In practice this turns schools and educational systems into Procrustean beds, whereby every pupil must be provided equal educational fare, dressed up as a common, core curriculum to be taught in mixed ability classes. Whether this is 'grammar school education for all' or a diet of 'community studies and the expressive arts' for all, the result is the same: indifference and hostility on the part of pupils. Minority and majority pupils alike find themselves offered a programme which has no appeal and less relevance. Therefore we ought to welcome some of the newer initiatives in schooling — TVEI for instance — which provide a chance for schools to begin to take notice of differing needs and abilities amongst their pupils, and to attempt at last to answer them.

References

BATLEY, R., O'BRIEN, O. and PARRIS, A. (1970) *Going Comprehensive*, London, Routledge and Kegan Paul.

BENN, C. (1976) *Comprehensive or Coexistence — 'We must Choose Which we Want'* London, National Union of Teachers.

BURGESS, R. (1983) *Experiencing Comprehensive Education*, London, Methuen.

COHEN, B. (1981) *Education and the Individual*, London, Allen and Unwin.

COLBECK, J. (1984), 'Private schools in the perspective of a reasonable egalitarian' in *Journal of Philosophy of Education*, 18, 1, pp. 129–32.

CROSLAND, A. (1956) *The Future of Socialism*, London, Jonathan Cape.

CROSLAND, S. (1982) *Tony Crosland*, London, Jonathan Cape.

DENNISON, S.R. (1984), *Choice in Education. An Analysis of the Political*

Economy of State and Private Education, London, Institute of Economic Affairs.

DES, (1979) *Aspects of Secondary Education in England. A Survey by HM Inspectors of Schools*, London; HMSO.

DES, (1965) *The Organisation of Secondary Education*, Circular 10/65, London, HMSO.

FLEW, A. (1976) *Sociology, Equality and Education*, London, Methuen.

FLEW, A. (1981) *The Politics of Procrustes. Contradictions of Enforced Equality*, London, Temple Smith.

HARGREAVES, D.H. (1982) *The Challenge for the Comprehensive School: Culture, Curriculum and Community*, London, Routledge and Kegan Paul.

HOLT, M. (1978) *The Common Curriculum, Its Structure and Style in the Comprehensive School*, London, Routledge and Kegan Paul.

ILEA, (1984) *Improving Secondary Schools*, London.

JAMES, P.H. (1980) *The Reorganisation of Secondary Education*, Windsor, NFER.

KOGAN, (1971) with BOYLE E. and CROSLAND, A. *The Politics of Education*, Harmondsworth, Penguin.

NEWSOM REPORT (1963), *Half Our Future*, London, HMSO.

PARKINSON, M. (1970) *The Labour Party and the Organisation of Secondary Education 1918–1965*, London, Routledge and Kegan Paul.

PEDLEY, R. (1978) *The Comprehensive School*, Harmondsworth, Penguin.

REID, M.I. *et al* (1981) *Mixed Ability Teaching: Problems and Possibilities*, Windsor, NFER.

ROYCE, R.J. (1982) 'Public schools: private privilege — a reply to Brenda Cohen' in *Journal of Philosophy of Education*, 16, 1, pp. 105–13.

RUTTER, M., *et al* (1979) *Fifteen Thousand Hours: Secondary Schools and Their Effects on Children*, London, Open Books.

SARAN, R. (1973) *Policy-making in Secondary Education*, London, Methuen.

SCHOOLS COUNCIL (1981) *The Practical Curriculum*, HMSO.

SHAW, B. (1983), *Comprehensive Schooling: The Impossible Dream?* Oxford, Basil Blackwell.

SHAW, B. (1984) 'Sameness and equality: a rejoinder to John Colbeck' in *Journal of Philosophy of Education*, 18, 2, pp. 283–85.

SHAW, B. (1983) 'Procrustes and private schooling' in *Journal of Philosophy of Education*, 17, 1, pp. 131–35.

STEVENS, A. (1980) *Clever Children in Comprehensive Schools*, Harmondsworth, Penguin.

VAIZEY, J. (1983) *In Breach of Promise*, London, Weidenfeld and Nicolson.

Order in an Age of Rebellion

Roy Kerridge

In order to understand the problems that teachers, headmasters and teenage schoolchildren have to face, it is necessary to examine the prevailing idea of our age, which is rebellion. The inventions, discoveries and explorations of the nineteenth century gave the British an exciting sense of anticipation as the century drew to a close. Hitherto, the end of a century had always seemed the obvious time for Doomsday. Now, in an 'age of science', superstition broke through the bonds of Christendom, and a new century promised a new era of 'freedom', a Heaven on no-longer sinful Earth.

However, the dream of progress ended with a jolt, when England awoke to the real-life nightmare of the First World War. When the dust of battle had settled, the magic land of the future had moved, mirage-like, from England to Communist Russia. The idea of progress and perfection was severed from peace, security and stability, and became allied with the warlike notion of revolution. A 'thinking man's orthodoxy' of patriotism to Russia and lip-service to revolution became entrenched in this country during the 1930s, later to be greatly strengthened by sympathetic reportage of Russia's belated role as our ally against Hitler.

But as the dust, radio-active in places, of a Second World War also settled, ideas changed once more. England's faith in Russia was destroyed by the invasion of Hungary and the denunciation of Stalin in the mid-nineteen fifties. The make-believe Russia of Soviet propaganda was still copied in the name of progress. But as it became acknowledged that the Russian revolution had gone wrong, the ideal of rebellion as an absolute good became separated from its base in Communism. Rebellion for its own sake became the orthodoxy, and the vague feeling arose that to rebel, fight and struggle for no definable purpose represented the highest virtue. This idea had an enormous attraction for young people, offering endless scope for a sense of adventure unencumbered by morality. A rebel industry, with films such as 'Rebel without a cause', grew into prominence overnight. Pop singers and film stars presented an up-to-date image of doomed young men — war poets and Rupert Brookes no longer — but heroes destroyed by society for dabbling in violence and crime.

Rebellion, felt deeply by some young people and crammed down the throats of others by rebels in authority, has become the starting point of most young people's adventures into adulthood. Normally the rebel declares a commitment to a gang or group. Diversifying wildly, those possessed by rebellion seize on causes and crusades almost at random, or as current fashion dictates. 'Liberation Fronts' can encompass the whole range of human activity, given a little imagination and gunpowder. Being Irish, a woman, a vegetarian, a person who thinks fur coats are immoral, being opposed to the use of pesticides in farming, being opposed to colours of skin, colours of football teams, styles of hairdressing — every human situation imaginable has its violent supporters or rebels.

The virtue of rebellion is unquestioned. Of late, rebellion has been satirized on stage and screen, but always from the standpoint of a superior rebel. Activists and cultists are sneered at for being 'weekend rebels', 'secretly middle class' and not true rebels at all. Rebel saints die young, whether by drug overdose in England or by firing squad abroad.

Most schoolboys, especially those who delight in laughing at mortar-boarded Teacher in 'The Bash Street kids', must imagine that teachers are opposed to rebellion. But this is not the case. The teaching profession is in a serious dilemma, for while a secondary school teacher may be very much opposed to rebellion against his own authority, he may be equally strongly committed to rebellion in the abstract. The teacher is a child of his time, vulnerable to orthodoxies and ideas which his demanding job leave him no time to investigate thoroughly. Rebels of a thousand causes have been with us so long that they have formed an Authority, very often an Education Authority. In this age of authoritarian anarchy, a teacher disobeys them at his or her peril. The efforts of the Fabians and other socialists have made this not only the Age of the Rebel, but the Age of the Expert. All too often, the expert is a rebel.

Dreams of socialism and progress often become, in reality, jobs for the boys. In order to build a perfect society, it was once reasoned, trained experts of every kind should be created, in order to improve every facet of modern life. In practice, this has meant that virtually anyone involved in a practical task has acquired a paid expert to breathe over his shoulder. Moreover, if advice followed leads to promotion and advice ignored does not, then 'advice' grows teeth and becomes an order. In the field of secondary education, every idea mined from the bottomless pit of rebellion took flesh and became an expert sent out by the Master of the Pit to bedevil teachers. Why and how experts came into being has long been forgotten. They are a fact of life, and in state education, where parents cannot call the tune, the expert reigns supreme. Parents sometimes curse at teachers, but the poor teachers must not heed them, for the expert, or educationalist, holds the purse strings and the promotion ladder. A good teacher must give sops to experts, and placate them, if he is to go on teaching.

Stability, not official rebellion, is necessary if school education is to succeed. Grammar and secondary modern schools (neither by any means perfect) were abolished, and new schools opened, and a chaotic and violent era of unrest was the result. Teachers who had been dedicated to bringing out and fostering talent in young people, with high examination marks and pupils taking up brilliant careers as a reward, simply left the profession. Such teachers felt that small, carefully selected classes were the only ones in which higher learning could take place. Faced with large, noisy, frightening classes, the remaining teachers often saw their role as simply keeping young people happy. Again, the function of a teacher, one who teaches, seemed to have become lost.

'Projects', or homework set by pupils for themselves, at first seem an ideal teaching method from an anti-authoritarian teacher's point of view. Here too the mood of the age has spoiled matters, for mischievous experts are at hand to suggest to baffled pupils the kind of subjects they should tackle. 'So you've chosen drugs for your project?' glares the headline of a pamphlet placed in a public library where schoolchildren sat doing their homework. 'A project guide for teenage pupils who are doing independent projects on legal and illegal drug use as part of a general social studies or other school leavers' CSE or O Level course', I read, and noted the name of the publishers, Release. The Release organization, once master-minded by Caroline Coon, was set up in the sixties to help those accused of drug charges to get off Scot free.

Even the books set as classics of English Literature by the GCE boards are heavily influenced by the rebel industry. Some of them are works that I read surreptitiously beneath the desk lid during my own schooldays. It makes you wonder what books, or comics, will be set in the forthcoming 1990s. Here are some books that have been used as O Level texts in the past few years: *Kes, Catcher in the Rye, Brighton Rock, Billy Liar, Roaring Boys*, and *Bang to Rights*.

Every one of these books deals with rebellious young people, at odds with the world around them. All are set in modern times, and tend to lead the reader into dream worlds of rebelliousness. *Bang to Rights* glorifies the life of a young Soho criminal. It is very readable but relies on the 'gimmick' of wrong spelling. Books such as these are not without merit when read beneath a desk lid, but when made 'official' must induce a feeling that rebellion or naughtiness is a virtue, approved by those in authority. No one brought up on such a diet is likely to turn to the works of Scott, Dickens, Stevenson, Shakespeare or Jane Austen. 'Don't tell your parents', one teacher warned a class as he read some of the fruitier O Level passages aloud.

Such books are only taught to the older children, those in the sixth form, if there is one. For the others, those who are being 'kept happy', there is the fearful Topliner series of text books, ostensibly on social studies, but actually rude, sensational paperbacks, making use of cartoons and clippings from the gutter press. They appear to be addressed to inmates of 'Grange Hill' school, as portrayed on television. In Birmingham last year, I saw three noisy fifteen year old girls, playing truant from school, sitting in the children's department of a public library. They were reading picture books meant for children of seven. If they had been at their desks instead, their reading matter might not have been so innocent.

As a result of having to question everything that they once took for granted, secondary school teachers are in a dilemma. What is their function now? Is teaching immoral, an evil force that makes children lose their class and their 'culture', or grow ashamed of it? Have not the prophets said that capitalism will end, that the world itself will end, or that the Tories have ensured that no one will ever work again? What is the point of teaching at all?

My advice to teachers is simple. Take no notice of the experts. Teach on. If you are a good teacher, one who can make a lesson interesting, you will know the excitement of imparting knowledge, and seeing the stimulating effect of your words on the growing minds before you. One who is taught gains knowledge, and knowledge is a glory in itself, a consolation even if the world *is* ending.

'Anti-eurocentric information packs' used in history lessons at some secondary schools (such as Aylestone School, Brent) produce very dry accounts of African and Indian historical events, taught to English coloured children who would rather learn about England. This does not mean to say that anti-racist experts are wholly wrong. History lessons gain half their impact from the feeling of involuntary patriotism shared by everyone who has lived for years in one country. It is your country, so you are interested in finding out what happened to it and how it became what it is today. Multicultural approaches to history become boring because they treat Britain as being twelve or fifteen countries at once. This does no service to *other* countries. A possible answer is to have *two* subjects in future, English History and World History. English History acts as a counterbalance to the uneasy vacuum conjured up by rebellion. It places the child's feet firmly on the ground, on its own soil. *World History* stimulates the sense of wonder, adventure and appreciation of distant peoples. In some classrooms it might bring a delighted cry from a boy or girl: 'My Dad comes from there!' Something is lost when the histories of all nations are jumbled together — a sense of security.

The dilemma of teachers of English Literature is that so little is being produced, and experts demand that contemporary works be studied. Again, an international touch could bring classic novels and plays to the classroom. Why not interpret English Literature as being literature *in English*, including translations of Russian classics by Constance Garnett and contemporary novels from West Africa and the Caribbean? Wholesome, inspiring tales can evidently still be written in India, by R.K. Narayan among others. Such writers, unlike modern English pygmies, can hold their own with the classic novelists of the past. Ideally, a Literature O Level would require knowledge of two pre-twentieth century authors and one modern. This is a mere dream on my part, of course, as the two subjects, English Language and Literature have long been merged into one. Correct answers can be obtained to many questions by the lottery of ticking the right box.

I well remember the manner in which my once-cosy grammar school went comprehensive, and the agonies I suffered as a result. It would be hard to bring back grammar schools, but many of their good qualities could easily be re-introduced to any school, with the minimum of effort.

A product of the age of rebellion, comprehensive schools often have a swirling, turbulent and bewildering effect on well-behaved pupils. In some cases, life at school can only become bearable for a child when he or she forgets about education and joins in with the rowdy horseplay of the others. This is what I liked about school: having my own classroom, my own desk with a lid, my battered schoolbooks with their familiar authors ('Get out your Ronald Ridout') and my own little place of order in an age of rebellion. All these delights were snatched from me.

First of all, it was the streams themselves. Instead of having one classroom, or one concerted move from one room to another, we all were separated into different categories for every subject. Every bell (or electronic bleep, as time went by) sent every one of us scurrying in a different direction. I was always lost, unsure of which crowd to follow, and left wandering disconsolately in a maze of corridors. My classroom became a mere home base, and late for every subject in turn, I burrowed in my desk for missing books while a strange boy sat in my proper chair, glaring at me! Everyone was shuffled around. Soon our beloved old desks with much carved-on lids were replaced by flat, lidless desks with a shelf below a table-top. This meant that you could not see your books, but had to reach down and fumble for them blindly. The boy in your seat had to be persuaded to get up while you dug about frantically for a ruler, reprimanded by a master who was not even yours! More horrors followed — belongings kept in lockers in the corridor, so no room felt like your own. Tables and chairs in circles and other shapes, so you did not face the person teaching you. Amid chaos and woe, my sense of security was eroded, and no feeling of friendship between teachers and taught had time to be developed.

After I left, so I heard, the dear old dog-eared text books were taken away (good riddance to the Geography book, though) and a new generation of boys now make do with Information Packs that can never be friends. No one ever said 'I don't know what to make of that boy, every day he's got his nose buried in an Information Pack.' These packs are shiny information sheets, loose and unbound within a folder, and offer instant information, highly disposable, leaving no more to think about afterwards than do last years's holiday brochures.

These complaints may seem trivial, but it is by a multitude of little worries like these that a boy's life can be made unbearable. Social engineering and rebellion should not be *inside* the school. If the insecurity and anarchy of rebellion must exist at all, it is better for it to howl outside the school gates than to prowl in the class-rooms and corridors. I think a school ought to be cosy, not bewildering, with no Social Studies lessons to let 'expert' opinion in.

Just how far my old school has fallen may be seen by the remarks made by the present day Head of English when I returned on an Old Boys' visit. After making clear to me how forward-looking he was, by talking about his 'live-in girlfriend', the elderly master began rooting about in a cupboard in the tiny teachers' room. When I had been a pupil, I had often wondered what this room was like on the inside. My suspicions that masters made cups of tea in there were confirmed. I waited for a while, expecting to be told of some sporting triumph, and at last the master emerged with a newspaper clipping. 'Here we are, our school was in the news again recently', he said, straightening up and proudly showing me a head-line, '"Sixteen Year Old Boy Dies of Glue Sniffing".' I felt hor-rified, the more so when I learned that this was the second such tragedy to have taken place at my old school. Teachers should be encouraged to have confidence in themselves, and in their ability to defy this rebellious age and its experts and to rediscover their original function, teaching. I was greatly encouraged by what I saw at Willesden High and South Kilburn schools in Brent, and hope my old school and others in ILEA and throughout the country will soon cease to be intimidated by experts. Our rebellious century is reaching its end, and the next one might be better.

A Case in Point: Multicultural Madness

Now that comprehensive schools have become part of the English scene, our equivalent of American high schools, their routine might be supposed to have settled down somewhat. Not so. Just when academic life seemed to be growing peaceful, a new furore rocked education, the idea of a 'Multicultural Society'. Teaching working class children had once been regarded in some circles as 'brain-washing them into accepting middle class values.' Nowadays teaching coloured pupils is often seen as 'robbing them of their culture.' The key hate-word is now 'Eurocentric', which means imparting a 'European' (or English) point of view in a lesson. With all due respect to other nations, it is very hard for an English person to feel anything other than English. However, the experts inform us that we now live in a 'multicultural society', and must have 'multi-cultural education.' What does this mean?

Jargon is notoriously hard to penetrate, but as far as I can understand, a multicultural education is one intended to fit the child of an immigrant for life in the most remote peasant village of his parents' country, a village where nothing from the outside world is ever to be seen. Ideally, the child will be further removed from English life than his grandparents or great grandparents who remain in Asia, Africa or the Caribbean. A battalion of experts, with a mountain of multicultural documents written in English jargonese, are needed to badger teachers who have never lived outside England into becoming beings capable of performing this educational task. Nothing of English corruption (or education) must harm the coloured child. Parents who have endured great sacrifices to establish themselves in this country, in the hope that their children may win academic honours and become respected citizens of Britain, would be horrified if they understood the implications of multiculturalism. Under the guise of 'anti-racism', the new experts, some of whom may themselves be the sons or daughters of immigrants, are in reality saying 'You do not belong in this country and we are not going to give you our education. It isn't good for you.' Such a message has to be well coated in jargon, as this is still to some extent a land of fair play, and teachers would not swallow it otherwise. Indian and West Indian parents, like white working class parents, are bemused and respectful in the face of education, and seldom have much inkling of what is going on. 'Multicultural inspectors' harass schools with impossible demands, and force teachers to turn to deception. From deceiving inspectors, deceiving parents is only a short step to take. Multicultural education is an impossibility, and the reality is an education interrupted and marred by various nuisances.

In most cities, white children have their share of foreign grandparents, Greek, Polish, Spanish and so on. Seemingly because of their colour, they are excused from multiculturalism.

For all the talk of multiculturalism and ethnic minorities, the most obvious service, that of teaching English to Indian-language speakers, is noticeably absent from many schools. Nor are lessons taught in Urdu or Gujerati. Indian children often have to pick up English by themselves, which makes their often-quoted achievement, outstripping white and other coloured children in examinations, all the more remarkable. As Indians have the reputation of being peace-loving, they suffer far more from attacks by hooligans than do Caribbean youngsters. At Holloway Comprehensive School, North London, I was pleased to learn that first form boys of Indian origin received special English lessons.

Marxist thinking has drifted away from seeing life as a battle between the Workers (good) and the Middle Class (bad) and now tends to a view of black versus white on the same plan. It is difficult to see how repentant whites can become blacks and so worthy of Marxist salvation. However, the white people who dream these dreams always hope they themselves can be accepted by the Black Community before the holocaust. Such ideas, when absorbed by coloured people, can lead to a Hitlerian racial pride. When presented to non-Marxist teachers, they work differently. Teachers who used to despise the working class and say 'You wouldn't *believe* the homes some of these children come from' now speak in exactly the same way of their coloured pupils.

'Black culture', as taught in both primary and secondary schools, often boils down to a grovelling admiration for a rebellious Jamaican pop singer, Bob Marley. Incredible as it may seem, Bob Marley has virtually been made a school subject.

A chapter in a text book entitled *Steel Bands and Reggae* by Paul Farmer (Longman's Music Topics) ends with this suggested exercise: 'Write in your own words the story of Bob Marley's rise to reggae stardom.' I have been shown numerous exercise books from London schools whose pupils had been set this task. The most careful and grammatical Marley essays are those by Indian pupils. Presumably for the benefit of white children, Elvis Presley has a whole text book to himself. Ah, the groves of Academe!

Children of West Indians in English schools are made to study endless books on the slave trade as part of Black History. Having their remote ancestors' slavery repeatedly thrown in their faces must be the most upsetting experience these youngsters have to suffer at school. The same wounded, shocked expression can be seen on their faces as their parents or grandparents wore when they found that England was not a welcoming mother country. Yes, coloured children *do* have a hard time in our schools. Here are some extracts from a Social Studies text book designed for sixteen year olds, *Being Black* by Roxy Harris (New Beacon Books, 1981).

> *Questions.* Black people are outnumbered in Britain. So how much good do you think it would do to try to defeat prejudiced white people just by using violence? (Picture of coloured youths throwing petrol bombs at a car.)

> How true is it that only a stupid black person thinks that all blacks are our brothers and all whites are our enemies?

> What are black Uncle Toms?

Roy Kerridge

> What should a black person do if he becomes rich and
> famous? Should he (a) behave in a way that will please white
> people and make them think better of blacks, or (b) behave
> in a way that will please black people but make white people
> angry and scared?

Can this really be England? Cannot the writer see how degrading it is to divide humanity into whites and blacks, nor how dreadful and contemptuous the word 'blacks' appears? The very title, *Being Black*, is an absurdity. As West Indians from former British territories and their English descendants alike speak English, there is no need for a teacher to make any difference in his approach to pupils on grounds of colour. Note also the premise of the last question, that a rich and famous person can only please black or white people but not both, and that he can please black people best by upsetting white people.

Roxy Harris was born in England, though his parents come from Sierra Leone, West Africa. Most of the book is not his own work, but extracts from George Jackson's *Soledad Brother* and Eldridge Cleaver's *Soul on Ice*. The writings of both these American Black Power fanatics betray a lunatic self-loathing and an obsession with race that is becoming fashionable only now in educational circles in Britain. Social Studies seems to be a catch-all subject for anything that is unpleasant and that divides man from his neighbour. Should young people be exposed to a science which depends on making class, race and religious differences more important than they ever were in the Middle Ages?

Black Power writings, of course, are not the exclusive prerogative of secondary school text books. Primary schools have to endure them also. The violent fantasy 'dialect' (i.e. wrongly spelled) poems of Linton Kwesi Johnson, a Jamaican now living in London, are taught to eight year olds in some London schools. Johnson's poem, 'Sonny's Lettah', about a fight in which a policeman and a youth are killed, inspired one tiny pupil to write a copycat verse, 'Sonny's Fight', about a battle to the death between nine year olds in a school playground. In districts where there are no coloured immigrants, such books are seldom used. Is this not a true example of prejudice and a denial of education?

If these are the books 'Experts' like the children to read, what do they foist on the teachers? Pamphlets from the Primary Curriculum Development Project for pupils of Caribbean Origin, as it happens. Addressed to the head teachers of *primary schools*, one

192

pamphlet asks: 'Is there included in the curriculum an examination of the history and continuing impact of racism on contemporary black struggles?'

The ILEA Centre for Anti-Racist Education sends directives to secondary schools in London calling for 'black' or 'anti-racist' mathematics, among other subject. With surprising frankness, the Centre declares that its aim is to 'show that racism permeates all aspects of life.' A poor example to London's beleaguered teachers of English, the Centre states that 'a growing pattern of in-service provision is taking place.' Here are some extracts from the directive entitled 'Anti-racist education in the secondary school and further education.'

> Anti-Racist Education Through Mathematics. It is constantly asserted that mathematics as a school subject is politically neutral. We believe, however, that Mathematics like other areas of school life reinforces the political status quo by omission, by accepting the limits of a traditional, unchanging subject matter and by encouraging particular ways of thinking. Initially we are interested in developing approaches and materials which may help to undermine racist attitudes.

Use of 'non-European units of measurement' is suggested, though the European ones are bad enough, and good old English feet, yards and inches seldom get a look-in these days. Teachers must question 'sexual superiority' and 'the unfair nature of the economic and political dominance of the West.' Poor teachers! They are ordered to do so much questioning that the normal school syllabus is being whittled away, subject by subject.

My conclusion, after reading the anti-racist literature carefully, is that the tide of opinion is taking us towards a policy of organizing either apartheid or race war. Nor is this mood confined to the field of Education. A West Indian barrister of my acquaintance recently earned a large fee from the Commission of Racial Equality by scribbling out a pamphlet on 'Black Women and the Law.' 'I know very well that it's the same law for men and women, black and white, but I have to pretend that it isn't', she explained.

Most teachers want to give the same education to boys and girls, black and white, but thanks to the education authorities they have to pretend that they don't. If the good of the children were put before abstract ideas on race and culture we could build an England to be proud of.

The Elusiveness of Youth Policy

John Ewen

This chapter is written from Australia, and illustrates that the problems outlined by earlier contributors are not confined to the United Kingdom. It rehearses and updates an analysis of structural problems in youth affairs; and seeks to define a new role for youth education in the context of continuing (and probably permanent) high levels of youth unemployment.

When this contributor wrote *Towards a Youth Policy* in 1973, his diagnosis of the problems of effective youth policies was a structural one. That book explained the dilemma in effectively responding to youth around the world in terms of the failure of Governments to adequately correlate their approaches, in failing to respond holistically instead of merely tangentially to young people's lives. Twelve years later, and overshadowing all such structural weakness, is the bewilderment of societies and their governments, in trying to understand the death of full-employment economies, and to find new roles for increasing numbers of young people who are surplus to market requirements.

Structural weaknesses still persist, and Governments today find it no easier to stitch together sectoral responses to youth. By way of illustration, this contributor has, during the past six weeks alone, submitted policy advice on three major debates currently taking place at Australian Federal Government level: the issue of youth income support through a single payments system subsuming unemployment benefit and the range of educational grants and allowances; a training guarantee based around a three day work/two day study pattern; and the concept of an Australian Youth Service co-ordinating local policy and service delivery. Each of these issues is being considered within a different Government Department, and through different consultation channels. Yet all the issues are intrinsically intertwined. Fortunately we at last have the key structures in place at Federal level to effect the correlations.

At the more local level we are not yet so organized. Within the past ten days, the State Government of Victoria has issued two major Youth Reports, each of which has been two years in preparation and has involved massive public consultation. The first has reviewed post-compulsory education; what is in Australia termed Years 11 and 12, and in UK would be post GCE O level. This review, the Blackburn Report, has proposed the biggest changes since the establishment of public education, dealing with the structure of schools (comprehensivisation of technical and high schools, and the formation of post-compulsory community colleges); a major overhaul of curriculum; and the adoption of a new examination system, not geared merely to the 12 per cent who go on to higher education. The second, the Carney Report, surveys the whole area of child-care and welfare services, and the jurisdictional frameworks of such services. As if this were not enough for one week, the State Employment Department has announced its Youth Guarantee scheme to provide relief for the 24 per cent of young people under 21 without jobs; the Community Services Department has set up a Task Force to consider the future of its Youth Training Centres (high and medium security provision for young offenders); and the Housing Ministry has expanded its single-shares accommodation program. Not surprisingly, the Blackburn Report scarcely mentions child welfare, and the Carney Report only touches upon educational issues.

Giving impetus to much of this activity is International Youth Year, with its 'highfalutin' concepts of youth participation, peace and development. As part of this activity we have seen the shift of the Federal Government's Office of Youth Affairs to the Prime Minister's Department (its sixth change of Department since it was established in 1977); the shift of the State Government's Bureau of Youth Affairs to Employment from Recreation (where it has lain moribund for the past three years); a national consultation on youth worker training; an OECD report on youth in Australia, a major Federal Government Review of further education and training (the Kirby Report) an Australian Bureau of Statistics survey of young people, a Special Minister of State's survey of young people's attitudes; a national drugs summit with considerable focus on youth; a Health Commission report on increasing suicide rates amongst the young; and so on, and so on.

In many ways this host of activity can only be welcomed.

Australia must now be the best informed nation about its youth in the world. There cannot be any group that is more studied, and talked about. The dilemma now is what to do with all this information, how to make sense of it, and how to build some frameworks in which to apply it. Even if that policy exercise can be achieved, *can a pluralistic and highly complex society be persuaded to agree on some common goals, and can the politicians maintain a commitment to pursue them?*

In my 1973 *Towards a Youth Policy*, two things were argued: firstly that the concept of youth affairs needed to be established, and secondly that the consequent co-ordinating structures needed to be set in place. It was pointed out that the traditional Governmental structures were organized on vertical policy and service delivery lines; that is, that the Department of Employment dealt with employment matters and services affecting all age groups, as did the Department of Housing in relation to its functions, and so on. It was argued that we needed a horizontal grid across these verticals to co-ordinate the impact of these disparate policies and services on specific target groups, in this case youth (though a similar case can be put in relation to women, the elderly, and so on). The approach was essentially a structuralist one. In particular it argued that the optimum chance of effective policies and programs with and for youth lay with an Office of Youth Affairs directly responsible to the Prime Minister, assisted by a committed Ministerial colleague, the task of which was not to separate out and administer all youth policies and programs, but to actively co-ordinate the contributions of all the Departments concerned, so that there was a coherent and holistic approach.

That is precisely the structure that Australia has now adopted. It has an Office of Youth Affairs, with some 50 public servants, with its Director appointed by the Prime Minister personally, and an Assistant Minister in day-to-day charge. There is an Inter-Departmental Committee, and there are liaison officers in each of the major Departments. There is a Ministerial Committee on the major issues reporting to Cabinet. There is a mass of data available on which to formulate policies and programs. Yet, it is by no means certain that improved outcomes will emerge. They are more likely, but they are not guaranteed. Which is why this contributor's 1984 book, *Youth in Australia in the 80s*, began to move from structuralist solutions towards political and conceptual responses. The problem in Australia now is that the structures are in place, but how do we find the agreed conceptual frameworks within which the structures can deliver? Above all, can they deliver in a context where a quarter of young Australians under 21 have no work (and our problems here are as nothing to those in UK)?

It cannot be assumed that a nation's youth policy is simply a matter of conglomerating all the individual policies and programs emerging from Government Departments, and providing the co-ordinating machineries to glue them together. What we are therefore now seeking to do in Australia is to work out what is an appropriate wrapping paper to put around the conglomerate which makes some total sense to the community, to Government, and to young people. We seek to define the 'x' factor which makes the whole more than merely the sum of the parts.

If we were living in an autocratic or statist form of Government that would not be difficult. In an autocracy the label on the wrapping paper presumably reads 'how to ensure all young people love the autocrat'; in a communist country or a theocracy, it reads 'how to ensure all young people are good communists, good fundamentalist Moslems', or whatever is the controlling creed or political theory. It was on such an approach that the Hitler Youth Movement thrived, for not only did it meet the needs of the single-party state apparatus, but it also spoke to the hearts of the young through some very attractive slogans such as full-employment, and nationalism. Similarly, countries experiencing revolution have no difficulties in attracting the young to the cause of change; but they have much greater difficulty in maintaining the commitment of the young once revolution has been attained.

For pluralist societies such as the United Kingdom and Australia, decisions about the wrapping paper and what to write on the label are not so easily come by. Society as a whole is confused and quarrelsome about its destiny. It has none of the certainties that victory gave it in 1945 about the directions in which it wants to proceed. Above all it is perplexed by the apparently insoluble problems of unemployment, and the social divisiveness which results from it. If that were not enough, it still struggles to live with the nuclear bomb, which not only refuses to go away, but which spreads more and more oppressively. Quite apart from these macro-problems, the individual also strives to deal with a whole range of micro-revolutions: with shifts in gender definition and in sex roles; with disruptions in commonly assumed fundamentals such as the protestant work ethic; with less constant life-long relationships, and many varieties of living experience other than the traditional nuclear family; with the loss of prevailing religious beliefs and the obligation to work out a personal ethic by which to interpret and engage in social relationships.

Given these general uncertainties and confusions, adults have tended (particularly during International Youth Year) to expect that young people themselves will be able to offer some clues. Television specials all round the globe have presented viewpoints of young people. Unfortunately we find that young people are no more a homogeneous group, able to offer us clear cut directions, than we adults are. They are as much divided by class, education, family experience, income distribution, race, and creed as the rest of us. They are equally confused, and equally divided about directions. In the context of these uncertainties, ambivalences, and disparaties, where might we start in seeking to establish some satisfactory frameworks for national youth policy?

Youth in Australia in the 80s attempted to correlate two themes: at the individual level, the hypothesis that people cannot satisfactorily exist without *role and status*; and at the societal level, the evidence of history that if political systems cannot give young people *appropriate power*, they will seize *inappropriate power*. The 1981 riots in Toxteth, Moss Side and Brixton and the new riots of 1985 were warnings to us that when these two themes coincide at any time and in any place, there will be severe social disruption. Given the current level of power of the State, the initial outcomes will be certain wins for the ruling elites (of whichever political flavour), but the long-term damage to stable societies may be irremediable. Established groups in society (not by any means restricted to the rich) will reflect their fears of disruption by seeking greater social controls of the young, whether through education, welfare or correctional services. The young, however immediately contained, will store their experience for the future. No amount of counter-balancing palliative programming is likely to assuage their underlying sense of anger at our failure to offer them role and status.

Since this book is concerned with youth and education, what are the implications of a national youth policy of which role and status are the themes? Society's expectations of schools have always been complex and often contain a mix of paradoxical demands. These include socialization of the young (rules, uniform, the school song, playing the game, identification with a hierarchical social structure, prefects); teaching (principally in the elementary skills of literacy, numeracy, and — latterly — articulacy); child-minding (especially important with the increase of women's participation in the work-force); sifting and sorting (through testing machineries which establish future social position); training (in the sense of preparing for entry into the labour market with knowledge and skills which will enable the child to bargain and compete); and sometimes education (in the sense of Rennaissance man — a privilege reserved for only a minority). Some of these expectations are increasingly difficult to meet, especially at a time when society seems to expect them more strongly. For example how does a school socialize the young in a context of little agreement on mores? How does the school train, when there is no clarity on what it is training for? For what purpose and on what basis is it sifting? How do you mind children when they are no longer children?

Nonetheless the one expectation which schools will increasingly have to meet is child-minding, but translated now into *adolescent minding*, and eventually into adult minding. This function could become increasingly a custodial one, a perpetual purgatory between infancy and death; or a form of universal entertainment centre to provide us with occupational therapy to fill in our workless lives.

Our principal unresolved dilemma of the future of work requires that we both scapegoat education as the root cause of our perplexity, and place an unrealistic onus on it to provide the solutions. (Though to antipodean eyes, there is an elegance in the British resolution to this paradox, by which one education system is elected as scapegoat, and an entirely new one created in parallel to it called the Manpower Services Commission. This at least demonstrates that, if it has lost all else, Britain still retains political style and finesse. There can be few other countries that now have two alternative education systems simultaneously.) In Australia, we have not yet rejected the old system completely; but we do expect it to resolve the labour market difficulties in two ways: we want it to contain more young people longer so as to keep the unemployment figures down, and thus we want it to be more 'relevant' (i.e. more entertaining); and we want it to stress the 'basics' so that young people are subsequently more employable, though in what and as what we are decidedly unclear. Unfortunately, we seem unable to convince many of the young of the virtues of such policies. Although a few more are being retained in the system longer, many choose unemployment benefit as a better alternative to more of what they are already disillusioned with. Moreover they are now highly suspicious that the traditional middle-class virtues of deferred gratification are not the blue chip stocks that they were. 'Stay on for what?', 'Train for what?' are the not unreasonable questions.

Our other policy approach is to diagnose the youth unemployment problem as being the fault of young people's own avarice. The employers claim that young people have priced themselves out of the market, and, if youth wage rates were lowered by forty per cent, youth employment levels would immediately rise. One of the largest junk food outlets which relies for its very considerable profits on cheap part-time youth labour promises to create 1000 new youth jobs if the wage rate is cut. Immoral, cry the unionists, noting that cheap youth labour will almost certainly result in the displacement of adult high-cost labour. In no way can we agree, says the socialist government, however, we will introduce a youth training scheme by which young people work three days a week and 'train' for two, and then of course it is quite fair to reduce their income by forty percent. Yet again, we run into difficulties in persuading young people that International Youth Year should be celebrated by reducing their income by two-fifths. The young always are so unreasonable.

In the last century and a half, role and status have derived from education, work, from the income that work earns, and from the things that the income buys: the house, the car, the holiday in Spain. Take work away and the whole house of cards collapses. Not least the carrot with which education wielded the stick disappears. Yet education still operates as though the cards were intact. It maintains the old assumptions. Education was the escape from the mines, the greening of the valley, the route to upward social mobility, to fame and fortune. It was not dissimilar to the football pools or the tatslotto ticket; it was worth the investment in case your number came up. It inculcated the protestant work ethic because that ethic demonstrably paid subsequent dividends. The house (and the mortgage), the car (and the HP), and the fortnight on the Costa Brava legitimized the effort. But when large numbers of young people (across the ability range) have no work or no guarantee of continuing work, an education system based on these old assumptions is in grave danger of not only being perceived as a sham, but is in reality a gigantic confidence trick. The charade becomes even more transparent if the political answers to an over supply of labour are merely the prolongation (albeit in a variety of more subtle styles) of what is already a dubious exercise. To the young it may well sound rather too like the doctor with a very uncertain diagnosis recommending that one keeps on taking the pill.

Yet, although sometimes questioning the validity of its assumption base, education is somewhat of a harlot, easily seduced. More education is more resources. The extension of education may not be the answer to the problem, but education is damned if it's going to admit it. With some blind masochistic determination, it suffers the politicians' scapegoating for 'another fine mess you've got us in', and sets itself up for further inevitable failure and the discomforts of growing customer resistance. For qualitative or quantitative changes in a 'pre-reformation' education system will not 'solve' unemployment. Nor for that matter will monetarism of Keynesianism. Nor will the current single-minded passion for the restructuring of the manufacturing base. Nor will the slogans about the right to work. Nor will neo-Luddites smashing the computers. We have now wasted fifteen years on this merry-go-round of panaceas.

The only significant role for education is to help us to understand the world we live in and how we can best relate to it. In particular, at a time of change and confusion, it must help us understand the nature of the revolution in which we are caught up, and which, unless understood, will continue to cause us misery and social dislocation. Nor will it suffice for education to draw inappropriate parallels from the nineteenth century industrial revolution, and to extrapolate these into our present circumstances. Of course that revolution caused dislocation and unhappiness, particularly in moving societies from a basically agrarian pattern to urbanized living. But that revolution created infinitely more employment. Indeed (with Victoria and Albert's example) we were urged to breed extensively (if not enthusiastically) to provide the manpower for the new labour demands. Our current revolution is of a quite different ilk. By some unfortunate quirk of fate, two major events hit us simultaneously: the loss of an empire on which our manufacturing and trading wealth was based, and the subsequent world-wide redistribution of economic power, the ownership of resources, and the means of production; and the discovery of new technological processes which have destroyed labour-intensive production. Cycles of boom and recession, to which politicians still pay so much attention, are as nothing compared with this great roller-coaster wave of change.

Education has the responsibility not to perpetuate the outdated nineteenth century assumptions on which it is based, not to sell its soul for the sake of the new program, course, classroom, or computer laboratory, not to be reactive to the whims of frightened politicians forever seeking to buy time in the hope that somehow it will all come right, but to be pro-active in establishing the arenas, the forums, in which our societies and we as individuals, and particularly our young people, can seek new definitions of life-purpose, of role and status, new means of wealth distribution other than through work or pension benefits, and new inter-relationships between the means of production and the community in which the production takes place.

For nearly one hundred and fifty years education has served the demands of industrial and commercial production. Its new role must return to its old role. It was education which dragged civilization from the dark ages, and created Rennaissance Man. It has the responsibility to begin that process anew. To argue thus is to argue against all the directions in which the policy debates are running. For the politicians only reflect the bewilderment in which all of us wallow. They, like us, need to cling to past experience as a security blanket for dealing with the present and the future. Somehow, they and we believe, we can find exciting new products and services that someone somewhere will want to buy — if only we could work out what they are, and if only someone else wasn't making them more cheaply already. The present difficulties are only temporary, and if we restructure, and invest in more education and training, then all will come right. Or, they and we believe (because we need to), the answer lies in the expansion of the servicing industries. A few of us will need to be highly technologically trained and will produce the wealth, which the few will then spend on employing the rest of us to service them. There will be the new patricians, and the new plebs. This scenario assumes enough patricians to provide secondary employment for an awful lot of plebs, and that such an arrangement will be socially acceptable to both of the new classes. Apart from these two approaches, the political menu for the future looks just a little barren. And, because it does, there is a further trend taking place. The centre is becoming increasingly aware that it does not have satisfactory answers, and it is tired of taking the blame. Gradually it is shifting the onus of problem solution to the edges of the system. If there are answers to be found, they must be found locally, and preferably amongst the people in most urgent need of finding the answers. The centre is absolving itself of the responsibility.

Whilst the motivation might be suspect, the movement away from centralism is probably the only way to go, if only on the grounds that centralism has little left to offer. Yet there are more positive reasons for welcoming this shift, and they have profound implications for education.

Much earlier in this chapter, we noted that the problems with which we wrestle are not merely of a macro type. Each of us as individuals is trying to come to terms with new relationships, new sex role definitions, new living units, as well as with the micro effects of the macro changes in work. If the centre has no answers, we have no alternative than to seek our own solutions in re-defining our individual relationship to our environment. Here too we will be tempted to cling to the safe familiarity of historic models; or, when they are destroyed, to lapse into despair and withdrawal — symptoms already too visible in so many.

If we are to redefine our micro links with the reality of our environment, we will need education of a quite different nature than the high-tech models often postulated. We will need frameworks in which to sort out our self-value and our role with quite different criteria than in our recent past. Such an education will be more concerned with being than doing, with mutually supportive relationships rather than with competition, with self-image built more on the satisfaction of appropriate contribution than on 'what's in it for me'. Role and status are likely to stem from quite different judgments, and to depend upon quite different bases of assessment. This is why youth education is so important, and why it has to be increasingly distinguished from the current child models of education (which have been pervasive even in the education of adults).

For the social value of youth is that it is less encumbered by the security blanket of past experience. It has less to lose from change. The adolescent can leap along Helvellyn's Striding Edge without care or fear, knowing that he or she just will not cannot fall. The twenty-five year old with the wife, two kids and the mortgage, clings on hard to every hold the rock permits, and contemplates the awfulness of his fall, which is only too possible. To be irresponsible is youth's great advantage. Youth's second assett is to be able to discern black from white. Maybe Adam and Eve's adolescence was at its highest when their eyes were opened and they beheld good and evil. Their successors have certainly learnt how to fudge the edges ever since. That combination of irresponsibility and clarity of focus is now at a premium.

Yet our current child-modelled education directly destroys these social values of youth. It trains youth for the past, yet youth knows that the past is over. It offers no room for an optimistic future, in which people can more effectively relate to each other and to their environment; and hence it breeds fear and conservatism. The assumption that education makes is rather like that of those sad

Chekovian characters who solace themselves with the repeated slogan 'if only we work, it will be alright' whilst the whole world is turning upside down around them. Maintaining that the future has to be a repeat performance of the past can only bring despair and hopelessness for the young. And for the adults it is absurd posturing. The good old days were never as good as we like to pretend.

What, Then, Might a Post-Reformation Youth Education Look Like?

It has to first assume that the child education which precedes it has provided the basic skills of writing, reading, and communicating verbally, and that the child education has at the very least not damaged a willingness to think, explore, question, imagine, and risk. If these assumptions are ill-founded then it will have to start by putting them right.

It will seek to engage in a learning transaction, rather than a teaching supermarket. It will therefore not imply a one-sided ownership of experience, though it will demonstrate a respect for empirical data. It will distinguish between fact and viewpoint, but will treasure both. It will encourage interpretation, originality, and eccentricity. It will respect the individual and the individual's right to individuality. But it will seek to engage the individual in group inter-actions, in order to exemplify the value to the individual of exploring and testing ideas and relationships, and the value to the group in working towards common learning goals. (It is here where the earlier contribution of Leslie Button described in Chapter 3 is so valuable.)

Its prime concern will be to hold the ropes around an arena in which the two essential questions to be faced are 'what kind of person am I?', and 'to what purpose am I going to put the me that I am?' Lest this sound all too abstract and philosophical, the contexts in which the two questions are explored can be as concrete as Wembley Stadium. Indeed it is only from being exposed to a variety of very real situations that such questions even begin to be formulated, let alone resolved. (The proposals explored by Alec Dickson in an earlier chapter are excellent examples of one set of such experience.) The bias towards being rather than doing does not imply that one can 'be' in a vacuum. The constant revision of self-image only transpires from interaction with others in the greatest variety of practical contexts. If we have to find new ways of defining role and status other than through the traditional definitions associated with work, we have to find it from a measure of ourselves in every possible admixture of surroundings and groupings. Self-worth can only be tested and proven by inter-action with others; it is their assessment which offers the potential for our role and status; and it is a reciprocal process.

Post-reformation education will need to break the nexus between schooling and work, the reverse of current education/training policy in the OECD countries, which is still based on nineteenth century dictates of national economies. It is clearly absurd to maintain economic pressures for more training, more job-related skills, more vocationally oriented education, in a context of diminishing demand for such products. Yet, current re-accentuation of these 'desirables' is making it less easy for society to adapt. It re-enforces traditional child and parent expectations that the prime value of education is job-getting, and dooms them to a disillusionment with a system that has cheated.

Post-reformation youth education will become real education. It will value discovery, analysis, choice, engagement, and above all it will be enjoyable. Once the nexus between education and work is broken, education ceases to be a sub-set of work, needing to adopt all the worst features which 'work' suggests. It can regain the pure joy of renaissance exploration. The education = vocational preparation model can only lead to disilliusionment and despair; post-reformation youth education can restore optimism in the sheer enjoyment of life.

For well over a hundred years education has sold its soul to the work market. Its curriculum, methodology, and above all the demands of its market interface through assessment systems, have been dominated by commercial interests. The ascendancy of the Manpower Services Commission over the Department of Education and Science during the past decade has even further re-enforced the economic dictatorship of education. Post-reformation youth education must in a sense be also post-colonial education, seeking to establish new cultural and value bases, representing a concept of education as 'humanity holding a great continuous discussion throughout the ages and across the world'.

Within such terms, the extension of educational opportunity for youth becomes valid in its own right. It is not merely another knee jerk re-action to economic vicissitudes, a means of soaking up spare labour capacity and decreasing the length of the juvenile dole queue. It is not a device to increase personal competitiveness in a shrinking job market. It is a valid extension of youth moritorium, of time-out for becoming a person and working out how best to be a contributor to the well-being of others through discovering valid social role and status.

The context of the post-reformation youth education will be most unlike school in its generally accepted sense. Its essence will be experiential, being through doing. It will depend on contractual relationships between 'student' and the community. It will be highly complex and very untidy, depending on a myriad of opportunity choices, many as yet totally unexplored. It will not be owned by teachers, but assisted by youth educators. Some of it will look like Alec Dickson's model, but a lot won't. It will permit the widest exploration of art, culture, sport, life-style. It will be based on the premise that anything is possible rather than nothing can be done.

What Are the Conditions For Such a Concept of Youth Education to Become Realizable?

Firstly, the politicians of the OECD countries will have to stop deluding themselves (and decreasingly deluding their electorates) that the post-industrial revolution has not arrived. To continue the pretence that this year, next year, sometime the clouds will roll back, and life will be as it was, is a monstrous lie. It leads to the continued exploration of the wrong questions, and prevents the address of the right ones. It breeds cul-de-sac organizations like the Manpower Services Commission.

Secondly, advocates for youth will need to forego self-indulgent ostrich-like slogans such as the 'right to work', as if work were the be all and end all of life. It is a peculiar irony that such advocates have become the die-hard defenders of the protestant work ethic, which was created as a value system to control labour.

Thirdly, educational institutions will need to stop playing the strumpet; to resist the blandishments of additional resources to do the wrong things; and to be pro-active in leading society's awareness of the implications of a post-industrial era, and the new definitions of education which such an era will require. In particular, education systems and institutions will need to break the century-old nexus between education and work, and reverse the current Gadarene rush towards pointless 'vocational' orientations.

Fourthly, we have all to combine in tackling the close of century conundrum, how to distribute wealth other than through 'work' and government charity?

Fifthly, we have to accept the cost of providing young people with the moratorium through some form of youth wage, to offer reasonable income security in which youth education can take place.

The combination of these five conditions may permit us to make a new beginning in formulating a youth policy, and in particular to begin to evolve an appropriate post-reformation youth education. The structural approach to youth policy has to date delivered little in positive outcomes. What we now need is a quantum leap in concept development.

Yet, even as this chapter is concluded, here in Victoria in Australia, the State Government (under an extravaganza headline of Youth Opportunity Guarantee) announces 575 work/study positions, of which the largest group is 120 station assistants (in an industrial sector notorious for 'over-manning' and which has seen persistent strikes over the past few years as successive Governments have tried to cut back labour-intensity!). It is not clear how the 'study' element will improve on platform sweeping techniques. If the poverty of thinking and the debilitating outcomes for young people were not so sad, such enterprises are so Monty Pythonesque as to provide comic relief for the rest of the century. Yet they are being seriously entertained and funded throughout the OECD as 'solutions' to the youth problem. On the same day the *Australian* national newspaper (owned by no less than *The Times*' Rupert Murdoch) prints an editorial under the headline 'A chance for youth' welcoming a Western Australian Arbitration Commission ruling that employers can negotiate with unemployed young people to accept below industry rate wages in return for a job offer. Presumably a return to the exploitation of child labour would be equally welcome and perceived as yet a further example of society's eagerness to increase youth opportunity (rapidly becoming the decade's most misused phrase).

The quantum leap seems scarcely at the warm-up exercise stage. It will inevitably come. The cost of delay will be in individual young people's lives, and potentially in major social disruption. The 1977 UNESCO report *Youth in a Changing World* contained this warning:

> Where the political forces in adult society appear to be immobilized and incapable of responding to growing social contradictions, young people may not wait to become adults

before assuming their roles as historical actors but may intervene, as youth, by unconventional means. Such interventions may remain ineffective for a long time but eventually they may trigger off major political and social upheavals.

Post-reformation youth education can only arise from much wider debates about youth in our society and about that society itself and its future directions. Education itself has a responsibility to be pro-active in such debates, and escape its current role of whipping-boy and servant.

References

AGPS (1985) *Report of the Committee of Enquiry into Labour Market Programs*, Canberra.

BUREAU OF STATISTICS (1985) *Australia's Youth Population 1984*, Canberra.

EWEN, J.R. (1984) *Youth in Australia in the '80s*, Centre for Youth and Community Studies, Phillip Institute of Technology, Melbourne.

GOVERNMENT OF VICTORIA (1985) *Child Welfare Practice and Legislative Review*.

GOVERNMENT OF VICTORIA (1985) *Ministerial Review of Post-Compulsory Schooling*.

NATIONAL YOUTH BUREAU (1973) *Towards a Youth Policy*, MBS Publications, Leicester.

OECD (1984) *Review of Youth Policies in Australia*, Paris.

UNESCO (1977) *Youth in a Changing World*, Paris.

Notes on Contributors

Dr J.C. Coleman trained both as an educational and a clinical psychologist. Until 1980 he was Senior Lecturer in Psychology at the London Hospital Medical College (University of London). In 1980 he became Director of the newly formed Sussex Youth Trust. He is also Visiting Fellow at the University of Sussex and Editor of the *Journal of Adolescence*. Books he has written include *The School Years*, (Methuen, 1979) and *The Nature of Adolescence* (Methuen, 1980).

Michael Day trained for professional youth work at Swansea University and worked for several years in a variety of posts in the Youth Service before being appointed Research Fellow in the Brunel Training Consultative Unit in 1973. He became its Director in 1984. He teaches group work in the Postgraduate Diploma in Youth and Community Studies at Brunel University, and has developed practical group work in the training of voluntary youth workers. He was joint editor of *Black Kids, White Kids: What Hope?* (National Youth Bureau, 1979), and is currently directing a DES funded project on management development in the Youth Service.

Dr Alec Dickson, CBE worked until 1939 as a foreign correspondent and in refugee relief in Central Europe. After wartime service in East Africa, he pioneered new approaches to rural development and youth training in West Africa and Iraq. In 1958 he founded Voluntary Service Overseas, and in 1962 Community Service Volunteers. He is Hon. Consultant to International Baccalaureat Schools. He has advised numerous governments and university authorities on the involvement of students in community service.

John Ewen is Principal Lecturer and Head of Department at the

Phillip Institute of Technology, Melbourne. Previously he was a Detached Youth Worker, Head of the Berkshire Training Agency, Head of the Youth Service Information Centre, and from 1973 to 1976 founder Director of the National Youth Bureau. He has advised governments in various parts of the world on youth work and youth affairs. He is the author of *Towards a Youth Policy* (MBS Publications, 1973), and *Youth in Australia in the Eighties* (Centre for Youth and Community Studies, Melbourne, 1984).

ROY KERRIDGE is an author and journalist. He writes regularly for *The Spectator* and other magazines and newspapers. He is the author of *Real Wicked, Guy: View of Black Britain* (Blackwell, 1983) and *The Lone Conformist* (Chatto and Windus, 1984).

PROFESSOR DAVID MARSLAND works in the Department of Human Sciences and the Youth Service Training Consultative Unit (of which he was founder-Director), both at Brunel University. He is Assistant Director of the Social Affairs Unit. He was until recently a member of the UNESCO Social Sciences Board, and is a former Honorary General Secretary of the British Sociological Association. Author of *Work To Be Done* (Youth Call, 1984) which argues for radical action on youth unemployment, and other books and papers including *Sociological Explorations in the Service of Youth* (National Youth Bureau, 1978).

ERROL MATHURA has worked at the United Nations and as a civil servant, and taught in primary, further, and higher education. Most recently he has been a senior educational administrator in London with responsibilities for the Youth Service and Further Education.

DR DENNIS O'KEEFFE is Senior Lecturer in the Sociology of Education at the Polytechnic of North London. A member of the Advisory Council of the Social Affairs Unit, he is editor of *The Wayward Curriculum* (Social Affairs Unit, 1986) and a frequent contributor to academic journals and newspapers.

BEVERLEY SHAW is a lecturer in the School of Education, University of Durham. He has taught previously in a secondary school, at a regional college of technology, and in adult education. He is the author of *Educational Practice and Sociology: an Introduction* (Martin Robertson, 1981), *Comprehensive Schooling: The Impossible Dream?* (Blackwell, 1983), and papers on various aspects of education.

DAVID M SMITH teaches in the School of Sociology at Middlesex Polytechnic. His main research interest is in the sociology of youth. Currently engaged as Research Associate of The Institute of Community Studies in research on part-time adult education and on generation and ethnicity in the inner city. Author of several papers including *New Movements in the Sociology of Youth* (British Journal of Sociology, Vol. 32, No. 2, 1981).

HOWARD WILLIAMSON is active in youth work and social research. He has written widely on delinquency, youth unemployment, education and training, and youth work. His interest in the transition from school to work began in 1979 in the course of a study conducted by the Social Research Unit, University College, Cardiff, where he has recently completed a research project on inter-agency approaches to youth and community work. With P. Williamson he wrote *Five Years* (National Youth Bureau, 1981) and contributed to the study of research on youth *Look At What You're Doing* (National Youth Bureau 1985).

Index

Index

Pedley, R. 174
peer groups 2–3, 12, 42–7, 58
  class and 49–50
  ethnicity 56–8
  girls 55–6, 59
  parents and 47–9
peer relationships, adolescent need
  100
Perker, H. 150
personal education 90
personal failure, sense of 162
personality theory, group work and
  102
Petersen, A. 28, 29, 30, 33, 36, 38
physical development, puberty
  26–8
physical education, community
  service and 82
Piaget, J. 6, 7, 30–1, 32, 33
Picasso, P. 124
planning schedule, developmental
  group work 107
Plato 127–8
police, help from school pupils 74
political education 101
political thought, development
  34–5
post-compulsory education 195
post-industrial revolution 206
Postman, N. 65, 66
pre-vocational education 138, 140
Preparation for Life courses 155,
  199
Primary Curriculum Development
  Project 192–3
privacy, group work and 105
private education, demand for 139
private schools 175–6
  abolition 176–8
Procrustes 167
producer-shaped curriculum 133
protestant work ethic 200, 206
psychoanalysis 6, 7
psychoanalytic approach, to
  adolescence 2, 22–4
psychological effects, puberty 26,
  27–9
psychological perspectives, youth
  11

psychology
  adolescence 2, 6
  group work and 102
psychotherapy 87
puberty 2, 6, 11, 22, 24, 26–30
public examinations 168, 169–70
public schools 55, 173, 175
Public Schools Commission 178
pupils
  community service projects 71–9
  conformity 54–5
  lower-ability 132
  personal aspects 103–4
  rejection of schooling 167
  relevance of school for 53–4

race, peer groups and 56–8
racial inequality, education and
  training 156–7
Radler, D.J. 48
reasoning, adolescent 32
rebellion 4–5, 23, 183–93
recession 150
reciprocity 73
Rees, T. 146
regional inequalities, education and
  training 157
regression 23
Reid, I. 149
Reid, M.I. 174
relationships, exploration in groups
  111
Release 185
relevance, education 145, 148–9,
  161–2
Remmers, H.H. 48
resources, for new technology 154
responsibility 11
retarded patients, preparation for
  discharge 77
Ridge, J. 147, 149
riots 198
Roberts, K. 151, 157
Robins, D. 52, 53, 54
role
  education 201–3
  personal 198, 200
role change, adolescence 24–5
role models, adults as 2, 37–9